A Ram in the Thicket

Idaho Yesterdays / A Series Edited by Judith Austin
          IDAHO STATE HISTORICAL SOCIETY

The Robertson Family

A Ram in the Thicket

THE STORY OF A ROAMING HOMESTEADER
FAMILY ON THE MORMON FRONTIER

FRANK C. ROBERTSON

Introduction by **CHARLES S. PETERSON**
Retrospective by **GLEN E. ROBERTSON**

UNIVERSITY OF IDAHO PRESS   Moscow, Idaho 1994

© 1978 Glen Robertson © 1959 Frank C. Robertson
Copyright © 1950 Frank C. Robertson
Introduction by Charles S. Peterson and Retrospective by Glen E. Robertson
© 1994 University of Idaho Press

Idaho Yesterdays is a reprint series developed by the Idaho State Historical Society and published by the University of Idaho Press, Moscow, Idaho 83844-1107

Printed in the United States of America.
All rights reserved. No part of this publication may be reproduced, stored in a retrieval system, or transmitted in any form or by any means, electronic, mechanical, photocopying, recording, or otherwise, except for purposes of scholarly review, without the prior permission of the copyright owner.

Cover design by Caroline Hagen

98 97 96 95   5 4 3 2 1

Library of Congress Catalog Card Number: 59-7373

To my son, Glen, and my wonderful
Czech daughter-in-law, Vera

A Ram in the Thicket is Frank C. Robertson's account of his salty father and the life of a Mormon family as late pioneers in Idaho. Although it has been some time since I read the story, it sticks in my memory a little like a burr to a sheep, and quite a bit like the flavor of chokecherries, special and sweet, and a little puckery.

There is something of the Old Testament patriarch about this Latter Day Saint father, and a lot of the old time horse trader and snake oil man. Indeed, pioneering seems to have changed very little during the thousands of years between. Certainly the life was never for the mild, the amiable and the gentle. Gentle folks had a way of fleeing back to the in-laws at the first onslaught of hot winds and blizzard cold, or plagues, whether locusts or Mormon crickets.

It seems increasingly important that we understand as much as possible about the men and the events that made our country, not only about the generals and their battles, the politicians and statesmen and rascals, but about the ordinary settler and his family. Perhaps the true color of our country comes from those who went out, or were pushed out, to follow on the heels of the bold frontiersmen as they moved on to the excitement of new game to kill, new aborigines to marry or to fight.

While Mr. Robertson is no stylist, he tells his story with considerable frankness, wry humor and off-hand understatement, even in some of those appalling situations that were so common in the lives of the High Country.

Mari Sandoz

October 10, 1958

Introduction

On the dust jacket of the 1959 edition of *A Ram in the Thicket: The Story of a Roaming Homesteader Family on the Mormon Frontier*, Nebraska writer Mari Sandoz predicted that Frank Robertson's family biography would still be "good reading fifty years from now." *A Ram in the Thicket*, she continued, combines the particulars of one man's time and place with the universals of the human experience to create a work of broad interest and lasting value. Almost immediately, *The Reader's Digest*'s decision to offer Robertson's "fascinating story" to its "millions of readers" confirmed its broad appeal, and now, nearly a half-century after the initial edition appeared in 1950, the University of Idaho Press reprint edition is convincing evidence that in this as in so much else Sandoz was on target.

Robertson's *A Ram in the Thicket* was then and still remains a significant contribution to what might be called High Country regionalism. Portraying the Robertson family in honest and graphic detail, *A Ram in the Thicket* is conscious of place, exceptional in candor, and penetrating in insight. The warp and woof of pioneering is there. It is the chronicle of a poor family in what Robertson's father called "a poor man's country." It is a story of failed dreams, of elusive comfort, of status that won't jell, of sacrificed schooling, of sickness and injury, of unremitting toil, of frayed nerves, of chronic anger and eruptive conflict, of exploitation, and, at times, of abuse. But it is also a testament of good will, of personal growth, of family loyalty, of community, of deep faith, and of satisfaction in service. Finally, it is an affirmation that tolerance, gentleness, and a penchant for getting on with life can prevail. In evidence, too, is Robertson's ability to characterize individuals, groups, and events and his sense of the cultural character as well as the physical makeup of the region in which he lived.

Frank Robertson was raised at the high tide of the Progressive Era. Frontier doctrines of masculinity and Anglo-American predominance were ascendant. But in *A Ram in the Thicket* he wrote with surprising modernity. His father, Will, is shown to be nearly as determined a male chauvinist as Jules Sandoz, Mari Sandoz's father, if not quite as successful in making chauvinism stick. Conditioned by the dominant role of her father, about whom she wrote in *Old Jules* (1935), Sandoz's introduction to the 1959 edition of *A Ram in the Thicket* is couched in masculine terms. Will Robertson, she held, was partly an "Old Testament patriarch," partly a Mormon "father," but mostly an "old-time horse trader and snake-oil man." Beyond this, the point of Sandoz's introduction is that *A Ram in the Thicket* helps readers understand more of the "men," more of the "ordinary settler." Nothing is said in Sandoz's introduction about Mary Robertson, who looms large in Frank Robertson's own accounting. The son saw his mother as a "man's woman" who, without an ounce of sex appeal, attracted close confidants among the community men, won lasting respect in homestead district debates, and enjoyed a wide reputation as a redoubtable Bible scholar and country preacher. In no way does Robertson present her as a secondary figure or member of a less endowed class. Other women are also shown to good effect in *A Ram in the Thicket*. This is especially true of prostitutes who treated young "Slim" Robertson with kindness and compassion in his most footloose days. Similarly, Indians and ethnic groups are treated with surprisingly modern tolerance and real appreciation, if only incidentally, since the Robertson story is clearly about the homestead and the Mormon frontier.

As a Mormon biography, *A Ram in the Thicket* is strikingly different. To begin with, it is slightly out of synch in its degenderized "ram in the thicket" title, which is used as a metaphor for something-will-turn-up rather than as a patriarchal idiom, its common Mormon application. Less subtle distinctions appear in its penetrating characterizations of Mormon businessmen as materialistic and in its indictment of Mormon young people as overindulged, worldly, and lacking in humility. An even more striking departure appears in Robertson's suggestion that Mormonism was a culture of two faces, one pious and Christian for world consumption and a home face that was sometimes profoundly status conscious, if indeed not contentious, coarse, intolerant, and uncharitable.

Equally important in setting *A Ram in the Thicket* apart as a work of Mormon biography is the fact that it strips away much of Mormondom's isolation. In Mary and Will Robertson, Campbellite persuasions and old style religion continue to play an important part even after their conversion to the Church of Jesus Christ of Latter-day Saints. Although Mormonism was a special blessing to the least-admirable member of the family, Will Robertson, in whom it gradually produced something quite like the metamorphosis portrayed in Mormon convert lore, Mary Robertson accepted the Mormon scriptures and Joseph Smith as a prophet and reluctantly "gathered to Zion" without undergoing any great change as the gospel light worked upon her. The sons found much to resist in both the society and the doctrine of the new religion. Belonging far more to the restless High Country work force than to the Church's isolated community, the Robertson boys nevertheless had more in common with a large fraternity of backsliding Mormon youngsters than the folk history and biography of Mormondom has admitted. Moreover, the homesteading Robertsons were part of the moving frontier in a most un-Mormon way. Indeed, at times they appear to be more like wagon tramps, after the fashion of the turn-of-the-century characters in H. L. Davis's superb regional novel, *Honey in the Horn* (1935), than like the ordered Mormon columns of earlier days or the Mormon Country water promoters and land speculators of the early twentieth century. Finally, the bonds of kinship find an altogether different expression in Frank's honest assessment of self and family than in the filiopietism that characterizes much Mormon biography. Less ostensibly touched by God and less consciously the founders of a noble generation, the Robertsons emerge as more believable if less infallible than the subjects of many Mormon biographies.

All in all, *A Ram in the Thicket* is a superb piece of work. Good reading when it first came to light, it is among a class that University of Oregon historian Richard Maxwell Brown calls "grassroots biography" that retains its appeal after many years. It is a fitting capstone for the career of one of the High Country West's many remarkable sons and daughters. As Sandoz was perhaps aware when she wrote in the 1950s, it is a work that rivals her own *Old Jules* as one of the West's great pieces of regionalism.

Frank Robertson's background as it unfolds so effectively in *A Ram in the Thicket* could hardly have better prepared him to speak for the High Country region. Born in 1890 at Moscow, Idaho, he homesteaded, hoboed, and "pillared and posted" his way over Idaho and Utah before literally writing his family through the hard times of the post–World War I collapse, the Great Depression, World War II, the Cold War, and into the agony of post-Vietnamese adjustment that was changing so much about how America viewed itself when he died in 1969. From the first short story in 1922 until his death, Robertson authored upward of 150 books and uncounted short stories, which sold as well in Europe as in the United States. This productivity brought him a five-digit income year after year, which allowed him to live in comfort as well as to provide a financial umbrella for the extended Robertson family.

The bread and butter of his literary output was western fiction that followed a fixed romantic formula. A sampling of his vast output suggests that most of it was aimed at a continuing interest in the mythic West. Through it violence ran rampant, lives were casually taken, and right and wrong were sharply distinguished. Not surprisingly, little attention was given to mere matters of conscience, guilt, or the complex mix of human impulse and character that play such an important role in *A Ram in the Thicket*. During the high tide of this productivity, Robertson took pride in the fact that he repeatedly published one million words a year. In time he came to be an important figure in western and Utah writing circles and for decades published a regular feature in the *Provo Herald* that attracted a devoted readership and led many to call him "the Sage of Mapleton." Under pressure he was known occasionally to turn out novels in as little as a week. This industry he plied from headquarters near Chesterfield in southern Idaho and then successively in Ogden, Salt Lake City, and finally Springville and Mapleton, south of Provo, Utah. He worked through book agents and was published in perhaps a hundred periodicals, which varied from the pious and staid *Improvement Era* of the Mormon Church to the socialist outlets of his radical youth and pulp westerns, as well as by scores of publishing houses. Many of the latter were in England, Germany, Holland, and elsewhere in Europe. His own experience and a family gift for a well-turned yarn stood him in good stead, providing new adventures to exploit and giving an extraordinary accuracy to his treatment of geography and place.

In addition to the regionalist's instinct that kept him close to what he had experienced, he had a keen sense for markets, and after the day of the successful television westerns, he turned an honest dollar from books with titles such as *Rawhide* (1961) and *A Man Called Paladin* (1963), which apparently were first printed by American publishing houses and must have been authorized by the television series in whose momentum they trafficked.

Now housed at Brigham Young University, his personal library of his own works runs to many feet of shelf space and nearly fills a card index drawer. Yet for all his industry and the impressive shelves of books, Frank Robertson is little known in the West of the 1990s. How does one account for it? In part it may have been the man's utter unpretentiousness. Or perhaps it was that after all he was a Robertson, still a family member, before he was anything else. In part it may also have related to his lack of connection with any established institution or intellectual community. He completed no more than eight grades in school, and part of that was apparently by default. What he knew was acquired from his parents and the school of hard knocks, from radicals met along the dusty workingman byways of the West, or from personal reading of anything he could lay his hands on. He had no mentor to mold and direct his mind or to sponsor and promote him as he entered professional or learned circles. Influences that were shaping generations of young Westerners at universities throughout the land at best had an indirect influence upon him, or, more probably, passed him by entirely. Exposed to socialism during his bindle stiff years, he lacked travel abroad or experience in any intellectual group that might have allowed socialist ideas to jell and become a lasting influence. Because his career was well advanced, he was passed over by even the Federal Writers' Project of the 1930s that did so much for the development of other regional writers, including Vardis Fisher and Dale Morgan, respectively project directors in Idaho and Utah.

In addition, Robertson's status as a writer was influenced by the fact that he broke from the workaday reality of the western romance in only a handful of more serious regional works. Of these, there can be little doubt that *A Ram in the Thicket* is the most important, but three others seem equally important in understanding what made Frank Robertson tick. A brief discussion comparing them with other works of regional significance may help place him in perspective.

First to appear was *The Rocky Road to Jericho* (1935), a work in regional fiction of an almost documentary nature in the adherence of its plot and development to the Mormon experience. Published by Hillman-Curl Inc. of New York, it appeared under the name of Frank Chester Field, which at this distance seems an effort to proclaim his Mormon ties locally but obscure them on national and international markets. Set around the tensions of the Mormon migration, *Rocky Road* follows a Mormon convert through various experiences in the Midwest, including a love affair that founders in the sinister schemes of a materialistic and lustful elder. Once in Utah, the protagonist stumbles into the deepening shoals of conflict between brotherly love and the harsh authoritarianism of Mormon culture. Ultimately, his blood is spilled by a fanatic neighbor in a ritual killing to atone for the protagonist's lapses in obedience. Together with Robertson's later connections with Springville, this outcome suggests that he was responding to certain unsolved murders at Springville during the tense times of the Utah War, when the United States sent an army to repress alleged Mormon disloyalty in 1857 to 1858.

Serious artistic and social commentary though it is, *Rocky Road* signaled no great change in Robertson's career. Other Mormon fiction did not follow, and no shift to writing for what might be called the public discourse occurred. Fuller research will reveal just how the book was received in the mid-Depression years. Certainly it failed to make the splash that fellow Idahoan Vardis Fisher's *Children of God* (1939) produced four years later when it won the Harper Prize. In retrospect, it seems fair to say that *Rocky Road* was undeserving of a prize. The plot is neither polished nor particularly convincing, and Robertson's command of the Mormon past, while sound in the general sense, errs in some of its detail to the extent that it flaws the book seriously. It is worth noting, however, that to a history-interested reader of the 1990s, Fisher's *Children of God* suffers from the same shortcomings, to a degree that seems roughly comparable to Robertson's *Rocky Road*. On the other hand, Robertson's story is more narrowly construed, addressing certain tensions within Mormon society rather than undertaking a general portrait of the Mormon saga as Fisher's work did.

If *Rocky Road* was flawed, Robertson's *Fort Hall: Gateway to the Oregon Country* (1963) is sound factually and well reasoned. It seems likely that it also lay much nearer the man's heart. It was at nearby Chesterfield and on the ranches, irrigation projects, and railroads of the Fort Hall area that Frank Robertson spent his formative years. Indeed, his own life is something of a metaphor for the way in which he sees Yankee and British competition for the Northwest converging at Fort Hall. As his cowboy father's Texas, his mother's stable Nebraska, and his poor man's beginnings in the Moscow area lay before the Fort Hall bottoms of his boyhood, and the sheepherding, High Country roughnecking, writing, and Utah living lay ahead, Fort Hall formed the meeting place for the "course of empire." More than a mere junction on the way west or even a gateway, it was the chief pawn in a regional chess game played out between the Hudson's Bay Company and American development. Robertson traces this interpretive point through the fur trade, the opening of the trail, the development of missionary activity, overland migration, the Gold Rush, Indian relations, mining and livestock frontiers, and the introduction of dry farm and project agriculture.

With this carefully developed interpretation, *Fort Hall* impresses one as legitimate history, although it is offered in a popular format, as Colorado state historian and Brigham Young University professor LeRoy Hafen noted in his forward to the book. In *Fort Hall,* Robertson depends heavily upon the anecdotal as he serves up secondary accounts and personal observations. He substitutes textual citations for footnotes, and mistakes appear here and there (like calling P. E. Connor a general before 1863). Furthermore, *Fort Hall* avoids the heavy prose that often characterizes scholarly treatises. In looking for comparables that combine historical soundness with popular appeal, one is tempted to place *Fort Hall* in pretty distinguished company. Often Robertson's writing smacks of a Bernard De Voto or a David Lavender, and he clearly possesses their penchant for romantic narrative, well-turned phrases, and precision and grace in word choice. His mix of personal involvement, broad regional interpretations, accepted nostalgic sources, and popularization of his topic make *Fort Hall* good history.

Moreover, Robertson characterizes people succinctly and vividly. Once having struck an image, he successfully maintains it as the book proceeds, embellishing and enlarging rather than lapsing into redundancy or losing impact. John McLoughlin, who contacted most Americans as the chief factor at the Hudson's Bay Company's Fort Vancouver, is sustained as true aristocrat and company loyalist, but first and last he is responsive to Christian duty as a man. Again and again this leads him to treat the invading Yankee settlers well. His superior, George Simpson, on the other hand, comes across as churlish and narrowly procompany. Nathaniel Wyeth, Boston iceman and original builder of Fort Hall, is broad-gauge, stable, and effective and possesses a strong sense of regional strategy. The Grants, who manage Fort Hall after the HBC takeover, are savvy in Indian relations, dependable, and fair in trade. Captain Bonneville, about whom Washington Irving wrote, is portrayed as loyal American, far ranging but playboyish, if indeed not foppish. The Blackfeet are characterized as fierce warriors. The Bannocks are less renowned but able to give a good account of themselves. And the Shoshones are Robertson's close friends; survivors in their own right and often wise, they are almost always admirable. Presbyterian missionaries Narcissa and Marcus Whitman come off well, as does Methodist Jason Lee. Other Protestant missionaries do not.

Robertson's treatment of Indians is surprisingly enlightened, well ahead of the times for 1960. He seems reluctantly willing to write about their raids and murders in the pejorative parlance of the early 1900s, but always one finds sympathy and understanding—for example, at one point he attributes their survival to a determined sense of humor that softened the almost impossible reverses they experienced. Robertson's Native Americans coexist with the HBC fur trade, which was synonymous with British Indian policy, because it leaves them in possession of the land. They resist the American approach because it involves settlement and loss of the land. This, of course, is not news, but for the early 1960s it is tellingly set forth in *Fort Hall*.

Brigham D. Madsen, the University of Utah's distinguished historian of "the Snake River Country," sums up the book effectively: "This is not an account that gives the reader a detailed picture of life inside the Fort . . . but [one that] is written from the vantage point of Boston, Washington, D. C., Fort Vancouver, and Sutter's Fort. It is a wide-ranging, deep-probing narrative, concerned with Fort Hall as the junction point of the Oregon and California Trails." In it, Robertson "paints on a broad canvas, with Spaniards, Russians, English, and Americans all vying for control of a vast, rich, and fertile land with only Mcloughlin, among the Britishers, apparently aware of the importance of farming the soil." The trouble with other Britishers, as Robertson astutely points out and Madsen wryly quotes, "was that their fur caps came down over their eyes, and they could see nothing but fur." As Madsen concludes, "Robertson goes far beyond the typical fur trade history of the area to give a new interpretation of Fort Hall as playing a significant role in the struggle of the British and the Americans to gain control of the Northwest. And he does so while at the same time avoiding pompous and dry history. . . . Many readers may not realize that they have been introduced to a scholarly treatise; it is so far removed from typical dull and academic studies." High praise indeed but well deserved.

Brief reference may also be made to a third departure from the West of romance and myth, *Boom Towns of the Great Basin* (1962). Robertson was nothing if he was not independent. This shows up especially in his writing, but on occasion he did jointly author fictional works with his brother Oba, and in the early 1960s he worked with Beth Kay Harris, notably collaborating with her on *Boom Towns*. Shifting from Robertson's High Country orientation to pair Utah with Nevada, *Boom Towns* is a tour guide and a popularly directed impression of the little-known and rarely traveled region that was beginning to be triangulated between Salt Lake City, Las Vegas, and Reno, cities which were coming into their own as a postwar industrial vacationland center on the one hand and gambling mecca extensions of California's millions on the other. Like *Fort Hall* and Robertson's literary response to the popular television westerns, *Boom Towns* reflects a highly individualistic kind of economic imperialism on the authors' part and defines a vast desert region in terms that responded to what the Great Basin was becoming culturally.

Like *Fort Hall*, Robertson and Harris's *Boom Towns* spreads a broad net. It is fast paced and journalistic in style—often assuming something of a *National Geographic* tone and is not too concerned with its sources and ultimate soundness. Salt Lake City journalist William Smart takes exception to mistakes made in dealing with the Salt Lake City end of the Basin (Bingham, the Cottonwood Canyons, Park City, Garfield, and Magna and other smelting towns) but assumes that the two authors hit their pace as they move west and south through Tintic, Frisco, and Silver Reef in Utah and Pioche, Delamare, and the other boom towns of eastern Nevada, as well as the grand strikes of Washoe and Comstock. No question, it is a rollicking account. Calculated to maintain motion as visitors drive desert distances, it is highly anecdotal—a good story never languishes in the file no matter how it stretches credulity. On the other hand, the serious reader detects an interpretive sophistication even here. "Boom towns," as a phrase and as anchored by the Great Basin's triangulated centers, rings surprisingly like the "instant cities" of University of California urban historian Gunther Barth. In significant ways it also foreshadows the provocative insights advanced in *East of Eden West of Zion: Essays on Nevada* (1989), edited by University of Nevada at Reno history professor Wilbur S. Shepperson. But looked at more generally, *Boom Towns*, like most guidebooks and impressionistic responses, was probably not expected to have more than a half-life of a decade or so, after which it could rightly be relegated to the growing pile of rarely-referred-to state and regional guides. In fairness, however, it should be said that in qualities that make for staying power, it doesn't lag too far behind the state guide volumes of the Federal Writers' Project, not even the often praised Utah and Idaho volumes to which Dale Morgan and Vardis Fisher contributed heavily.

In sum, it may be said that Robertson's life story is a kind of regional history in itself, and his writing is surely grounded in those experiences. He worked diligently; he found what would sell; and he was ultimately read by American and European audiences. Yet little attention has been given him since his death. Without disciples to celebrate his work and with few institutional attachments, he has been virtually unremembered, a dilemma confronting regionalists generally in the post-Vietnam era of global interests and concern with current relevance, in contrast to the escapism and romance of the Wild West narrative of which Robertson was a master. Now, with a vigorous resurgence in western regionalism underway, one hopes that the reprinted *A Ram in the Thicket* will attract a wide readership; that Robertson's work will receive appropriate scholarly attention; that a biography of Robertson is in the offing; and that at some future time, courtesy of the University of Idaho Press, we may see Fort Hall in a new edition and, perhaps, a sampling of Robertson's best romances. Here's to the Chesterfield sheepherder turned western writer and sometime biographer. May his works enjoy a second "half-life" that extends far into the future.

CHARLES S. PETERSON
Professor Emeritus Utah State University
Professor of History Southern Utah University
October 21, 1993

1

My father and mother considered themselves farmers, but they seldom owned a farm. During a good share of my boyhood our home was a covered wagon. Mother was a former schoolteacher, and Father an ex-cowboy. Neither would have felt at home anywhere except on the fringe of the frontier. From the beginning of their marriage they seemed doomed to failure, and financially they were; yet, success has many faces.

My father was driven from one move to another by the twin devils of restlessness and discontent, and my mother accepted each move with the hope that it would be the last, but fortified by faith that whatever happened could be endured. She believed that in the last extremity the Lord would provide a ram in the thicket.

From her preacher father she inherited not only deep religious faith and a fine sense of justice and fair-dealing, but an instinctive culture which kept her, in spite of discouraging hardships, from ever becoming hard, coarse, or cynical. She grew old gracefully. My father started to grow up when he was about seventy-five.

My parents were strong people. They lived in a period of the frontier that has been generally overlooked by the historians of the West. This is largely their story, although they did raise three sons, including me.

My father, William Hugh Robertson, was born October 6, 1852, at Alton, Illinois. Of eight children, only he and two younger brothers grew to manhood. His grandfather, Hugh Robertson, had been born in the ancestral home in North Carolina, in 1794, resided in Tennessee and Kentucky for a time, and died in that part of Illinois known as Little Egypt. Old Hugh's wife was supposed to have brought with her a small strain of Cherokee Indian blood.

My grandfather, John Robertson, was for his day a successful farmer. He raised corn and hogs; selling the corn to the whisky distilleries in St. Louis and fattening his hogs on the sour mash they gave back to him without charge.

Father, then, was a stranger to the poverty with which he was to become so familiar in later life. His boyhood was completely normal. He learned to ride a horse almost as soon as he could walk, and excelled at swimming and skating.

Unfortunately, Grandfather Robertson had a liking for the whisky which his corn helped to make. Easy-going when sober, he became quarrelsome when drunk and my father got many a thrashing. One stormy night Grandfather put Father on a horse and sent him to town for a bottle of whisky. The horse fell, Father's foot was caught in the stirrup, and he was all but dragged to death. Frightened by this event, Grandfather swore off whisky for good, but he and Father never became friends.

Father always believed that Grandfather was partial to one of the two younger boys.

My father cherished another grudge against his father. Once during the Civil War when one of the children was sick, Grandfather, an ardent Southerner, got into an argument with the doctor, an equally ardent Union man, and so delayed things that by the time the doctor arrived in the house the child was dead.

What with Grandmother and her people being damned Yankees, all was not peace and harmony in the Robertson household during those troublesome years. Father's two brothers spoke with a Southern accent all their lives, while Father shed the soil and the language of the South at the first opportunity.

Grandmother never let her husband have any peace, with a determined demand that they go West and get free land for the boys. The first venture was to Lawrence, Kansas, where Grandfather got involved in the pre-war struggle over slavery and got shot in the leg. Having previously been shot in the buttocks in the Mexican War—a feat he had difficulty explaining the rest of his life—Grandfather decided he'd had enough of violence and returned to Illinois.

In no manner discouraged, Grandmother kept after him with the lure of free land until the war was well over and Father was sixteen years old. The family then moved to Texas and settled near what is now Archer City. From the very first, Father shared General Phil Sheridan's opinion that given the choice between hell and Texas he would take hell. The first mesquite had scarcely been cleared away to build a house when Father and Grandfather got into a squabble, and Father left home, never to return.

Whatever his father had been Will Robertson seemed determined not to be. John Robertson had liked his whisky, so son William would never take a drink. Grandfather was a crack shot with a gun, so in later life Father would never have one in his house. Grandfather belonged to no church and never attended services, so Father reverenced religion. There was seldom a time in Father's life that he wasn't against something or somebody.

Those days saw the beginnings of the famous cattle drives from Texas, across the treacherous Red and Cimarron rivers through Indian Territory up to the notorious frontier towns of Kansas. Father hired out as a cowboy for the Belcher Stock Company of Henrietta, Texas.

How many trips up the cattle trails through The Nations Father made I am not sure. He must have made three or four in the period between 1870 and 1875, and was familiar with Wichita, Abilene, Hayes City, and Dodge. For the most part they were hell-roaring places, which he didn't like, but he always resented the claims that the cowboys were all hard-drinking gunmen. A few, he always insisted, gave the tag to many. I have heard him describe Wild Bill Hickok, who was no hero in Father's eyes. He was in Wichita at the time Wyatt Earp was marshal. He was well acquainted with Judge Ed Jewett there, and must have seen Earp many times though I never heard him mention Earp's name.

As a teetotaler and nongambler, something very rare for the time and place, Father looked with a disapproving eye upon all the frontier swashbucklers.

It was the hard work and daily danger of the trail that Father used to talk about most. Stampedes were of course a common occurrence and a cowboy occasionally got killed, but the real peril was getting caught in a mill in a swollen river: he saw more than one of his friends drown.

The danger from Indians he always claimed was exaggerated. At that time Father owned a six-shooter, but I doubt if he ever fired it. In fact, I remember his saying that he only got it out of the bedwagon on one occasion when a band of seemingly hostile Indians cut off the herd. Fearing that they were Comanches, everybody hustled to the wagon for the little used guns, but the Indians turned out to be Osages who were merely demanding a few cows as tribute for crossing their land.

When in later life Father became familiar with the life of the late Will Rogers he recalled having stayed overnight several times with the Rogers and Howard families as he was going back to Texas after the trail drive with his friend Luther Clark.

But the one time he considered his life to be in real danger, though he had no idea of it then, was when he and a companion stayed overnight with a family named Bender. As they sat at a long table he wondered why there was a calico curtain at their backs. The waitress was a husky girl named Kate. Father was shaken when he read later that more than a dozen men had been murdered at that place, the executioner being Kate Bender, who swung on the victims from behind that curtain with an ax.

Yearning for a more peaceful sort of life, Father quit the cattle trails and went to Wichita, where he and a friend invested their small savings in a photograph gallery. The venture, the only one in which Father ever held an interest in his life, was ill-starred and the amateur photographers soon went broke. One of the tintypes they took was of Father himself with his feet cocked up on a chair and almost hiding his bearded young face.

About this time Father became acquainted with Winfield Scott Matthews, starting a family friendship which carried over into my generation. Win Matthews became the closest friend Father was ever to have. Win and his father owned a flour mill, and Father went to work for them. Win was the son-in-law of Judge Jewett, though he was soon to be a widower. Father at this time was restless and fiddle-footed and needed Win's stabilizing influence.

The elder Matthews, however, was a restless, adventuresome type who could never stay put, and when he and Win moved to Nebraska Father soon followed them. The first winter sixteen of them lived in a one-room sod shanty. It was in Nebraska that my parents met, and my two older brothers were born there.

My mother was born July 16, 1850, at Shelbyville, Indiana. When she was three years old Grandfather Matthews—no relation to Win Matthews—moved to South English, a little town in Iowa where Mother grew up.

Grandfather Matthews was a tall, thin, gentle man who became a Campbellite preacher while still in his teens. The only picture I have of him shows a kindly, benevolent face with a long flowing white beard and a shaven upper lip. He was born in Kentucky in 1807, and early in life married a cultured woman who wrote poetry and died early, leaving him three small daughters. Soon afterward he married Harriet Stone, my grandmother; a plain, unpretentious farm girl who bore him four more daughters—my mother was the youngest—and a son.

Tunstal Quareles Matthews, who rarely received any money for preaching, practiced the trade of shoemaker and otherwise eked out his income by serving as postmaster and justice of the peace. Though a man of peace, Grandfather Matthews had the courage of his convictions. He belonged to Sons of Temperance in a day when a nondrinker was considered a milksop. He hated slavery and for many years helped runaway slaves to escape to Canada over what was called the underground railroad.

On one occasion during the Civil War a large body of Southern sympathizers called "copperheads," led by a man named Tally, invaded South English. As they paraded up the street three wagons abreast, Tally, a gun in one hand and a knife in the other, shouted, "Cowards! Cowards!" The Union men rushed to a blacksmith shop where their guns were stored and a battle seemed imminent. Grandfather Matthews walked out unarmed between the two factions urging them to avoid trouble. As he turned his back on the copperheads to address his own people he heard a shot fired by Tally, then another fired by a disabled Union soldier, and Tally fell dead. The copperheads fled and the battle was over, but Grandfather had risked his life trying to prevent bloodshed.

My mother had no opportunity to attend college, or even high school, but at the age of sixteen she passed a teacher's examination. Her first job was on the blizzard-swept prairies of South Dakota at a salary of twenty dollars a month.

Her father having grown old by the time she started to teach, she became the main support of her parents. Though one sister had died of "consumption," the others had married well: one to a doctor; the others to preachers or well-to-do farmers. Mary, the youngest, was the one on whom the burden fell.

Teaching in those days was not easy. The teacher had to rotate from family to family each week. Mostly, the food was poor, and often the teacher shared a bed with several of her girl pupils. When the blizzards came it was often necessary for the teacher to keep her frightened charges at the schoolhouse all night, or until help arrived. Mother never spoke of these things as unusual or out of the ordinary.

The years passed, and by the standards of her day Mother became an old maid. Her parents had moved to Nebraska, and it was there she became acquainted with Win Matthews and, through him, with my father.

Twice-widowed Win Matthews had brought his colorful cowboy friend to prayer meeting, and Will Robertson sat down beside Mary Matthews. Preacher's daughter that she was, Mother moved away from him as far as she could, having been led to believe that cowboys were tough characters. Their big hats and jingling spurs were symbols of iniquity. Yet she may have been secretly thrilled by her proximity to such a sinner.

Then the first hymn was announced and the quavery voices of the congregation, without benefit of organ or chorister, began the doleful strains of a favorite old hymn.

Suddenly, a loud, golden voice began to lead the singing. Startled, Mother and the others looked around, but they finished the hymn with more enthusiasm than their little church had ever known. That voice belonged to Father. He liked to sing and he liked to sing loud, and if in group singing the others couldn't keep up with him that was too bad for the group.

Whatever was to be between them probably began right there. Mother must have thought: *Surely, a man who can sing gospel hymns with such sincerity and enthusiasm must be a good man.*

Win introduced them after the meeting and left them alone while he went in search of Belle Stillman, the young widow whom he was then courting.

Father was something entirely new in Mother's experience. Undoubtedly her own quiet, peaceful life must have seemed dull compared to the one he had led. He thrilled her with tales of the range and the trails and the tough towns he had been around, of the drinking and fighting and gambling he had seen, and he made dark allusions to still greater vices, which, she knew, involved women.

He told her he had quit punching cows because of the rough and sinful life most cowboys led, and he won her approval by saying that although his parents had never belonged to any church he was religious by nature.

He had had very little schooling, but he was eager to learn, and that was where she could help him. At twenty-eight, she was intellectually mature; he, at twenty-six, in spite of his wider experience, was immature.

When she announced her intention to marry the former Texas cowhand, Mother was beset by her sisters and their husbands with dire predictions of disaster. But Mother had a will of her own: they were married.

Before long Mother realized that some of those warnings had been well founded. Father was a gadabout whose clutching fingers always missed success. Poverty she was used to, and didn't mind, but she wanted Will to settle down, and it just wasn't in his nature to settle down.

He was always an energetic and efficient worker and employers were anxious to hire him, but farm wages were not sufficient to support a family. With Win Matthews's aid he tried farming, but could never make ends meet. He built track for the railroad and had the misfortune to break a leg. He went from job to job, and was often out of work. Meantime, Grandfather Matthews had died, and Grandmother came to live with Mary.

Nebraska was still a pioneer state, and its rural population expected to make their fortunes by thrift and hard work and staying qualities. Father was short on the first and last of those virtues. He feuded with most of his neighbors and one move followed another.

Mother's well married sisters and their husbands, especially the sharp-tongued doctor, were critical of Father and loud in resentment. Each of the sisters counted Mother, with the possible exception of herself, the pride of the flock. Her poverty caused them to dislike Father even more, a feeling he returned with an unbridled violence which confirmed their misgivings about him. Father never expected to inherit the earth through meekness.

He had an ungovernable temper which could change him in an instant from a jovial, pleasant companion to a roaring incarnation of fury at the drop of a thoughtless word, and Mother had constantly to be on guard lest his tender feelings be hurt. Before my oldest brother Chauncey was born Father had become quarrelsome.

It was particularly bad when my brother Oba was born. Father was out of work, the weather was bad, and the doctor-brother-in-law was needlessly insulting. It seemed to Father that if the doctor was so well off he might have contributed to Grandma's support, even though she was only step-mother to his wife.

Mother didn't blame Father for losing his temper when everything seemed to go wrong, and she could endure his treatment of her, but it was hard to forgive him for taking it out on the baby. Obe was afraid of Father and cried every time he approached, which, of course, infuriated him. When Obe was little more than six months old Father tried to cure this flaw in Obe's character by giving him a whipping with a strap.

Mother started to leave Father then, even wrapping her personal belongings in a bundle, but she couldn't go through with it. Her religious training had taught her that the marriage relationship was sacred. Only weak women would resort to divorce. Like the Biblical Ruth she would say, "Whither thou goest, I will go."

She had practical as well as idealistic reasons for keeping her family together. If she left Father she would have to accept the charity of her sisters and pride would not permit her to do that. If Father had been a lazy man or a drunkard her decision might have been even harder to make—but he was not. For a man who was always willing to work there was hope.

Win Matthews had followed his roving father to the panhandle of Idaho in the far West. Both my parents missed their staunch friend, and his letters constantly urged them to come out. Conditions would never get better for them in Nebraska, they knew. When Father said, "I'm going, Mary. I'll send for you and the boys just as soon as I can earn enough money, and we'll start a new life," she said simply, "We'll come when you send for us."

It would be a wrench, she knew. In spite of Father's differences with them, she felt great affection for her sisters and their families, and worst of all she would have to leave her mother behind. Poor people didn't travel long distances just to visit, and she knew in her heart that when she left Nebraska she would never see any of her family again. It was breaking these ties that hurt, but she had no fear of plunging into the unknown.

They did without all they possibly could until Father saved enough to buy a ticket to Moscow, Idaho. A few months later he sent money to bring out Mother and the boys, and they were ready. The Robertsons were on the move. It was to become a chronic condition.

2

When my mother moved to Idaho, in 1888, a couple of emigrant cars were a feature of every train. The fare was low; the people brought most of their food and slept in their seats. Trains were slow and Mother and her two small boys were nearly a week making the trip.

The only unusual incident of the journey concerned my brother Oba, whose name by that time had been shortened to Obe. At Cheyenne the train stopped for an hour or so and the children of the emigrant car were taken for a tour of the station. A ten-year-old girl appointed herself supervisor of the group. Chubby little Obe, the youngest of the party, was the tail-end of the procession, except when being shepherded along by the leader.

Suddenly the engine whistled and there was a wild stampede to get back on the train. Obe, with his short legs, was left far behind. The whistle blew again. Convinced that he would never be able to make it he gave a wild cry and struck out down the tracks determined to beat the train to the next station, which was Laramie, about a hundred miles away. Fortunately, the ten-year-old supervisor saw him in desperate flight and overhauled him just as he was passing the engine.

Father was waiting in Moscow with a borrowed wagon to take them twenty miles back into the mountains to a place called Bear Creek, where he had spent the winter with the Matthews family helping Win chop cordwood. After a few days with the Matthewses, the family moved into a single-room log cabin by themselves. There were few neighbors, no school and no church. For the first time in her life Mother couldn't go to meeting on Sunday. But the change from the flat prairies she had lived on all her life to the rolling mountains covered by tall and stately pine, fir, and tamarack trees was pleasing rather than otherwise to her; it brought out a latent spirit of adventure and a desire to see new things.

That winter the snow had been six feet deep. Cougars prowled. Every night they could hear the weird howls of the timber wolves, but physical fear had never been part of the make-up of my mother and brothers and they were undisturbed. Sometimes Mother wished that Father had a gun but he would never have one in the house. Even when riding the range he had always left his six-shooter in the chuck-wagon.

As for the boys, they quickly found a pleasing manner of diversion—especially my brother Chauncey. There were numerous pine saplings close to the cabin. While one of the boys climbed to the precarious top the other chopped away at the base of the tree with a hatchet until the sapling bent gracefully to the ground, giving the boy in the treetop an exhilarating ride back to earth. Obe was always careful of his strokes so that the tree never fell too suddenly, but Chauncey was fond of giving one final, hearty blow, so that Obe's descent was often quick and violent. If he happened to be on the under side of the tree there was nothing to protect him from a hard and bruising thump. In a way this set the pattern of my brothers' lives.

Father's wages were small and he felt constantly frustrated. He talked of opportunities but never seemed to catch them, and the family rows soon began where they had left off.

Win Matthews moved back to the edge of the prairie, some six miles from Moscow, and thence Father soon followed him. The winter of 1889–90 found the Robertsons living near an abandoned sawmill site in a one-room slab shack, with a small lean-to in which my brothers slept. There I was born; unfortunately, I timed my arrival in the midst of a family row.

In the middle of the night Mother nudged Father, and said, "It's my time, Will. You'll have to build a fire and go get Belle."

"How long have you been havin' them pains?" Father demanded.

"Quite a while now. This is no false alarm."

"You're a fool, Mary Robertson," Father growled. "Always tryin' to keep things to yourself. That's why we never get along."

He jumped out of bed and pranced across the cold floor to the stove; he slept in his shirt and the red flannel drawers and undershirt Mother had made for him. He soon had the stove roaring. He always built a fire the same way, thrusting ready-made shavings into the fire-box, covering them with split kindling wood of pitch-pine, then dousing it all plentifully with kerosene and dropping in a match. It took him no more than a minute before he could hop back into bed. Mother always expected him to burn the house down.

Shavings and kindling always had to be ready the night before, a task assigned to my brother Obe. A couple of nights before he'd forgotten the chore; Father had jerked him out of bed, given him half a dozen licks with his razor strap, and sent him out in the bitter cold of the woodshed to split the kindlings while Mother cowered in fear that he would cut himself with the razor-sharp ax. She dared not let her sympathy overcome her, for Father insisted upon discipline. If she had interfered, Obe's punishment would have been worse.

This night Father did not go back to bed. In a jiffy he had on his trousers, his heavy German socks and rubbers, mackinaw coat and denim-faced mittens which Mother had knitted and faced for him. This night he needed all the heavy clothing he could get, for it was the night of January 12th, and the thermometer registered forty below zero.

He closed the damper, choked the stove full of wood, then asked gruffly, "You think you'll be all right till I get back?"

"I'll have to be," Mother said, "but you had better hurry."

He looked down upon her thin face. It was no longer young. She would be forty on her next birthday and her life had been hard. Her fine, silky light-brown hair was beginning to gray. Now her lips were blue and twisted with pain, but the hard, belligerent look in Father's blue eyes didn't soften. Many times he was kindness itself, but no such trivial thing as the birth of a child was going to interfere with a family row.

"It's your own fault," he said harshly. "What makes you act the way you do? You had that last miscarriage out in the privy, and if Belle hadn't told me about it I'd never have known you had it. It's a wonder you didn't die."

There, at least, he was right. Mother never tried any more to explain why she tried to keep her personal problems to herself. She knew that she would be sure to say something that would ignite the fire of his rage.

With a snort that plainly accused her of having picked out the coldest night of the winter in which to have her baby he grabbed the water bucket and went out to the well. She could hear the protesting squall of the pulley through the thin walls.

When he came in, she said, "Maybe you'd better put the baby's things to warm on the oven door and drag the bed over to where I can reach them."

He did this and filled the tea kettle. He had to walk a mile and a half to the Matthews' house over a snow trail through the timber; then he and Belle would have to walk back. Mother knew that her time was short.

Father gave her a final resentful glare. For a moment the doorway was filled with his angry back, then the door slammed shut behind him and the coal-oil lamp guttered crazily in the icy back-draft. She could hear his squeaking footsteps on the hard-packed, frosty snow for minutes after he had gone.

Father was not a bad man, nor willfully unkind. He would do anything for a neighbor, and many times surprised Mother with little unexpected acts of thoughtfulness. But when the temper was on him he could no more restrain himself than a spawning salmon could stop swimming upstream. He was a sentimental man, too: the trials of the heroine in a dime novel would bring tears down his bearded cheeks.

The stove was red-hot now. Light played along the old newspapers with which Mother had lined the pitifully thin walls against a rigorous Idaho winter. The room was cold everywhere except within the radius of a few feet from the stove; yet beads of sweat glistened on my mother's forehead. A pale, frozen looking moon hung low over the treetops, and my birth was celebrated by the wail of a coyote at the edge of the clearing.

Mother severed the umbilical cord with her scissors and lay back exhausted. When Father with Belle and Win Matthews entered the room they thought she had fainted or was dead.

Belle gasped when she saw me, and turned in fury upon Father. "Will Robertson, you ought to be ashamed! Mary here alone at a time like this! If you hadn't been so nasty with that tongue of yours Ida would have stayed here." Her fourteen-year-old daughter, Ida, had gone home in tears the day before.

Father shouted back, "She just wanted an excuse to get out of work. She's no good—just wait and see what she turns out to be!"

Belle paled with anger. Her temper was every bit a match for Father's. "Don't you dare say my daughter will be a harlot," she screamed.

They stood toe to toe, yelling at each other, their faces flushed and angry, until Win interfered. He was a sensitive man with white hair and a great prematurely gray, drooping mustache.

"Be still, both of you," he commanded. "Mary needs help."

"I'll not have my daughter insulted by this—this wood-chopper!" Belle shouted.

"If I had a wife like you—"

"You couldn't treat her like you do Mary, I'll tell you that!"

"Shut up, Belle, before I slap your mouth," Win said. "Will, you get out and bring in some wood and build up the fire. Why must you two fight all the time?"

"Stick up for him!" Belle cried. "If it was your daughter—"

Win turned away wearily. At his house it was a case of "my kids, your kids, and our kids."

Mother spoke gently from her bed, "Ida's a good girl, Belle. You send her down tomorrow. She'll want to see the baby anyway."

Belle apologized. Hot-tempered and quarrelsome as she was, Belle never became angry with Mother.

But no woman ever had the last word with Father. "You wait till Ida grows up," he predicted gloomily.

Ida did grow up, to become the wife of a successful contractor and the mother of a fine family. Father should have had his prophet's license revoked.

The storm passed until it became necessary to give me a name. Father had had a favorite brother named Thomas who died while quite young, and he always wanted to name one of his boys after that brother. But Mother had always been adamant: none of her sons should be named Thomas. What Mother had against the name I never knew, but I am sure that in my case she believed the name would cause Father to be partial toward me and thus work to the disadvantage of my brothers.

They finally agreed on Frank. The name Chester was tacked on as a compromise. Which one suggested it I do not know, but disliking it as I do, perhaps it is just as well.

3

Father was never entirely happy in his sons: Chauncey was too spirited to suit him; Obe was entirely too much like his mother; and I was a thin, gangling fumble-fingers with the knack of always disappointing him. Yet when he wasn't in temper he was affectionate and kind, and generous to the extent of his means.

Father was chopping cordwood for a living when I was born. Even when he worked every day, which he could not, he had to give up every other cord to the man who owned the timber. His earnings seldom exceeded a dollar a day.

Bad as it was, Mother had a congenital dread of change.

Every move her preacher father had made had led to something worse, and Father's destiny seemed to be the same. Father would have done well, she thought, to follow the example of Win Matthews.

Win had a team and had settled on eighty acres of part timbered, part cultivated land, where he was to remain for the next thirty years. Win was thrifty and Father was not. Unconsciously, Father followed the admonition of Robert G. Ingersoll, that if a man had but a single dollar he should spend it as if it was a withered leaf and he the owner of unbounded forests.

There were few times, I think, when my mother was entirely free from pain. She had been so frail as a child that her parents hadn't expected her to live. She would have been quite a tall woman had she not been so stooped. Her only personal vanity was her long, beautiful hair. Her fine gray eyes and mobile face and her seldom-failing sense of humor redeemed her from being a plain-looking woman.

Belle Matthews, on the contrary, had been a beauty, and though still a young woman, the rugged pioneer life and her own combativeness had taken its toll; but she still loved jewelry and perfume, and was a little disdainful of Mother for never having had her ears pierced and for never owning so much as a wedding ring.

"What's the use?" Mother would say. "A ring on my finger would only call attention to my red and bony knuckles." Her only jewelry was a simple gold breast-pin, a family heirloom that had been her mother's wedding gift.

She could see things with remarkable clarity and had long since learned to conquer fear. If her lot was a hard one, she had learned how to reconcile herself to it and make the most of the little she had. Her sense of pity was all-embracing, but she was ever a stranger to self-pity. Hers was a negative strength built upon the capacity to endure rather than to fight hardships. To her, God was as real a personality as if she could reach out at any time and touch His hand.

Father was as aggressive as Mother was submissive. He could never sit still for long. Even when he did his fingers were forever busy. His shirt collar always held half a dozen pins he used to dig at his ears, which were always itching. His skin was exceptionally tender. Sun or snow or dust and wind caused sores and scabs to develop, and he kept them raw from constant scratching. If he had a misery he multiplied it a hundredfold by dramatizing himself as the particular target for the devil's amusement.

In spite of the scabs he was a handsome man. Although his eyes were pale blue his hair was jet black. His beard and mustache were brown. He had a high, well-formed nose and high cheekbones, and he was proud of his small strain of Cherokee blood. His mind was alert and his bodily movements quick and efficient. He was wonderfully adept with his hands. He could chop three cords of wood a day or piece a patchwork quilt with more skill than most women.

He was a good though untrained singer. Knowing countless ballads, he simply opened his mouth and let the melody roll out. Often after one of his black moods when his expression indicated that never again would he be able to lift up his head and look his fellow man in the eye, when his few short sentences came in a weak and faltering whisper, Mother would hear that golden voice rolling over the hills in song five minutes after he left the house. And it would be the same husky, broken-hearted whisper when he crept back.

He was still attractive to women—Mother knew that—but it was the least of her worries. "He'll always manage to get involved in a quarrel before he gets involved in sin," she would say smilingly.

She was always filled with apprehension when he began to talk about getting a farm. But he argued that because he had failed in Nebraska didn't mean that he would fail here. This was a new country with farm land slowly eating into virgin timber. And just across the Washington state line lay the Palouse country, the best wheat land anyone had ever seen.

But Father wouldn't go there. The country was too settled. Here, where the prairie joined the timber, land was cheap, and if a crop failed a man could always chop cordwood.

With this Mother agreed. She accepted his philosophy that a poor man should stick to a poor country. But she had a horror of debt and knew that Father would never save enough to get a start. She told herself that some day the boys must get a piece of land, but the only means she had toward achieving that end was prayer. She didn't believe that even prayer could make a farmer out of Father.

One day Father stomped in and declared, "I'm goin' to buy me a team and git holt of some land."

Mother felt the dread of another failure, and without thinking she asked, "Where would you get the money to buy a team and wagon?" Her skepticism brought the old familiar hard glint into his eyes.

"I can rent the Gear place, and Win's father will go security for the equipment," he asserted confidently.

Doubtfully, she said, "I don't know, Will. My father always preached against going in debt."

Anger shrilled his voice. "There you go!" he shouted. "Always throwin' cold water on me, always bringin' up your father. Have you forgot how you used to support him?"

Mother protested, "I don't mean to throw cold water on you, Pa. I just hate debt. If I was sure you'd stick to it—but the first time you get mad you're up and gone."

"That's a lie! If you'd ever have any faith in me I could do something."

A family row was on and it followed an endless pattern. Father always switched the argument to Mother's folks, accusing them of thinking that he wasn't good enough for her—and making her believe it.

"My folks," he would orate, "were just as good as yours, maybe better. At least they had a-plenty of everything until a woman talked my father into givin' up his good farm and movin' out to the goddamned mesquite and gumbo of Texas."

"That woman was your mother," she reminded him.

"Yes, but she had no more business sense than any woman. I used to blame my father for everything and thought my mother could do no wrong until I got married. Now I know he was right. A man should be the head of his family."

Sometimes he became so interested in the oft-told odyssey of his family that he forgot the issue at stake, much to Mother's relief, even if she had heard the same story hundreds of times. More often, though, he returned to the attack.

At such times he gave her no peace, mouthing the moth-eaten phrases over and over until in desperation she would flee to the outhouse hoping for respite from the torrent of words. But that seldom worked. He would circle the privy shouting his denunciations, even if someone, either acquaintance or stranger, might pause to listen. Many times I have cringed in shame because of this, but how much worse it must have been for Mother! Always the quarrels would last until long after they went to bed, until exhaustion finally put Father to sleep.

Sometimes after a row he would disappear for a week or so—much to our relief, I am afraid—but this time his mind was set. Come hell or high water, he was going to be a farmer.

He was gone but a couple of days. When he returned he was sitting proudly in the spring seat of a new Studebaker wagon drawn by a span of fine colts he had named Barney and Roan. He had rented the Gear place, he announced.

His manifest pride melted Mother's heart. She gave him whole-hearted approval. She loved horses, and a man with a team and wagon was somebody, a man of means and capital. She assured Father that he would do all right.

They must have been really happy that night as she listened to Father's glowing plans. He would soon get a cow, some chickens and a pig. If the first crop turned out well they would buy the place. He would build a new house and become the kind of citizen he had always dreamed of being. He and the boys would work together. There was no doubting his sincerity.

Mother was particularly pleased about the cow. Her own folks had always owned a cow in spite of their poverty. She was tired of being given milk for her family by Win Matthews and other neighbors. No one would even think of selling milk, but there was never enough.

A farm, comfort and dignity for themselves, maybe even schooling for the boys. It was good to be able even to dream of such things.

4

Mother's dreams were short-lived. Father, when he should have been putting in a crop, was usually away on what he called "business." He had to negotiate for this and for that. Grain and hay for the team. Seed wheat. He had to borrow a plow or a harrow from this man or a drill from someone else. He was always on the go from four o'clock in the morning until dark. But Belle Matthews, the skeptic where Father was concerned, informed Mother with some little malice, that he would stand and talk with a neighbor for two hours where five minutes would have sufficed. The charm of his own voice, Mother knew, was a heavy handicap for Father.

When Mother ventured to remonstrate, he flew into a rage, and three days were lost as he followed her about the house or beat a path around the privy as he denounced her and her whole family, yelling the loudest when neighbors were passing by. He was a man to whom profanity never came naturally, but in his tantrums he would use blood-curdling oaths merely for their shock value to her sensitive ears.

The succeeding days were even worse, for then he went into a sulk and his air of injured innocence was harder to bear than his outbursts of abuse.

If Mother would say, "Will you have more coffee, Pa?" he would reply in a voice weak and pitiful from long suffering, "It don't matter whether I get any coffee or not."

The time slipped by until only a fraction of the land was in crop—and Mr. Gear would get half of that. The family lived even more frugally than before, Mother hoping there would be something left with which to pay debts. But Father had discovered that magic thing called credit, and because of it he was in debt most of the rest of his natural life. To him it was a measure of a man's stature, but to Mother it was an everlasting nightmare.

The unseeded land had to be summer-fallowed. After Father had finished the plowing he allowed Chauncey to harrow the ground. All the boy had to do was trudge along behind the harrow in a cloud of dust with Obe tagging behind.

Chauncey had a natural knack with horses and liked the job in spite of the dirt and the blisters that formed on his feet. He possessed resourcefulness and grit plus a bland disregard for consequences which was always getting him into trouble.

Father had told the boys they could ride Barney, the black colt, as much as they wanted to, but to stay off the roan—and for good reason. Father, the former Texas cowboy, had ridden many a bronco. I have seen him ride a bucking horse when he was well past fifty. He still owned his old flat-horned Texas saddle, and when no one was looking he had tried to ride Roan and got himself bucked off.

Notwithstanding these strict orders, Chauncey made ready to ride Roan, and though Obe bellowed in protest Chauncey led Roan out in the plowed ground, and using the harness hame for a saddlehorn scrambled to the horse's back. Roan's eyes rolled wildly. He whirled a few times while Chauncey clung to the hames and spoke soothing words and presently walked gingerly to the barn.

Roan was a strange horse. Never in his life would he permit an adult to ride him, but a child on his back was as safe as if in a rocking-chair. When Chauncey became fifteen or so Roan decided he had grown to manhood and tossed him so high in the air that Chauncey maintained a blackbird built a nest in his hip-pocket before he came back to earth. He never rode old Roan again.

But this time he was so filled with triumph that despite Obe's plea to keep quiet about it, Chauncey had to blurt the story of his achievement at the supper table. Father, seeing only the fact that he had been disobeyed, hurled his fork onto the table, dragged Chauncey outside and whipped him with a doubled-up halter-rope. Whenever Father whipped one of us he never stopped until he was out of breath. Fortunately for us his loud admonitions helped to get him in that condition, but many times he lasted long enough to make us wear our bruises for days. This was one of the worst lickings any of us ever received.

Mother sat listening to Father's panted warnings and Chauncey's screams, but not daring to interfere. She felt the injustice keenly. Chauncey had done most of the work—work which no eleven-year-old should be asked to do—and he had ridden the horse without harm to it or to himself. A whipping within reason would have been different; but where punishment was concerned, Father was without reason.

He came panting into the room, the rope still doubled in his hand, jerked Obe from his chair and dragged him outside. "You helped him!" he yelled.

"Pa," Mother protested, "you've done enough—"

"You shut up," he shouted at her in frenzy, "or I'll take this rope to you."

He wouldn't have done it—he had never struck Mother—but further protests would have made it harder on Obe. She could only shudder each time she heard the rope come down across Obe's young shoulders. But there was no outcry from Obe. Young as he was, he had stubbornly resolved that never again could Father make him cry. His flesh must have ached and burned unbearably, but he would have died before uttering a sound.

Father, panting heavily from his exertions, paused to extract a confession. "If you don't own up I'll wear this rope plumb out on you," he threatened. "I'll make you cry if I have to whip you all night."

"You can't ever make me cry!" Obe's thin voice was defiant.

The rope descended once more, then Father threw it away. "Ma," he demanded, as he returned to his half-eaten supper, "what's the matter with that boy? He just can't be conquered."

Obe received many whippings after that, but the results were always the same. Father retired from the field a beaten man. Yet Obe was the only one of his sons who never offered to return violence with violence; the only one who never cursed him secretly or openly.

"Pa can't help being the way he is," Mother would tell us. "We must pray for him; maybe some day he'll be better."

She did pray for Father, I am sure, but never in his presence, or ours. When she prayed it was in secrecy. She never insisted on her overly proud sons kneeling in prayer. Prayer was a condition of mind to her rather than a mumbling of words. She believed in a personal God and in a personal devil. God, she believed, knew what was in a person's mind without having to be told. He could recognize a humble and contrite spirit whether the body was on its knees or standing erect upon its feet. As for the devil, she, in her universal charity, was prone to remark that very probably he had his good points.

"Pa," she said, after they went to bed that night, "you should be ashamed of yourself. Chauncey told me that Obe did everything he could to keep him from riding Roan."

"Well," Father said sullenly, "he could have spoke up."

"You wouldn't have listened. How do you expect to govern your children if you won't give them a hearing?"

"I'll govern 'm all right," he insisted. "I wouldn't have no trouble if it wasn't for you always stickin' up for 'em. They'll hate me if you have your way." And so another family row was launched.

Father lectured all the next day, but in the evening, to the relief of his harassed family, he went away to see a neighbor. It was nearly midnight when he returned. Mother heard his clear voice ringing out in an old trail song as he walked through the timber. It stopped, however, before he reached the house. He undressed silently and crept into the edge of the bed.

"You've been to the Carles," Mother said. "Did Dora say how her mother was?"

His reply was so pitifully faint that she could scarcely hear him. "I didn't ask. I just didn't feel like talking."

With the summer-fallowing done, Father went into the Palouse country to look for work. Although times were hard and jobs scarce he was sure he could get work with the team. Meantime, he would sleep in the wagon box and cook his own meals. As always, when he was about to leave home, he was in high good humor. So were the rest of us, I am afraid.

Father was an emotional man. Tears were in his eyes when he kissed Mother good-by. "I'll send you some money just as soon as I can land a job," he promised. Mother knew it was a promise he would keep.

Many times, however, his absence was the best thing he could provide. It wasn't altogether conscience or religious training which had caused Mother to stick to him through thick and thin. She knew better than anyone how much he needed her. No matter how much he might revile her and her people she was the anchor of his existence. Without her and the children Father would have been a lost man. She never gave up hoping that some day he would make something of himself. She realized that much of his temper grew out of his failures. But her ultimate aim was to raise her sons to be just men, and live in the love, not the fear, of the Lord. She would expect them to be Christians, of course, but she would leave the matter of joining a church to them.

Soon after his marriage Father had joined the Campbellite church, and sometimes he was a faithful church-goer, while at other times he scandalized her by ribald attacks on religion. Mother's moral code was embraced in a single sentence: *Do what is right.* The pattern for her family she tried to weave into her daily living—but it was a little easier when Father was away.

Several letters came from Father during the next few months and no two of them came from the same place. One was from Walla Walla, down near the Oregon state line; another was from Pomeroy, a town south of Snake River; then another from Colfax, nearer home and in the heart of the Palouse country. Finally, he wrote that he was driving a header box on a big wheat ranch less than twenty miles from home.

His letters were poorly written, heedless of capitalization or punctuation, yet somehow he always contrived to make them interesting. They were full of terms of affection and endearment so sadly lacking when he was home.

He hadn't sent Mother any money but that was because he had none to send. His personal extravagances never took the form of dissipation. He was down on whisky though occasionally he would have a glass of beer with Win Matthews or some other crony. He loved to play cards for fun but never gambled. And he hated prostitutes so much that sometimes Mother would wink slyly when he got to ranting about them; then he would color up and snort, "You've got an evil mind."

He had found so little work that she knew he must at times have gone hungry, but now he was making four dollars a day with the team and everything looked rosy. He wrote with enthusiasm that he would be home in time to harvest the crop. She hadn't told him that there wouldn't be much to harvest.

The land adjoined some timber. Ground squirrels swept through the wheat in hordes, cutting off the stalks at the joint and leaving them to wither and die. Mother and the boys fought the pests with every means at their command. Win Matthews brought some strychnine to mix with flour. He suggested that it might be a little more efficacious if the stuff was mixed with ground glass, but this Mother couldn't consider; poisoning was cruel enough.

Win got a dozen steel traps that the boys used, each in his fashion. Chauncey would frequently have fun with the rodents before dispatching them and would bring about their demise with the sang-froid of a seasoned trapper. Obe, on the other hand, never wasted any time. With his nose crinkled in disgust for the job he hated to do he smashed the heads of the little varmints with a ferocity that made Mother shudder. Sometimes he made wild swings with his club long after they were dead.

Neither boy was cruel. To Chauncey it was merely a routine chore, but Obe never enjoyed hurting anything, so he went at the necessary job with apparent viciousness to assure that the victim suffered as little as possible.

Almost equally troublesome were the weeds on the summer fallow, which had grown so thickly that the ground was a brown mat sucking all moisture from the soil. The plowed ground in other fields lay black and mellow. The owner of the farm was dissatisfied—as he had a right to be. He never would have rented the land to Father, he told Mother, if he hadn't thought Will would stay home and take care of it. Mother and the boys tried pulling the weeds by hand, but it was like trying to hold back a river with the paddle of a canoe.

That summer we lived mostly on bread and milk and the products of the little garden which Mother and the boys tended carefully. There, they could keep the weeds down.

What staples we had Win Matthews brought out from Moscow where he "stood good" for them at the store.

Father arrived home in time to take care of the threshing. He was full of business. He rushed around giving orders to everybody as though thousands of bushels were to be threshed instead of three hundred.

On the big wheat farms of the Palouse the steam threshers always carried their own crew, with a cook-wagon and other accessories; but here in the timber where jobs were small the separator was horse-powered—a dozen weary horses going round and round, stepping over the tumbling-rod mechanically, while the driver stood upon his little platform over the gears and urged them on with his whip and a muleskinner's vocabulary.

Outside of the power driver, separator tender, and the sack-jig and sack sewer the other help had to be furnished by the farmer. That was usually a matter of trading work. The whole outfit had to be fed by the farmer's wife.

Mother would have them for one meal only, but Father had communicated some of his enthusiasm to her and she was determined that the harvesters would have as good a meal at her house as at any other. Men who worked like animals from before dawn until after dark would consume prodigious quantities of food.

Father bought some hens which were to be the mainstay of the meal. He cut off their heads and left Obe to guard the flopping bodies until Mother found time to clean them. We had potatoes and chicken gravy, squash, carrots and cabbage. Mother had dried apples that fall, and the dessert would be dried-apple pie.

After the meager meals of the summer that dinner was a banquet for us kids. Obe vowed that when he grew up he would spend his life following a threshing machine just for the good food that would be provided. Chauncey, however, was vastly more interested in the horses and machinery.

Life was good. Pa seemed glad to be back. He kissed Mother

frequently, and joked with the rest of us. He didn't even get mad when an over-curious Chauncey almost fell into the cylinder of the threshing machine.

In the evening Father talked about his experiences in the harvest field, while Mother listened eagerly. She loved the sound of his voice when it wasn't shrilled with anger. He was a natural storyteller. One of his fond illusions was that he was also a good listener, but when someone else seized the floor he would whistle in irritation until he found a chance to grab the conversational ball himself.

"Pa, you can listen about as well as a tomcat with its tail caught in the wringer," Mother used to tell him.

Father followed the thresher a few days to pay back the labor he had borrowed; but he always came home to sleep. Little by little the old irritability and jealousy came back.

At such times I believe Mother deliberately closed her mind to the questions that must have been moiling in her brain. Were they going to have to give up the place and move again? Could Pa pay for the team and wagon? Was he going to stay home now—would he be easier to live with? If he failed, would he ever make a start again?

5

We had to move. The farmer who owned the place apologized to Mother. "I hate to cause you trouble, Mrs. Robertson; you're a woman everybody respects, but I can't let the land out to a man who lets his summer fallow grow up to weeds."

It was the end of another dream in which she hadn't believed very strongly, but it brought its pangs. She couldn't blame Mr. Gear, but she had to voice some defense of Father.

"I think Will will do better another year. He had to work to pay for his team. It's awfully hard for a man without anything to get a start. Once Will gets out of debt—"

"I don't know about that, Mrs. Robertson. Dang few farmers

in the Palouse had much when they came here, but they were stayers. The trouble with your husband is that he gets mad and raises a ruckus over nothing."

She didn't need to be told that Father had already quarreled with Mr. Gear. She was a stayer, but Father wasn't. It was hard for her to quit anything she undertook. It was a prime reason why she would never leave Father. She gave herself no particular credit. She could see the same quality in her son Obe. As stamina, it was a virtue; as stubbornness, it could become a vice. In her own case she wasn't quite sure where the one quality left off and the other began.

Mr. Gear went on, "If Will was only like Charley Munsen. When he came here from Sweden ten years ago he didn't have a dollar and couldn't speak a word of English. Now he's got as good a farm as there is in the country. Charley stayed home and worked."

Mother knew Charley Munsen very well indeed. Often during the winter he had trudged over to our cabin to get Mother to help him with his studies. He spoke slowly and with an accent. His visits were not solely because he respected her as a teacher, but because she had understanding and fired him with an ambition not commonly found among farmers. He was so much younger than she that he could pour out his heart to her with complete freedom. She was very proud when a few years later Charley was sent to the state legislature. Now he had built a comfortable white cottage and a big red barn and had just brought home a bride—while Will Roberston was being dispossessed. Mother always seemed able to influence and help any man around her—except Father.

Father was not content to express his opinion of old man Gear; he insisted that Mother should join in his denunciations. When she refused he accused her of the old sin of throwing cold water on him. She let herself in for a row that lasted a week—a week in which he should have been out on the prairie hauling wheat and making good wages. Instead, his team idled in pasture while he followed her about the house or circled the privy.

"How can a man ever do anything if his own wife always takes sides against him?" he would roar.

"But I don't take sides against you, Will," Mother would remonstrate. "Sometimes I try to show you where you are wrong—"

"You always think I'm wrong! Just because your folks looked down on me you think I can't do anything right."

So it went, with Father hashing and rehashing the wearisome old complaints until, unable to stand it any longer, Mother would lug me over to a neighbor's a mile away while Father followed and shouted right up to the neighbor's front gate.

When finally she returned home Father's expression was that of a completely broken man. Had it not been for the many times she had heard him singing so happily in the midst of those emotional debauches she might have come to him on her knees to beg his forgiveness. But she knew from experience that asking his forgiveness made him ten times worse.

She had other reasons for doubting the genuineness of his suffering. Win and Belle Matthews, considered by Father as his best and most loyal friends, were treacherous as Apaches where Mother was concerned. Many times they told her how he had come to their house when he had a domestic tempest going in full blast, laughed, sung and joked, and played with their children who, incidentally, adored him. But when he came home his expression was that of a man who would never smile again.

Father's pouts would surely have moved a stranger to heartfelt sympathy. A mere word would leave his sensitive soul naked and shuddering to the wintry blast of a cruel, cold world. If either of the boys had kicked him on the shins he would have said, "That's right, go ahead and kick me—that's what your mother wants."

Mother could have said anything to him then without fear

of retaliation, but every word would have been treasured up and used against her in the next altercation. Father had an amazing memory for the things he wanted to remember, along with the ability to obliterate anything else by simply closing some inner gate in his mind.

Father finally drove his team out on the Palouse prairie. A week later Mother had a letter from him, which sounded as if they had never had a quarrel in their lives.

Three weeks later he came home. He had done very well. He paid something on his debts and he talked about buying a cow. They found a small house closer than they had ever lived to the Matthews family. They could get milk there, so they didn't have to buy the cow, much as Mother would have liked to have one.

That winter Father chopped cordwood for Charley Munsen, for which he received a dollar and a half a cord. He was good for three cords a day when the snow wasn't too deep to work. It was good money for the times but feed for the team was also high, so our standard of living didn't improve much. Potatoes and water gravy, known locally as "slitchet," was the backbone of our fare, with white beans and salt pork an invariable high spot on wash day. Father was a good country butcher, just as he was a fairly good carpenter, painter, cook and half a dozen other things, and was frequently called to help butcher hogs. He would never take pay for helping out a neighbor at this kind of work, but he always brought home a mess of liver or spareribs that was a welcome addition to our diet.

Mother enjoyed being where she could see Win and Belle nearly every day. Next to God, Win was her rock of refuge and her solace. When neither Father nor Belle was present they could sit for hours in perfect companionship without speaking a word. Win was still the only person with any influence over Father. Unfortunately, he was so conservative that he seldom tried to direct Father, only to restrain him. And it was not in Father's nature to brook restraint.

That winter there were debates at the local schoolhouse almost every week, with Mother and Charley Munsen usually pitted against Win Mathews and the local schoolteacher. Mother and her Swedish protege usually came out on top. Win was a slow, though logical speaker, and the schoolteacher wasn't well liked. The judges wouldn't have voted against Mother anyway, if she had tried to lose, although when Father was a judge his vote always went against her.

She had inherited the eloquence of her preacher father; she had a clear, cutting logic of her own tempered with gentle humor which made her a formidable antagonist and she enjoyed the stimulation of the intellectual conflicts. Father, who so enjoyed using his voice, was tongue-tied when asked to speak in public.

Then, suddenly, our little settlement was hit by that great scourge of pioneer rural settlements, diphtheria.

It was at times like this when Father was at his best. He went from house to house, wherever help was needed, sitting up with the sick or helping to bury the dead. He was tireless and went for days with little or no sleep. He was the bulwark of the community and many a child owed its life to him.

Unfortunately, most of the neighbors had an overwhelming dread of fresh air during the winter months. Usually every door in the house except one was nailed shut, and every crack in the house, including the keyhole, was stuffed with rags. No child could pass in or out without hearing the shouted command, "Shut that door!"

Father's first act was to tear out the rags and open the windows. So terrible was his wrath that few dared close the windows after he had gone. Those children, he told them savagely, had to have fresh air to breathe.

Belle Matthews fought him until one of her children died; then she yielded, and the rest of her children were saved. In sickness Father was better than Mother. He had skillful, tender hands, but he could be ruthless when necessary. No one could swab out a child's tormented throat so thoroughly and gently as he. He had little difficulty with the Matthews' children who trusted him, but with some of the Swedish and German neighbors he had to be firm.

The disease became epidemic, and Mother, too, did her part. She and Father trudged through the snow from house to house, sometimes together but more often alone. Neither had their clothes off for weeks except to change underwear. Mother stayed at home only long enough to bake bread.

Almost alone in the neighborhood, the Robertson kids escaped the scourge, although I frightened my parents by coming down with a severe case of croup. Mother worried, of course, but she was not afraid, although she recognized fear as a natural thing. To a neighbor whose meekness in the face of disaster irritated her, she said, "It's all very well to say that Christ promised the meek would inherit the earth, but he never said that applied to the cowardly. Get up and clean your house." It was probably the sharpest language she ever in her life used to a human being.

Far fewer children died in our community that winter than in surrounding ones. Mother was assured that God had been in our neighborhood that winter, for she had never felt so close to Him—or, for that matter, to Father.

Several unbaptized babies were among those who did die, and there were still ignorant preachers on the retreating lines of the frontier who preached infant damnation. For these, Mother had no use. No baby, she told bereaved and frightened parents, was going to hell because it had not been baptized, and what Mary Robertson said people believed. No long-haired, fanatical preacher ever came to remonstrate with her the second time.

When it came right down to it, she admitted pronounced doubts that there was any hell. Her reasoning was simple. There was no soul, however wicked, that she would doom to eternal fire and brimstone, and surely God was infinitely kinder and more merciful than she was. Therefore, hell was only the misery which men created for themselves with their own minds.

As for heaven, she hoped for it, with no real assurance that it existed as a physical location. If it was the solace of endless peace, for her, who had known so much turmoil, it would be ample.

6

When I was a little older and we went visiting around various parts of Latah County, I was constantly being surprised as Mother or the boys pointed out various cabins and shacks in which we had lived before I was old enough to remember. The method of our moving has always stuck in my mind, however.

All our worldly goods could be packed inside the wagon box, for Father knew how to utilize every inch of space. He did practically everything, even to packing away Mother's few china dishes in a barrel after wrapping them in rags. When the bottom of the wagon was full of boxes and trunks and sacks, our half dozen rawhide-bottomed chairs, which Father himself had made, and Mother's wooden rocker were inverted and the tops stuck inside the wagon box with the legs and seat protruding outside to make a projection to hold the lighter material, such as beds and clothes. Surmounting it all like a capstone was the feather-bed on which Father and Mother slept. From the grub-box in the front to the cook-stove in the back everything had its proper place. For our short moves we didn't bother about bows and a wagon cover, though a stout piece of canvas was tied over the load to protect it. In case of rain we kids could crawl under it. Mother had an umbrella to cover herself and Father on the spring seat.

The most important thing to me in our cargo was the green grub-box. Mother used it as a foot-rest as we rode along, and it was easy to reach. She could always dig a sandwich out of the box for me as we rode along, even as she scolded me for "piecing" between meals.

We had tin dishes for camping purposes and Father did most of the cooking. He could get a meal quicker than anyone I have ever seen and it always tasted good. In a sense, those moves were the only vacations Mother ever had.

Father and Mother each owned a trunk, battered and banged by many moves. Within them lay the divergent customs and traditions of the two families. Father's trunk was more often opened than Mother's, because her treasures were not for the public gaze.

Father's contained pieces of silverware that had been in his family for generations, most prized being a silver spoon with the firmly imprinted teethmarks of a brother who had died. There was a gorgeous patchwork quilt made of tiny pieces of silk sewn in intricate patterns, the workmanship of Father's grandmother. Mother loved the feel of that quilt, but not for anything would she have spread it on a bed. There were several quilt tops which Father himself had pieced, and my grandfather's huge mustache cup, rimmed in gold, which I still own.

Inside Mother's trunk was a very small wooden chest which her father had built. It was full of old letters, records, and fine leather wallets which Grandfather Matthews had made in his shoe shop. He even tanned the leather from the green cowhides, and in that little chest is still his own hand-written recipe for tanning.

There were old family albums with grim-looking ancestors looking with apparent disapproval on a sinful, Godforsaken world. There were a pair of my dead sister Lizzie's baby shoes, a lock of golden hair in an envelope cut from the head of my aunt Clarinda, a tiny beaded purse sent to Mother by her step-mother-in-law, and—most prized by Mother, and now by me—old family letters.

Also in Mother's trunk were her brown wedding dress and the leghorn hat she wore on that occasion. She kept them, not for sentimental reasons, but because they were still the best clothes she owned.

Those trunks carried homely histories of two vastly different families that had been united by the corners of a hymn book in a tiny Nebraska frontier settlement. Father's people had always been Southerners at heart, and I suppose it was natural for him to hate "niggers." Mother believed the Emancipation Proclamation to be the greatest document in American history. When Father lacked other material for the domestic wars he could always attack her views on slavery. His view was that Grandfather Matthews should have been imprisoned for helping slaves run away from their masters.

It never occurred to Mother that the people in the backwoods communities in which she lived were ignorant or drab. They were all God's people. Those in Idaho differed little from the folks in Iowa among whom she had been reared; a little more venturesome and violent, perhaps, but all impelled by the same impulses to love or hate, to do good or evil.

"Possibly," she would say smilingly, "the devil works a little harder on some folks than he does others because they are more worthwhile." Unlike most professed Christians, she looked with a lenient eye upon sinners, if not their sins.

In every community she found someone whose intellect she could respect. It was more likely to be some hard-headed farmer than it was the preacher or schoolteacher, who was supposed to be endowed with a certain amount of knowledge and culture. She could spot sham unerringly and valued an ignorant man's honest, carefully thought-out opinion more than a preacher's platitudes.

Although she got to read few good books, her respect for real learning was vast. Somehow she managed to keep abreast of the times. It gave her no feeling of superiority that she was recognized as the "best posted" member of her community.

She rejoiced that nearly all of her nephews and nieces had gone to college and become either preachers or teachers. It was my earnest desire to obtain a college education so that Mother could hold up her head and say she had a son who was a college graduate, but I never got beyond the eighth grade.

Mother liked practical men, even if they couldn't sign their own names, and she liked men who were intellectually alive, even if they didn't have a red cent. She was better informed than Win Matthews but, considering him wiser than herself, deferred gladly to his judgment. Her capacity for liking people made her, in turn, well liked.

Her attitude toward women was different from that toward men. Her close companionship with her father had made her "a man's woman." She was not often perfectly at ease with other women, unless she knew them intimately, as she did Belle Matthews. Broadminded and progressive as she was in other matters, she was unalterably opposed to woman suffrage. By her experience, women's outlook was too limited. Few women she had known had interests that extended beyond home, children and church.

The women she liked best were hardy and self-reliant, often coarse, vulgar, pipe-smoking women who gave themselves wholeheartedly to the business of making a home and took nothing from anybody. They, in turn, respected Mother for her wisdom and goodness, though sometimes with a shade of disapproval for the way she submitted so meekly to Father's tantrums. Yet the gulf between them being too great for any sustained conversation, she had few intimate women friends.

Most women, she felt, were lacking in both moral and physical courage—a quality for which she had great respect. Like herself, they were utterly dependent upon their men for security, but she didn't approve of their parading their dependence as though it were a virtue. Fear of adversity, she maintained, made them more selfish than men.

This personal courage of Mother's had been demonstrated quite typically the summer before I was born. There was in the neighborhood a huge, longhorned red bull belonging to a man named Haskins. This bull's belligerent propensities when on the loose had put brawny woodchoppers up trees and forced woodhaulers with their four-horse teams to turn out and surrender the road.

Returning from a neighbor's one evening with her two small boys, Mother found the bull roaring up and down in the clearing between her and her house, shaking the earth with his bellows and tearing up the sod with his hoofs and horns. When he saw Mother and the boys he put on a special display of fury for their benefit and threatened to charge. The only safety was up a tree, but Mother's sense of dignity revolted against being treed all night by an ill-mannered bull.

She put the boys, aged nine and six, up a tree, and arming herself with a small stick, set out across the clearing. Chauncey promptly slid down the tree, armed himself with a stick, and joined Mother. Obe, electing to remain in the tree, was sick with horror of the tragedy he expected to see enacted and wondered when he would be able to reach a neighbor's and tell them of Mother's and Chauncey's death.

Unable to make Chauncey go back, Mother walked straight toward the house, keeping between him and the bull, warning him to skedaddle for the house if the bull charged. The animal watched them as if it couldn't believe the evidence of its own eyes. It was accustomed to seeing people run for their lives when it lowered its head, and Mother and Chauncey were *sauntering,* coming nearer and nearer. The bull gored the ground, rumbling ferociously, pawing great clouds of dust over its back. But it didn't charge. Humbled by this affront to his majesty, perhaps, it turned and ambled away into the timber. Short-legged Obe got to the house almost as soon as they did.

Mother was not vain because of her exploit. She had simply been sure that the bull would not attack—as it undoubtedly would have done at the slightest indication of fear on her part. She knew that some would think her brave and some would think her foolhardy, but in her own mind she thought that she had only done the natural thing.

Father, of course, hit the ceiling when he came home and heard about it. She received no word of praise or admiration from him. "You were just lucky," he said. "I wouldn't have faced that bull with a double-bitted ax. You had no right to endanger the children."

He continued to berate her until she reminded him of the story of Abraham and Isaac. "Jehovah, that time," she said, "acted a little like you do once in a while by needlessly trying people, but He provided a ram in the thicket to save Isaac's life. I'm sure He would have provided one for us if it became necessary."

"Jehovah never commanded you to cross that clearing," he said with indisputable logic, but he couldn't shake her serenity. It was a cardinal point of her faith that God would never permit an extremity beyond her capacity to bear. There would always be a ram in the thicket.

That was the guide to her philosophy of life. If one would lean trustfully enough on God, one would never fall. The darker the hour the more she trusted Him. She never believed that God had let her down. The ram in the thicket she prayed for was always there.

"*Now* where's your goddamned ram in the thicket?" Father would cry out in times of crisis.

Undoubtedly she visualized Abraham's ram as a fine, brawny animal with magnificent horns, but to the rest of us it appeared to be a pretty puny, sickly little old lamb. But it always showed up in the nick of time; I'll grant that much. . . .

7

There was a sound reason for Win Matthews's conservatism. His father had been a born adventurer. When gold was discovered in Montana in the early sixties he had seen an opportunity to get rich by freighting to Virginia City and Bannack from Fort Benton on the Missouri. He had bought a string of wagons and a herd of mules, loaded the wagons with merchandise bought on credit and headed for Virginia City. He took his twelve-year-old son Win with him.

He had done extremely well on his first trip and hurried back for another load. The season was growing late and because the weather was cold he left Win in Virginia City until his expected return. Unfortunately, winter set in earlier than usual that year and he found himself snowbound at a place he called Disaster Gulch. He stayed until his provisions were exhausted and his mules starving. He couldn't go on so he returned to the Missouri, losing everything he had. When he went back in the spring all the mules were dead and all the goods were spoiled.

Meantime, the money he had left with Win was gone. To keep himself alive twelve-year-old Win swept out saloons and dance halls, his wages being what gold dust he could recover that the miners and the ladies of the night had spilled on the floor in their drunken revelries.

Win vowed then and there that he would find a place to settle down and stay there. Every move he made thereafter was made reluctantly. He was twice-widowed and had a son and daughter when he married Belle Stillman, who also had a daughter. They followed the elder Matthews to Idaho where he soon bought eighty acres of land, and there he remained some thirty years. His farm wouldn't support him but he was an expert judge of wheat, so he worked in a wheat warehouse in Moscow and farmed on the side.

Though the surrounding farms grew bigger Win was content with his eighty acres, and constantly urged Father to get a small piece of land. And so it came to pass that Father bought, and we moved onto that landmark known to the Robertson family thereafter as "The Forty."

That land was good enough, but far too small to support a family even in those days. For the first time Father moved onto his own land, even though it was mortgaged. Whatever misgivings Mother had she rigidly suppressed. There were a small but good house, a berry patch, and even a few fruit trees. Always she'd had to paper her houses with old newspapers, but now she could afford real wallpaper which Father put on after work. Her best dishes and silverware and linen came out of the trunks. The family put its best foot forward.

Our fare was still meager and we had the same old battered

furniture, except that the boys got their own bedstead and no longer had to sleep on the floor. We were surely on the way up. Father took us all to Moscow where we had our picture taken to commemorate the occasion.

"If Will can just stop speculating and tend to business he'll be all right," Win commented sagely to Mother. By "speculating," Win meant, of course, trying something new.

Father got in twenty acres of spring wheat and then went looking for work, leaving Chauncey to finish the summer fallowing with a walking plow. It was hard work for a small boy whose chin hardly came to the top of the plow handles, but Chauncey needed little sympathy. He had a well developed ego, and it was worth all the suffering when the men around the community began to talk about the skill and grit of "that Robertson boy." It gave him an opportunity to swagger before the unaccomplished Obe.

When the plowing was done the land had to be harrowed over and over. Those were Father's strict orders. Weeds were never going to take *his* farm.

But twenty acres of summer fallow couldn't keep a team busy all the while, and there was time for leisure and enjoyment. Nothing delighted Chauncey more than to drive Barney and Roan down the street of a village called Cornwall at a spanking trot with Mother in the spring seat beside him, hanging onto me, and Obe standing up behind. He would have preferred going to Moscow, but Mother dreaded the traffic in that bustling center of two thousand population.

Other times we went visiting on horseback. Mother was always a little afraid when Chauncey rode Roan, but to her indignation it was usually the gentle Barney who "acted up." Sidewise on Father's old Texas saddle, with me in her lap and Obe clinging on behind, she'd have her hands full for a time as Barney insisted on kicking up. I had an acquaintance with old Barney for more than twenty years, and I know that he had a well-developed sense of humor. He wouldn't have hurt one of us for anything, but he had to have his fun. Mother always gave him a good scolding. She was a great believer in firmness with children and animals, and never could understand why people howled with derisive laughter at the idea of her exercising discipline.

One of the homes we used to visit was that of Herm Mallory, the local infidel. He was a man of impeccable honor and great generosity; he and his wife Clara were among Mother's most loyal friends, but he loved to argue with Mother about religion. He couldn't make her believe he was serious when he claimed not to believe the Bible.

"But you do think I'm bound for hell, don't you, Mary?" he would tease.

"No, Herm," she would reply, "there'll be worse men than you in heaven. The Lord will know how to deal with your stubbornness, even if I don't."

For a really restful visit, though, Mother called upon Aunt Polly Tyrrell. Aunt Polly had been blind for more than fifty years, yet Mother often declared she had never known anyone so cheerful and contented. The old lady lived with the secret sorrow of having made what Mother would have considered the greatest sacrifice a person could ever make. Aunt Polly had to face the crisis of giving up her religion, or her husband, and she had chosen to keep her husband. Facing the same crisis, I doubt that Mother would have done the same.

Uncle Marsh, Aunt Polly's husband, was a holy terror even to Mother. A huge old man, nearing ninety, he seldom spoke without sprinkling every sentence with blood-curdling profanity. About twice a year he would go to Moscow, get fearsomely drunk and boast that he could lick his weight in wildcats; and in his younger days I believe he could. He always professed to marvel that Mother liked him, and was wont to declare fervently that she and Aunt Polly were the best goddamned women who ever lived.

Their sixty-year-old son, Leander, was in every way the antithesis of his father. He never drank, never used profanity. He did all the cooking and housework in his meticulously neat little white cottage and cared for his blind mother as tenderly as if she was a baby. A wounded Civil War veteran, he drew a small pension and also owned a good farm. He never attended church, but in Mother's eyes he was little short of being a saint.

In her later years, when she had the opportunity to read the best novels of the day, Mother was quite put out by the "serious" novelists who wrote of backwoods people as if they were all vulgar morons living stupidly in dirt and filth and given over to debauchery, incest and adultery. She thought back to such folks as Leander Tyrrell, Aunt Polly, the Mallorys, and Win and Belle Matthews and could find no prototypes for the fictional characters of the Faulkners, the Caldwells and the Fishers.

"Oh, pshaw!" she would exclaim. "They don't know what they are talking about."

Uncle Marsh had one violent pet hate—Mormons. Mother had never met a Mormon and he talked to her about them by the hour.

"Yes, by God, I helped run the sons-of-bitches out of Missouri, and I cheered when a lot of the bastards were massacred at Haun's Mill," he would boast.

"Marshall, you did no such a thing," Aunt Polly would remonstrate.

"I fought 'em from hell to bush," Uncle Marsh would maintain. "I knowed old Joe Smith. Many a time I saw him strutting around in a military uniform like a goddamned peacock."

"The Prophet Joseph was a good man," Aunt Polly would say mildly.

"Prophet, hell!" Uncle Marsh would yell. "Him and his Golden Bible, and his lyin' witnesses. Pack of liars, all of 'em! When a bunch of 'em would meet a man with a good team they'd stop him and say that all things belonged to the Lord, and since they were the Lord's servants they had the right to his team and wagon and they'd take it."

Later, Aunt Polly confided to Mother, "We were Mormons

once, but those were bitter times when many were carried away by their lusts and hates. Marshall fell into apostasy. I tell you, Mary, the Mormons are good people and their gospel is true. But for all his faults, I still love Marshall."

Harvest had started in the lower Palouse country, and about the Fourth of July Father came home to get the team and wagon. He praised Chauncey heartily, and declared that the wheat would go forty bushels to the acre.

"Wouldn't surprise me if we'd get a dollar a bushel," he said optimistically.

"Unless old Grover Cleveland brings on a panic," Mother said.

"There you go," Father shouted; "always lookin' on the dark side of things, never givin' me the least encouragement!"

"I didn't mean anything, Pa," Mother said hastily. "Heaven knows I hope we will get a good price."

Where some women cowered in fear lest their husbands come home drunk, Mother lived in constant fear of these emotional jags which were just as painful in their efforts as another man's intoxication. Father hadn't had a good row for months, and he was on the verge of a tantrum. If it happened he wouldn't go back to his job for a week and might even lose it. If he lost the job he would have to turn back The Forty. The situation was critical.

"You've been readin' them Republican papers," he accused. "If you'd ever believe anything except what you read in a book you might have more sense."

Mother pleaded guilty and he walked away. It had been a narrow escape. Mother didn't breathe easy until he left for Colfax the next morning. He hadn't spoken to her again and wore his injured manner as a beggar might exhibit his rags.

Mother used to take us kids in the evening to the top of a hill overlooking the field just as a breeze began to ripple the tall green wheat until it seemed to be a moving sea. Her hopes for happiness for herself and her family were bound up in that small, rolling field. Forty bushels an acre—eight hundred bushels at a dollar a bushel! The sum seemed fabulous. And this year Pa would have his wages besides.

But she still didn't trust Grover Cleveland. He was playing merry hob with the high protective tariff, in which she, as a good Republican, believed. Father, of course, was a Democrat.

She watched the wheat ripen slowly. It was like heaven's golden pavements in the sunlight!

We had a cow now, and there were two peach trees which had borne a full crop. At last Mother had something she could divide with the neighbors. So deeply did the luscious beauty of those peaches impress itself upon me that I can remember them overflowing from the two tin tubs after they were picked. I was then a little over three years old.

Then came the blow which Mother had feared. The Cleveland panic was on. Wheat dropped from eighty cents a bushel to twenty-five with no buyers. It would have been better for the farmers had their seed rotted in the ground, for most of the harvested grain rotted in the sacks.

It was grim irony that it was the biggest crop in years. The warehouses bulged; the chunky little steamboats which carried most of the crop down the Snake and Columbia rivers to be reshipped overseas remained tied up at their docks. The railroad cars stood empty on the tracks. Huge piles of sacked wheat rose like brown buttes in the fields. And then, piling catastrophe upon disaster, the rains came. Day after day it fell, and the wheat kernels sprouted and burst the sacks. Soon there was little left in many of them except a mass of greenish mold.

Banks everywhere closed. Farmers had no money to pay hired hands. Most of the men were transients. They had labored and sweated fourteen, sixteen hours a day, much of it by lantern light, and now they were broke and ugly. Mortgage companies, at first eager to foreclose, became chary when they saw how eager the farmers were to turn over their property.

Father had two hundred dollars coming and couldn't collect

a cent of it. He had bought another team so that he could outfit a header box, had planned to make big money hauling wheat down to the wharfs at Almoto and Penewawa. He came home to face his creditors without a dollar. His own little crop had been threshed and he owed a heading and threshing bill.

Mother forgot her own ruined hopes in her anxiety over Father. He was like a crazy man. Mother and the boys had covered the sack-pile with straw, but there was no let-up in the rain. When Father dug down into the sacks the wheat was hot enough to burn his fingers. He screamed curses at the weather until exhausted, then came into the house and sat silently for hours staring straight at the rain-drenched window.

Mother said timidly, "We'll get along all right, Pa. We've never starved to death yet."

He turned his blazing eyes upon her and shouted, "How'll we get along? No money and no job, and no credit. It's easy for you to say we'll get along, but I'm the one has to make the living. I've always been a good provider, but all you ever do is jaw at me if I complain."

"Well," Mother said, "I don't see what good complaining does. All we can do is trust in God."

"Trust in God? Jesus Christ! What's He ever done for us?"

She tried to hide the shock she felt from his blasphemous outburst. Other men could have cursed like that before her—though they seldom did—and she would not have minded too much. But Father didn't know how to swear. He was too conscious of the bad words. He handled them as awkwardly as a city man would handle an ax. But Mother still didn't like to hear God abused. She wondered if even God didn't get a little out of patience with Father sometimes.

"And you're the man who once told me you were naturally religious," she reminded him.

She expected nothing other than the long-delayed fuss, but to her surprise he got his hat and started for the door. He came back to ask for some salve. His lower lip was swollen and covered with cold sores.

"If you'd keep your lips dry, Pa," Mother told him gently, "they wouldn't get so sore."

"Who in hell do you and your Heavenly Father think I am?" he demanded; "Job?"

He didn't come home for a week. She heard about him from Win Matthews, who stopped on his way home from work in Moscow. It was still raining. Mother was mending as she sat on the opposite side of the fire from Win.

"Saw Will yesterday," Win said. "He tells me you are going to move."

The news struck into her like a knife. She had hoped desperately that some way we wouldn't have to give up The Forty.

"I suppose so," she said.

Win looked at her silently for a moment.

"Did he say where we're going to move?" Mother asked.

"Will said something about moving into Billy Buchanan's old house over in the Tim Bell district. He mortgaged the horses yesterday. I wish he hadn't done that."

Again the knife twisted in Mother's heart. She had hoped that at least we might keep Barney and Roan and the wagon in the clear.

Win stood up. "Before I forget it," he said, "Belle wants you all to come over to Sunday dinner."

She knew the invitation was a spontaneous idea of his own, but it didn't matter. Grateful as she was toward Win for all his unselfish kindness, it is possible, as she watched him go out in the drizzle and climb awkwardly upon old gray Dolly, that she couldn't help thinking that he cut a poor figure on a horse compared to her own still untamed and unpredictable ex-cowboy.

8

The new settlement into which we moved was a little older and more thickly populated than the one we had come from but it was still frontier and my people were not long in getting acquainted with the neighbors.

We lived within a stone's throw of the fine new house which our landlord, Billy Buchanan, had built for himself. Billy Buck, as he was familiarly called, was a fat, jolly farmer with a thunderous bass voice. He owned a good farm that he left largely to the management of a brother and a couple of hired men, while he spent considerable time in Moscow talking politics. Finding out that Mother was pretty well informed on topics of the day, he deliberately drew out her shrewd and often witty comments so that he could use them there himself.

In those days every school district had its literary and debating society, and Tim Bell was unusually well supplied with talent. It had two preachers, a schoolteacher, and several farmers with a flair for public speaking. A woman debater was something unusual, but with Billy Buck loudly proclaiming Mother as his protege, she was soon in nearly every weekly debate and usually on the winning side. Her features conformed to no standard of beauty and her clothes were cheap and often rusty with age, but when she began to speak nobody noticed how she was dressed. She spoke clearly and distinctly, without hesitation, yet slow enough to get the expression and emphasis she wanted.

It was Billy Buchanan who got Mother into the only debate that ever frightened her. She almost backed out when they told her the subject: *Is the Pope of Rome a menace to civilization?* Her opponents were to be the two rival Protestant ministers from the neighboring village of Cornwall—whose downfall Billy Buchanan very much wanted to bring about. Mother was permitted to choose her own associate; and she promptly selected the lone atheist of the community.

There wasn't a Catholic in the neighborhood, so the Pope had to rely upon a Campbellite woman and a man who professed no religion at all for his defense. It seemed that Mother and the Pope were destined to go down to defeat.

Mother didn't know much about Catholicism, although she had little use for "popery." Still, she believed that Catholics were good people, and the Pope and his priests no better and no worse than other preachers. Hers was not a popular viewpoint.

The first preacher brought down the house with a violent and passionate attack upon everything the Pope and his church stood for including a good many things which would have been news to them. Backwoods audiences loved a speaker who could "give 'em fits," and that was the chief stock in trade of the country preachers.

Mother, as the first speaker for the negative, began calmly, and pointed out that it was really a debate on tolerance versus intolerance, and as she warmed up she took the preacher who had preceded her to task for his lack of charity and blatantly intolerant attitude. This preacher was a Methodist and the one who followed Mother was a Baptist; he tore into Mother for being willing to compromise with sin. "Would Mrs. Robertson have us believe," he shouted, "that we should have tolerance for an individual who is leading millions of ignorant people straight to *hell*? I tell you, brethren and sisters, that there can be but one true church, and the test of whether or not a soul is destined for salvation or damnation is whether or not he belongs to that church. Does anyone here believe that old Anti-Christ, the Pope, is the leader of that true church?"

The crowd plainly showed that nobody did. Mother's atheist co-debater surprised everyone except Mother by the mildness of his argument. Twisting the tiger's tail was left to the two preachers. Then it came Mother's turn for rebuttal. She said quietly, "If it is true, as we have been told, that only members of one true church can go to heaven and the rest are destined for hell, we should get it straightened out right here which one it is. If Reverend Rutledge is leading his flock to heaven then it follows that Reverend Nelson must be leading his to hell. Or perhaps—" she paused with a twinkle in her eye as she looked around at the two uncomfortable preachers—"perhaps *my* church is the only true one, and *both* these gentlemen are leading their congregations to hell."

She got a big laugh, knowing well that being laughed at was the one thing country preachers as a rule could not stand. When the laughter subsided she said, "Since at least one of them must be wrong, he is certainly as bad as the Pope of Rome. But wouldn't it be better and kinder to assume that neither the Pope, nor Reverend Nelson, nor Reverend Rutledge wants people to go to hell?" She gazed kindly at the preachers and remarked, "It seems to me that you reverend gentlemen in your zeal to save souls are working together like a team of horses hitched to different ends of a wagon."

That was a dig her farmer audience could appreciate. Mother and her infidel friend had been sweetly reasonable; the preachers had overreached themselves by the fury of their attack. Mother and her partner received the unanimous decision of the judges.

Mother was soon being asked to debate against chosen teams from other districts and, though she didn't win them all, her reputation as a speaker grew—but it didn't promote domestic harmony. Until now Father had usually been rather proud of Mother's forensic ability, but this winter he sat in the back seat and glowered, ignored and almost unknown while his wife received the applause.

Adding to Father's disgruntlement was the fact that our only income came from our two boarders and the money Mother made doing theirs and Mrs. Buchanan's washing. It was hard for a proud man to take.

The boarders, Phil Carlin and Seymour Ivy, were waiting around to go to work for Billy Buck in the spring. We all liked them, but Mother appreciated them most for being around to play cards with Father. This provided a relief from the family rows, which otherwise would have been continuous.

There were plenty of them as it was, as Father followed Mother about the house with his charges that her lack of faith in him was responsible for our present plight. He went over their past life together with a fine-toothed comb—and his memory was phenomenal. Every molehill was made into a mountain.

Sometimes, when goaded beyond endurance, Mother would fight back, but she was no match for him. This was no debating platform but an arena where victory went to the one who could talk the loudest, the longest, and think of the meanest things to say.

Mother was never robust and, aside from constantly suffering from "female trouble," she had frequent attacks of pleurisy. The chronic family warfare caused her headaches, but she would rarely take to her bed. To add to her troubles she learned that Obe, the gentlest of her sons and the one most like her, was considered by his teacher and most of the mothers of the district as little better than a small beast in human form.

When the boys had started to school in Tim Bell, they found themselves hurled into schism and strife stemming from the religious differences of their elders. Small as the community was, it had two congregations, the Methodists and the Campbellites. The Campbellite preacher was a gaunt, one-eyed, part-time farmer with a nasal, singsong voice. The Methodist minister was a graduate of a sure-enough theological seminary, so the Methodists were confident that they made up in quality for what they lacked in numbers. The children, quite naturally, carried on a juvenile version of religious rivalry.

Obe had got off to a bad start in school. He was a shy boy, but always anxious to please. On his first day he heard the teacher address a redheaded urchin somewhat larger than Obe, "Sam Lowe, I wish some boy your own size would give you a right good whipping."

Obe stuck up his hand. "I will, teacher," he volunteered and punched Sam in the nose.

The teacher pulled them apart and gave each a sound thrashing. Later, they had it out with Obe emerging the victor, after which they became good friends.

The next day Obe and Sam were enjoying the schoolground seesaw when a larger boy, son of Nelson, the Methodist minister, arrived with a bevy of admiring girls and ordered them away. Obe, confident of the righteousness of his cause, resisted the efforts of the girls to eject him, while the Nelson boy was pushing Sam off the other end. Having finished with Sam, young Nelson stepped upon the end of the teeter-board and, being heavier, lifted Obe high in the air and stepped off. Obe hit the ground with a painful thud.

The Nelson boy's laughter turned to a whimper as Obe's

fist caught him on the end of the nose. Rallying, the preacher's son charged his smaller assailant.

Obe's nose was soon bleeding and his lips cut and swollen. His arms were too short to reach his opponent's face; he was forced steadily backward while the little girls applauded their hero.

Obe had withstood the worst punishment Father could hand out and was not to be conquered easily by any boy anywhere near his size. He knew that if he lost this fight the rest of his days in school would be miserable. Furthermore, win, lose or draw, he was sure to get whipped for fighting when he got home. In any fight he always expected to get the worst of it—for a time.

Tiring at last from his own efforts, young Nelson dropped his guard to ask if Obe had enough. He caught a short, jarring punch to the stomach that made him gag. Then he caught another and another. Having never encountered anything like this before, Nelson started to retreat, stumbled and fell. Obe was upon him instantly, raining blows while Nelson bellowed. The little girls screamed and belabored my brother with whatever weapons came to hand, but he wouldn't desist until he was lifted clear of the ground by the strong arm of Mr. Roderick, the teacher.

For the second day in a row Obe got a whipping from the teacher, who was just as baffled as Father by the boy's refusal either to beg or cry. Obe became a fiend incarnate in that teacher's mind.

But the fighting for that day wasn't done. No sooner were the children off the schoolground than they divided into groups according to their religious faith and began to assail each other with hard names and eventually with harder clods.

For a time the Robertsons, the Buchanans, the Lowes and the Marshalls were more than able to hold their own against the Nelsons and the Turnidges and a few others. Chauncey, having an unerring aim with a clod, was a tower of strength to the Campbellite cause, but Obe's efforts were half-hearted.

He'd had enough for the day and faced the certainty of a hard whipping from Father when he got home. Father didn't believe that children, especially his own, should fight. Moreover, Obe had the idea that Chauncey was carrying things a little too far, for the Methodist group included several large and athletic girls. He tried to warn Chauncey, but with the zeal of a crusader upon him Chauncey refused to listen.

Obe's premonition became a painful fact with bewildering suddenness as two of the big girls swooped down and made Chauncey their prisoner. He kicked and clawed but he was at the none too tender mercy of the female Methodists. Slowly but relentlessly, the big girls dragged him toward a fresh and fragrant pile of cow manure with the determined intention of rubbing his face in it. Chauncey screamed and cursed, rending the air to unavailing purpose. Retribution had him in its grasp.

Obe's stomach revolted as though it were *his* nose in jeopardy. Howling his rage, he picked up a handful of rocks and charged. The niceties of war meant nothing to his peace-loving soul when beset. One girl dodged a rock that grazed her face; another caught one in the stomach, and more were coming. They let go of Chauncey and fled with pigtails flying. Obe's reputation for viciousness was set for the remainder of the term.

Obe was endowed with a strong competitive spirit. Up until now he had gone to school very little, but thanks to Mother's home teaching from which we all benefited, he would have been able to stay at the head of his class had it not been for Mr. Roderick's dislike. His only real rival was Mr. Roderick's own daughter. Again and again Obe revolted at some palpable favoritism. He brought some of his papers home and Mother saw that Mr. Roderick had marked his answers wrong when they were right.

Unwilling to take sides against the teacher, she tried to make Obe believe that Mr. Roderick had only made a mistake, but Obe, knowing better, withdrew into himself. His interest in school lagged; he hated girls and his chief satisfaction was his reputation, shared by Sam Lowe, of being the most obstreperous boy in school.

Chauncey got along better. His black, curly hair, good looks and genial manner soon made him a favorite, even with the Methodist girls. He excelled at schoolground games and learned his lessons with no apparent effort, forgetting them with equal facility.

So we passed the winter. Spring came, and there was still no work for Father. He no longer had any interest even in a good family row. Phil and Seymour, our boarders, had gone to work, and Father couldn't even play cards. Some days he would get on Barney and ride around the country hunting work, but there were no jobs. Other times he would merely sit staring out the window. When Mother spoke to him he wouldn't answer. She would have welcomed even a fight—anything to get him out of the black mood which had descended on him. When he did speak it was to utter vague threats or to voice despair.

Then one day he put on his shabby best suit and told Mother he was riding into Moscow with Bill Buchanan. He didn't come back; it was many months before we learned whether he was dead or alive.

Kindly Billy Buchanan broke the news to Mother. "Will didn't come back with me," he said. "I'm afraid he never will."

"He isn't dead—" Mother said weakly.

"Oh, no. Last time I saw him he looked fine. He'd just bought himself a new suit, new shoes and everything. I brought back his old clothes."

"But how could he?" Mother exclaimed. "He only had a dollar and a half."

"I don't know, Mary. I only know that he bought them, and he left town on the train."

I doubt if in her wildest imaginings Mother had ever dreamed that Father would desert her and us children. She had been ironing Phil's shirt, and in her perplexity and anguish she had been leaning on the hot iron. "I've ruined Phil's shirt," she said dully.

Billy tried to make a joke of it. "He'd just as well buy a new shirt as a bottle of whisky." He leaned forward, his fat, jolly face suddenly sober. He said, "If Will's left you, Mary, you've no call to worry. A lot of us have thought you'd be better off if you left him. Your friends will stand by you. With your ability there ain't a job in the county you couldn't fill. If you'll run for county superintendent of schools—"

Mother smiled her thanks. She knew that Billy was only talking. Thus far he hadn't been able to get himself elected sheriff, although later he did accomplish that goal. She said, "Will must have gone away to look for work. We'll hear from him."

"I hope so," Billy said. "In the meantime, you stay here as long as you like. You've still got four good horses. I've been thinking that Chauncey is a mighty handy lad with a team. He could work for me. When he does a man's job I'll pay him a man's wages, though God knows that won't be much these days."

Mother must have been remembering her eldest son's chapped hands and lips, his blistered feet, and the way she had lain awake nights listening to him screaming hysterical curses at his team in his sleep—but the family had to live.

Where, she kept asking herself, had Father got the money? He didn't have credit enough to buy a sack of flour, let alone a new suit of clothes. He couldn't have sold the horses, for they were running in Billy Buck's pasture—and they were mortgaged for as much as they were worth.

I was too young to understand, but when the older boys came home from school she explained to them gravely that we probably wouldn't see Father again for a long time. She tried not to notice how relieved they looked.

"Don't worry, Ma," Chauncey said. "I can make a living for us."

She patted his shoulder. "I know you can, son."

No word came from Father. Chauncey was working but the panic was still on and Billy could afford to pay but little. If the hard times lasted another year he would face bankruptcy himself. It broke Mother's heart to have to rouse Chauncey from a sound sleep and send him out with a lantern to feed, water, curry and harness his four horses while she prepared his breakfast. Often she could hear him screaming curses at Pete, the big, unruly bay with the sore neck who fought against being harnessed. Again and again Pete would buck the harness off and trample it underfoot before Chauncey could fasten the buckles.

Once the team was hitched to plow or harrow, Pete's energy departed and his tugs went slack. Chauncey fought the horse all day and in his dreams at night. Sometimes the oaths he screamed in his sleep made Mother's blood run cold, but she could not bear to chastise him.

When the crops were in, there was no more work for Chauncey and the team. Mother used part of the money he earned to pay interest on the mortgage on the horses.

For a while Billy Buchanan paid the boys a little for poisoning squirrels, but it wasn't enough to live on. Then sacks of flour or potatoes began to appear mysteriously on the porch when Mother opened the door in the morning. Herm Mallory, the atheist, drove ten miles to bring a sack of apples he insisted would otherwise rot. He also brought a huge cured ham sent by Leander Tyrrell.

Mother accepted the gifts in the spirit in which they were sent because she didn't want to hurt the feelings of the donors. But she felt that she had found another ram in the thicket when George Poe, a man she scarcely knew, dropped by to tell her that he had owed Father ten cords of wood for many years. He was a big, slow-moving fellow with a great drooping mustache stained by the pipe he was never without.

Mother couldn't remember having ever heard Father mention such a debt, but she couldn't call the man a liar.

"You have your boys come up and get it, and I'll help 'em

load," Mr. Poe said. That wood, delivered in Moscow, would bring twenty-five dollars in hard cash!

Chauncey was entranced by the thought of becoming a woodhauler, but he howled when Mother refused to let him drive a four-horse team; all woodhaulers drove four-horse teams, he wailed. Mother reminded him that none of the Swedes who hauled wood past our house ever drove more than two horses.

"You think I can't drive better than a *Swede?*" he demanded indignantly.

Mother was even afraid for him to drive the high-spirited Roan and Barney in the strange city, but she yielded on that point—and the very first day they had a runaway. Thanks to Chauncey's skill and pluck nothing more serious happened than the fright of a couple of men they almost ran over, an incident which enhanced rather than detracted from my older brother's reputation as a horseman. Mother didn't find out about it until some ten years later.

The boys didn't always see eye to eye about their operations. Always, after the load was sold, Obe wanted to hurry home to show Mother the fruits of the day, but Chauncey insisted upon hanging around the burly, horse-talking teamsters until dark; this was mostly inside the saloons. Not much attention was paid to minors in those days, but if Mother had known that her sons were loafing in saloons there would have been no more wood hauled. Obe, of course, wouldn't tell where they spent their time. It wasn't the first or the last time Obe had to yield principle to expediency to keep his older brother out of trouble.

Mother lived in constant dread that the man who held the mortgage on the horses, the same Mr. Gear with whom Father once had trouble, would foreclose, and it was as much because Barney and Roan had practically become members of the family as it was that they were our only capital.

At this time Mother wondered if she might not be able to get a school. She knew herself to be a more competent teacher than most of those she had seen in northern Idaho, but she had no certificate. And then she had me—still too young to go to school, too little to be left behind.

Everywhere men were out of work, and it was little wonder that a child like Chauncey couldn't get a job. He and Obe rode around the country and often got into fights with other boys. One evening Obe came home with the inside of his thumb laid open to the bone by a sharpened buttonhook wielded by a boy he'd been fighting.

Mother couldn't blame them for not staying home when there was nothing to do. They were looking for work; still, she thought they needed the firm, guiding hand of a father. Though it hurt her pride to do so, she took the initiative to find out what had become of Father.

Among Father's people was a wealthy old aunt for whom he cherished a sentimental regard. At his request Mother had carried on an intermittent correspondence with her over the years. From Aunt Nancy's letters Mother had built up a picture of her somewhat at variance from that of the saintly old lady Father remembered. Aunt Nancy had married at sixteen, lost her husband two months later, and never remarried. Now past eighty, she lived with a niece who expected to inherit her not inconsiderable fortune. If anyone would know Father's present whereabouts it would be Aunt Nancy. Mother wrote her.

Promptly, she received this letter: DEAR MARY: *Yes, I can tell you where Will is. He is down in Texas visiting with his two brothers and his step-mother. You see, my old bachelor brother Malcolm, who was quite a rich man, died last winter, and Will's share of the estate was about five hundred dollars. That's where he got the money.*

I'm not surprised that he deserted you. Will's trouble was that he was a spoiled brat. His mother called him Willie, and all Willie boys are spoiled. If I were you I wouldn't put up with it. I'd write and tell him you know how much he got, and make him send you enough to pay your debts. If you say so I'll write him a letter that will scorch his ears. Don't worry about him not coming back. He will when the money is all gone. He tells the folks in Texas he is making up his mind whether or not to send for you. If you are in actual need let me know and I'll send you some money. Don't let Will, or anyone else, trample on you, Mary. That's the lesson I've learned. Your aff. aunt, NANCY A. PIERS.

None of the children could understand why Mother laughed so heartily. But she wrote neither to Aunt Nancy nor to Father.

Perhaps during that trying summer she considered writing to him after she knew where he was, but she realized that if he didn't come home of his own free will life with him would be unbearable. She could endure, and she could wait.

She missed the comforting talks with Win Matthews; at times she was tempted to drive over and see him and Belle, but refrained because she feared they might think she had come for material help.

Then one night she awakened to find a light shining in her eyes. She blinked, wondering if she had fallen asleep with the lamp burning. Father leaned over and kissed her.

He had come home!

9

Sleeping with my mother, I was awakened too. She has told me that I sat up in bed, a big smile on my face as I yelled out, "Pa!" My father wiped tears from his eyes, and said, "Gosh, how he's growed."

Up until then I had seldom felt Father's anger, except for an occasional light slap, but I did remember often sitting on his knee while he sang the old trail songs, or such old English ballads as *Bonnie Black Bess* and *Andy Bardeen*. And I remembered the striped candy sticks he used to manage to bring home, no matter how lean he was in pocket. The vividness of my recollection of his homecoming indicates I must have missed him sorely.

Mother smiled at Father and he smiled back. He had three faces that we all knew; the truculent one, the humble one, and a kindly one, which in those days we saw far too seldom. This was the one he wore now, to Mother's vast relief, for she had feared that he would come back either belligerently, or in shame.

"How've you been, Will?"

"Fine. I brought back some Indian pictures from Oklahoma that'll tickle Frank. How're the other boys?"

"They're well. Hungry, Will? There's some bread and milk."

"Believe I am. Walked all the way from Diamond today. Been working for Jim McConnell down there. No, don't get up, I'll fetch it."

We watched as he got out the crock of milk, crumbled in an entire loaf of bread, and ate it to the last morsel.

He was not wearing the new suit he had bought in Moscow when he went away, but overalls and cotton shirt which showed signs of wear. But like anything he ever wore, it was neat and clean. He could do his own washing, and mend as well as any woman.

Mother treated him no differently than she had the many other times when he'd been away working. She must have felt bitter against him, but she had thought things through and come to understand. He had felt himself crushed and hopeless. When he got the money from Uncle Malcolm it had seemed to be the only chance to escape he would ever have. Doubtless he had told himself that he would use it to look around and find something better for his family. Then, before he knew it, the money was gone.

There was something on his mind. "Where's the horses?" he asked.

There was relief on his face when Mother replied, "They're running in Billy Buck's pasture."

"Old man Gear ain't tried to take 'em away from you?"

"No, I managed to pay something on the interest."

"Listen, Mary, here's what I want you to do. I can make good money hauling wheat for McConnell, but if Gear found out I was back he wouldn't let me take the horses and wagon across the state line. In the morning you and Chauncey pack up without saying anything to anybody and take the Uniontown road. I'll meet you as soon as you git into Washington."

It was a penitentiary offense to take mortgaged property out of the state, and he was asking her to be an accessory to a crime—not that he stopped to think of it as such.

Now Mother could understand better the agony of decision which her friend Aunt Polly Tyrrell had once undergone. If she refused Father's request he would go away in a huff, and this time he wouldn't come back. She must go against her life-long rule always to do right—or lose her husband.

Maybe I had something to do with her decision, for she had seen the joy on my face at Father's return.

She said feebly, "Are you sure it's the right thing, Will? Wouldn't it be better if you saw Mr. Gear and explained things to him? I'm sure he would understand."

"And lose the horses?" The old familiar anger blazed out at her. It faded in a moment and he became pleading, almost tearful. "It's not like I meant to cheat him out of anything. I'll pay for the horses, but I've got to have time. Just as soon as I can git the money I'll send it to him."

So the five hundred dollars was gone, as she had thought it would be. Squandered, as only Father could squander money—without wasting a cent of it on women, liquor, or gambling.

"All right, Will," she said finally. "This violates every moral principle of my life, but if that's what you think is best, me and the boys will meet you."

"You'll never be sorry," he promised her. "I've still got a little time; I'll help you pack."

He went away long after I fell asleep. In the morning Mother told the boys about his return and what was up. Then she went up the hill to Billy Buchanan's house. She was not going to sneak away like a thief.

"Well, Mary," Billy said, "I think you're making a mistake. You'd be better off without him."

"That may be, Billy," she admitted ruefully, "but I married Will for better or worse—and this does look like the worst."

Billy laughed. "All right, Mary, I'll help you load up. But it won't do me any good when I run for sheriff if the voters ever find out I helped smuggle mortgaged property out of the state."

"You're a good man, Billy," Mother said.

He said, "I'd rather hear those words from you than anybody I know. I'm not much on religion, as you know, but—God bless you, Mary Robertson."

Without any sex allure whatever, and without ever trying, Mother had a way of winning men to her side—all men except Father. It was the men, not the women, who had rallied to our support that bleak summer, and among them were the two preachers whom she had discomfited in debate.

Father was in fine fettle when he joined us just over the Washington state line. He greeted Chauncey and Obe boisterously, ousted Chauncey from the driver's seat, for it was a great pleasure to him to be driving his own team again. As we went along he sang the new cowboy ballads he had learned in Texas.

He had no sense of wrongdoing whatever. It was part of his nature that he could always justify himself. Whatever he did was right or he wouldn't have done it. Whatever he said was true or he wouldn't have said it. He was the eternal adolescent.

We were now well into the Palouse country about which Father had talked so much. One hill rolled away from another as far as you could see, with never a tree in sight. The landscape was a vast checkerboard of golden wheat stubble and black fallowed land. The soil produced wheat at an unbelievable rate of bushels to the acre.

Most of the houses were big and white. The barns were

enormous and all painted red. Most of the buildings were wedged into draws or gulches between the hills. Where the gulches widened out they were called "hollers," and if the hollers leveled out enough they were called "flats." Thus in the years of our sojourn in bondage in the Egypt that was called the Palouse country we lived variously in such places as Union, Rebel, and Alkali Flat, and Tom Smith Holler.

In the distance—I remember it as always surrounded by purple haze—was the great eminence known as Steptoe Butte. Off to the south the mighty Snake cut a great chasm through basalt bluffs on its way to junction with the Columbia.

Whenever we were on the move Father did the cooking. Our regular fare was usually helped out by cheese, crackers, bologna, and sardines—things which we never tasted at other times. It was the best living that I could remember.

When we reached the McConnell ranch we moved into a small abandoned homestead shack and we lived in it for more than half a year. Moving here with the greatest misgiving she had ever known, Mother was to admit later that these were some of the best years of her married life.

It was lonely. There was no church or school within reach, and no debating or literary society; the big scattered wheat ranches with their thousands of acres made such things impossible. The rich farmers could afford to send their children to school in town; their tenants and hired men could shift for themselves. But there was peace and a reasonable amount of plenty, and these things my mother had come to value above all else.

Outside of the McConnells, we had few neighbors, but Mother had never been a great visitor; mostly, she left that to Father. Jim McConnell was a prosperous farmer, but not one of the wheat barons, and didn't think it hurt his dignity to have an employee in his house. Father was often there, but none of the rest of us was ever invited. I doubt that Father was either; he merely dropped in when he wasn't working. There were several pretty McConnell girls about whom he talked a lot, but as always Mother wasn't worried about the women in his life.

It was characteristic of Father that he never cared to associate with men of his own age or older, with but two or three exceptions, and the older he grew the more he sought the companionship of the young. There were three McConnell boys who became Father's boon companions. They were wilder than young mustangs and at times almost led Father astray. He never played cards for money and never drank anything stronger than beer but he spent many evenings in the saloons of Colfax with them and joined in their pranks with the gusto of a teen-ager. They liked him because of his wide experience and the stories he could tell. Father was always "good company."

Once they got into a scrape which, while quite innocent in its conception, almost landed them all in jail. The McConnell boys knew where there was a watermelon patch. They thought it would be a lark to go there with a team and wagon and swipe a few dozen melons. Father was all for it and with Barney and Roan hitched to the wagon they approached the melon patch on a dark night. They left the team tied to the fence and, with Father leading the way, explored for the ripest melons.

Father must have felt the cold chill of iron bars closing around him when he heard Dell McConnell yell, "Boys, they're cutting up the harness!"

The strategy of the farmer was masterly. By cutting the harness off the horses he could capture the wagon and obtain ample evidence against the culprits.

By the time Father got back to the wagon the McConnell boys and the farmer and his hired men were engaged in a knockdown and drag-out fight. Father found that the lines and one tug had been cut. He quickly tied a knot in each of the lines, improvised a temporary tug with a halter-rope, and springing into the wagon yelled for the McConnells to come on. With their foes clawing at their coattails the boys landed in the wagon, and Father lashed the team into a dead run.

They had escaped but they knew that Father's team, famous in the country as pullers, had been recognized. Besides, his harness bore cuts and slashes that could not be explained. The McConnell boys bore plenty of evidence against them on their faces.

Fred, the eldest of the McConnells, said, "They know it was us, and they know it was Will's team, but they couldn't have recognized Will. No use dragging him into it. We'll say we swiped his outfit. Dad can fix it up some way."

One of Father's most oft-repeated phrases was, "I hate a liar," but on this occasion he was grateful for the stout lying of the McConnell brothers. I think he must have felt pretty sheepish when Mr. McConnell insisted on paying for the damage to the harness, though.

In general Father's disposition was better than it had been for years, but once in a while he would fly off the handle. I was the astonished object of one of these outbursts. Up to now I had viewed the whippings received by my brothers with more curiosity than alarm. But one day, having borrowed Father's jackknife, I climbed high up on a great rick of grain sacks in the yard and accidentally slit a long hole in one of the sacks. A couple of bushels of wheat made a golden cascade to the ground. Father yanked me off the sacks and gave me a thrashing which left me sore in body and mind for several days to come. The days of my immunity were over.

Chauncey was delighted by the licking I got, and even Obe offered no sympathy. I'd been riding the horse of Father's favoritism a little too high, they thought, and was overdue for a fall.

In the late fall Father and Fred McConnell went on a fishing trip far up the Clearwater river in Idaho. When they returned a couple weeks later Father had two washtubs full of trout and whitefish which he had salted down. He also made a forty-gallon barrel full of delicious sauerkraut, into which, after it had properly fermented, we boys were allowed to stick our fists and withdraw dripping, succulent handfuls which we ate raw and with relish.

The Robertsons lived better that winter than they ever had in their lives. During the long winter evenings we gathered around the stove while Mother read aloud to us boys, and to Father if he happened to be at home. She had a fine, expressive reading voice. We liked to watch her as well as listen, for she had a trick of getting an entire paragraph at a glance and could deliver most of it while looking at her audience instead of the book.

We took two newspapers, which contained the writings of such homespun humorists as Bill Nye and Josh Billings. Chauncey and Obe were partial to the novels of H. Rider Haggard: *King Solomon's Mines, She,* and *Allan Quatermain.* I best remember, however, a hair-raising serial recounting the adventures of one Captain Bearcolt, a loyal officer of the Crown, against the upstart Oliver Cromwell. I'd give a lot to know now who wrote it, or why.

But to Mother the best of all the books we were able to borrow from Mr. McConnell were two of Mark Twain's: *Innocents Abroad* and *Roughing It.* She had long been an admirer of Mark Twain, but this was the first time she had been able to read anything but fragments of his work. Never a day passed that she didn't read aloud a chapter from the Bible. Her copy was an old and battered one which her father had used for many years in the pulpit.

Aunt Nancy Piers had added to the winter's supply of reading material by sending each boy a story book which she deemed suitable to his particular age. Since the Robertson boys were somewhat precocious, the good old lady missed the mark by about five years; but for many years I was the pleased beneficiary of her bequests to my older brothers. I cannot remember when I learned to read, but it was long before I started school. Those books and the various large volumes of *Stories from the Bible* which Father bought from wandering book agents were my textbooks. I've had a pretty fair knowledge of the Bible ever since.

The best thing about our new home for Chauncey and Obe, I believe, was that there was no school, a fact which bothered Mother no end. She also experienced real tragedy that winter when she received word of the death of her mother. She knew that Grandma had always considered that she was just visiting around among the other daughters until Mary could send for her. It had been a long, unrewarded wait.

Good as the life was in many respects, Mother never felt any permanent roots there. She wanted to be where there was a church and school for the children, and she missed the loyal neighbors she had known in the timber. Not gregarious like Father, she still had a passionate regard for friendship. But not for worlds would she suggest to Father that we move again. She knew the urge would soon strike him again, and she could wait.

Then one day he made her supremely happy when he laid before her the canceled mortgages against the horses and the wagon. Once again Mother could hold up her head. This confirmed what she had always believed, that Father was fundamentally an honest man.

She could not have been too surprised when Father announced that he was quitting his job to rent a place of his own in Tom Smith Holler. He had been discontented for weeks, ready to jump down her throat at the slightest provocation. Grover Cleveland was still president and times were still hard. Mother doubted the wisdom of the move, but kept her doubts to herself.

Father gave up the farm in Tom Smith Holler soon after he got the crop in, just about the time Mother finished papering the house with newspapers. The place was literally overrun with the great gray Columbia ground squirrels, and at times the whole earth seemed to be moving. The grain stalks were cut down and eaten as fast as they got above the ground. Now

Father understood why he had been able to get such good terms on the place.

I have one vivid recollection of Tom Smith Holler. I had followed my brothers and some other lads to an old deserted house where they proposed to hold a potato roast. No sooner were the potatoes in the hot ashes than we were invaded by a larger party of boys from another holler. At first our forces tried to hold them off with the hot potatoes, but these were soon exhausted.

Whoever had last lived in the two-story house had abandoned a flock of chickens. There were nests of eggs in every conditions from fresh to rotten all over the place. Obe, the general, ordered all of us to fill our hats with eggs, the rottener the better, and take refuge on the top floor of the old house. From there we bombarded our enemies until our ammunition was exhausted. They had superiority of numbers and supplies, but we had the advantage of position, and Chauncey rarely missed a target. Many a boy went home that night bearing the effluvium of rotten eggs.

Toward evening the besiegers withdrew and the besieged went home. The way my brothers treated me for having followed them, one would have thought that I was the enemy. I was warned of the dire consequences that would follow if I ever told Father what had happened, but Father took one sniff, and extracted the truth from them. They got a few extra licks for having taken me along.

One move followed another, each equally unfortunate. Finally, Father heard of a place in the mountain area where the states of Washington, Oregon, and Idaho joined; there, he was told, a poor man would have a chance. The place was called Peola, and when improperly divided appealed greatly to Chauncey and Obe's misguided sense of humor.

As usual, Father had been misled. The country was in truth poor enough for anybody, but despite this there was no opportunity for a poor man. Once more he was without work and without money in a land of total strangers. They were not the kind to give a helping hand to a family of wagon tramps.

In the short time we were there Mother received the scare of her life, which was to reoccur in her dreams for years to come and wake her up in a cold sweat.

Many tall pine trees still stood in the clearings and were heavily infested with hawks which lived fatly on the overabundance of ground squirrels. It was fine sport for the boys to climb these trees and break up the nests, often after a vigorous battle with the defending hawks, which were more dangerous than they realized.

One day Mother saw Obe at the top of a tall pine which had died the summer before. Its boughs and needles were dry and brown. Suddenly, to her horror, she saw the tree wrapped in a sheet of fire. Some mischievous, unthinking boy on the ground had applied a match to the lower boughs.

If Obe had hesitated a second he would have been roasted alive. He had but a single chance, to drop from branch to branch, out at the very tips before the flames could reach that far. If he missed a branch he would be killed by the fall. To Mother it appeared that he was falling anyway, so swift was his descent; but he managed to hold on to the limbs long enough to check himself, and when he finally plummeted to the ground he was only stunned and slightly singed. When he got to his feet it was with his fists doubled up to fight the badly frightened boy who had all but cremated him.

A few weeks of Peola brought us to the verge of starvation. Father moved into an old abandoned shack, just above the south rim of Snake River. He could find no work for himself. Unknown in the vicinity, he could get no credit. Never lazy, never inactive, he crossed the river looking for work with his team.

Meanwhile a wheat farmer on the rimrock hired Chauncey at fifty cents a day to drive six half-broken broncos on a harrow. Ten hours a day the boy had to plod through the soft plowed ground in a perpetual cloud of dust, tend his horses, then walk the mile and a half home. His feet in the ill-fitting brogans he had to wear were practically parboiled from the heat and dust and sweat. But the family was living on that fifty cents a day and he didn't complain.

After a few weeks Father returned to move us to Alkali Flat, the poorest country so far as productivity was concerned in which we had ever lived. There we spent the winter and most of the next summer.

It was as though the low, sprawling hills were too dispirited to stand erect. In place of the good black loam of the Palouse country there was a thin, sad, sour soil encrusted with dirty white alkali. There were but few settlers in the better corners, men who, like Father, believed in a poor country for a poor man. Even the ground squirrels, of which there seemed to be millions, were of a dwarf variety.

We moved into a bleak, unpainted frame shack on an abandoned homestead which hadn't been lived in for years. Half the shingles were off the roof and the weather-boarding banged and rattled like dead men's bones whenever the wind blew—which was most of the time. At that, it was better than the hovel on Alpowa Creek from which we had just moved.

Again there was no school or church within reach, and few neighbors with whom to visit. We had practically nothing to eat except bread and the eternal "slitchet." The family row that went on was never-ending. Father couldn't be satisfied until he had baited Mother into uttering some bitter remark upon which he seized triumphantly to accuse her of wanting to set the children against him. He became a master at the art of twisting words to make her most innocent comment seem in some way a reflection against him.

Spring came at last, and he went looking for work. Hundreds of migratory workers of all kinds lined the roads or tramped the fields. People no longer differentiated between honest workingmen like Father and the bums who were only looking for a handout.

One evening we saw Father driving up the road with someone. When he stopped, an ungainly fat man climbed laboriously down over the wagon wheel. Mother, too near sighted to recognize even members of her own family at any great distance, stared at the stranger with perhaps as much resentment as she ever permitted herself to feel. It was like Father to bring home a stranger when there was nothing in the house to eat except cornmeal bread and water gravy.

Then the fat man gave a great shout. "How are you, Mary?"

For a moment Mother hesitated, then with a cry of "Milam!" she went into the fat man's awkward arms, sobbing while he muttered, "Mary, Mary, Mary." His name was Milam Burnham, a man from *home*. A man who had known her when she was a young, unmarried schoolteacher; who had known her father and mother, and sisters, and who was but a few years younger than she.

This was one of the few times I ever saw my mother lose her self-control. The long bottled-up homesickness she had fought back successfully for many years had burst forth at last.

Milam, it turned out, was looking for work. He and Father had met accidentally in Walla Walla, but he had a few dollars and a team and wagon which he had left at the nearest town. Forthwith, this good man declared himself a member of the family, and we were able to eat again. For several years, off and on, Milam made his home with us. His heart was as big as his huge, unwieldy body.

Milam could tell Mother much more about her sisters than she had gotten from their letters. All of them were doing well. Some of their sons were already high-toned preachers. Most of their daughters had gone to college, or were going. Only her children, it appeared, were destined to grow up in poverty and ignorance.

Milam's words must have seared Mother like a branding-iron when he said, "Mary, I never knew anybody so well thought of as your father. Everybody back home says you are most like him, and the smartest one of the family."

Father and Milam went back to Walla Walla looking for work, leaving behind a big, awkward sorrel mare belonging to Milam, and a little brown mare called Lena and her colt, Dot, which were Father's. Chauncey and Obe rode Blaze and Lena down to the Penewawa ferry almost every day, where they learned to swim in the Snake and made friends with an Indian family. While they were gone Mother and I played endless games of "pigeon draw" with a dog-eared pack of cards, the only game simple enough for me to understand.

Once the boys reported that cherries were ripe in the orchard of Mr. Simpson, owner of the ferry, and he had sent word that Mother could pick some on shares. So we all started out, the boys on Lena, and Mother and I on old Blaze.

All went well until we started down the steep dugway from the rimrock to the river. Then Chauncey lashed Lena to a swift trot, more with the idea of making Obe beg him to stop than anything else. Averse to being left behind, old Blaze swung into a lumbering, earth-shaking trot. Mother couldn't hold the old mare back, nor could she force her into a lope. She tried to call out to Chauncey to pull up, but the breath was being jolted out of her and she couldn't shout. Soon Mother was coming down as the saddle was going up, and finally she missed it altogether and landed in a heap in the middle of the road with me still in her lap.

When Chauncey looked back and saw a riderless old Blaze thundering along behind him, he wheeled round and galloped back, not knowing what tragedy he would find. Mother was still sitting in the middle of the road laughing so hard that she couldn't get up. Unhurt, we climbed back on the old sorrel mare and resumed our journey at a more sedate pace.

Mr. Simpson's was the first real orchard I had ever been in, and I could scarcely wait to get there. We had two varieties to choose from: Royal Annes and Black Republicans. Even the names were gloriously dramatic. We had all the cherries we could carry home. I couldn't understand why my foolish brothers took time out to go swimming, and to row back and forth across the river in a small boat belonging to Mr. Simpson when there were cherries to be eaten.

Chauncey and Obe were always able to find something of interest in every community in which we lived, even in a place as drab as Alkali Flat. Once while exploring they came upon an old trail that had been trodden three or four feet deep in places; it ran as far as they were able to ride. Their Indian friends at Penewawa told them it was a trail that had been used for centuries by the horse tribes of the Northwest, that one of those who had used it was Chief Joseph of the Nez Perce, whose ancestral home had once been not so far distant in the Wallowa valley in northeast Oregon.

When they told Mother about it, she told them the story of Chief Joseph, the great leader who had fought the last major Indian war against the whites. During her girlhood Mother had lived almost within echoing distance of the war whoops of the Sioux, but with her instinctive sympathy for the underdog she had believed that the Indians had always gotten a dirty deal. She had a pronounced admiration for Chief Joseph. Shabbily and unjustly treated, Joseph had led his people, women and children included, over trackless mountains for hundreds of miles, outmaneuvering and outfighting greatly superior forces of the United States Army, although showing mercy to the white non-combatants he could have destroyed. He had given up almost within sight of his goal, the Canadian border, because he could no longer bear to see his people suffer.

The American generals opposing him had called him the Indian Napoleon, and pronounced him one of the greatest military geniuses of his time. From somewhere, Mother had got a copy of the short speech Joseph had made at the time of his surrender. It began, "From where the sun now stands I shall fight no more forever." Mother believed that speech was entitled to live forever in the pages of oratory, along with Lincoln's Gettysburg address. It had purity, power and simplicity, and the sincerity of a broken heart.

Unknown to us children we were approaching one of the major crises in our family hegira. We were to see our father, one of the few times in his life, a broken and defeated man.

He and Milam returned without having found any work. Finding the teams too expensive to feed, they had put the animals out to pasture and traveled on foot from Pendleton, Oregon, to Spokane, Washington, detouring whenever they heard of a possible job, without making a single dollar.

Father's lips were swollen and the scabs on his face raw and bleeding. The soles of his shoes were worn out and his feet blistered. For the first time in his life he looked downright seedy.

"Mary," he said, "I've had enough. We're going back to Moscow."

10

Neither broken heart nor empty belly could keep Father from singing when he was driving his team, and he sang now, though there was hardly enough cornmeal in the grub-box to last us to Moscow. But in token of his humility and out of deference to Mother he sang, not the old trail songs, but began with the one hymn in which she never failed to join her voice with his.

> "*Sweet hour of prayer, sweet hour of prayer,*
> *When shall I thy consolation bear?*

And cast on thee my every care,
And wait for thee, sweet hour of prayer.
In seasons of distress and grief,
My soul hath often found relief.
I'll cast on thee my every care,
And wait for thee, sweet hour of prayer."

I shall never forget the evening we drove into Leander Tyrrell's yard. Uncle Marsh, now past ninety, was the first to see us. "Well, by God, if it ain't Will and Mary!" he yelled, and hobbled out to help Father and the boys unhitch.

His warwhoop brought blind Aunt Polly out to the porch to hug and kiss Mother when she came up the steps.

When Leander arrived, he said, "Now, Will, don't bother to unpack a thing. You're all going to have supper and breakfast with us."

And what meals they were!

After supper Herm and Clara Mallory came up. It was past midnight before anybody thought of going to bed and, as usual, Father did most of the talking. As Mother snuggled down into her wagon-box bed, she thought, *Nothing in the world is so wonderful as friends.*

We had no money and no place to live, but Leander and Herm both volunteered to lend Father money. Our housing problem was solved by George Poe, who had once remembered a non-existent debt of ten cords of wood. He remembered now a vacant cabin back in the woods near his own place which wouldn't cost us a cent; Father and the boys could chop cordwood for him. Poe, who was notoriously lazy, wouldn't mind hauling the wood to town.

Mother was not one who thought her boys too good for honest labor, and she didn't object when Father took them into the timber to help make a living. But she protested vehemently when he refused to let them go to school. For three years none of us had been inside a church or school, but hers was a losing battle. Father didn't believe schooling was necessary for boys who would have to make their living with their hands. If they were old enough to become full-fledged woodchoppers—Chauncey was going on fifteen, Obe on twelve—they were too old for school. They spent ten hours every day dragging a crosscut saw or swinging an eight-pound sledge.

For me, however, those were heavenly days. The Poes had a little granddaughter living with them who had an impediment in her speech, and even her grandparents were often at a loss to understand what she was saying. In a couple of weeks I could understand every word Nellie said.

In the Poes' back yard was a great, glistening snow-white pile of mica from a near-by mica mine. There Nellie and I spent many happy hours in the merchandising of what Nellie called "shug" and "fow," perfectly understandable to me as sugar and flour. A very polite little girl, she always referred to my parents as Mr. and Mrs. Robertson, but both came out alike: "Me Ya," and "Me Ya."

A year or so later, after I had started to school, Nellie came to enroll for the first time. The teacher tried to question her but couldn't understand anything she said. The other children laughed uproariously. I could understand every word she uttered, but now, timidly shy and bashful myself, and fearful of ridicule, I remained silent. Nellie went home that night and never came back to school. After all these years I can remember few things for which I blush so much for shame as for my moral cowardice on that occasion.

George Poe developed a fatherly affection for my brother Obe, and the two frequently spent long, quiet hours together in philosophical discussion. George didn't treat Obe as a child, but as a human being, an equal. Obe never married, but all his life he had a way with children. It was what he had learned from George Poe. I remember George's wife Nancy best for her generosity to me, and because she was seldom seen without a corncob pipe in her mouth. And, to my further shame, it was from these good people that I did my first and, I guess, my only stealing.

Going to their house once, I found them away and, looking through the window, I saw a crate of fresh peaches and another of tomatoes. There was, of course, no lock on their door. I went inside and temptation overcame me. I filled my pockets with peaches and tomatoes and fled to the woods to eat them. They must have missed the fruit and guessed who was the culprit, but they never mentioned it to me or my parents.

Mother's interest in current events revived. The country flamed with excitement over the presidential campaign of 1896. William Jennings Bryan, the "boy orator of the Platte," had just won the Democratic nomination with his famous Cross of Gold speech. Mother admired Bryan immensely for his oratory, his high moral character, and his views on temperance, but she mistrusted his economic theories.

Father, on the other hand, was for Bryan, lock, stock and barrel, and jeered at Mother's prediction that McKinley would be elected. He fondly believed that he was "getting her goat" by constantly singing the most popular of Bryan's campaign songs:

> "Bryan's gallant Western boys
> Will never win the day.
> So the 'goldbug' Shylocks said,
> And slyly turned away.
> But they counted not the thousands
> With their loyal hearts aflame,
> Who put their trust in Bryan,
> And the silver man from Maine.
>
> "Hurrah! Hurrah! for William Jennings B.
> Hurrah! Hurrah! 'tis silver makes us free.
> Thus we'll sing the chorus
> From Nebraska to the sea:
> While we go marching to vict'ry."

Those were good days, with much visiting around among the Matthewses, the Poes, and the Robertsons—although Father was usually at outs with either Belle Matthews or Nancy Poe. The latter could remove her pipe from her mouth and cut Father to the quick more easily and devastatingly than Belle could with a half-hour diatribe. Mother and Win were back on the old friendly footing, neither of them ever saying much, but quietly enjoying each other's company.

It was inevitable that Father should feel a returning of his old longing for land of his own, but the prairie frightened him and he felt safe only in the timber. He had made the acquaintance of a domineering Tennessean by the name of Ira Lee, who lived a few miles away in what was known as the Zeiglar school district. What Father didn't know then was that the district was inhabited almost exclusively by tough refugees from the law, particularly former moonshiners from the Blue Ridge mountains of the South.

Ira Lee, one of the toughest of them, bragged of having killed a man or two, and was destined to die with his boots on years later after he had returned to his native Tennessee. A poor judge of character and easily flattered, Father was led to believe that Lee's sole interest was in seeing Father established in a home of his own.

Said Lee, "There's a hundred and sixty acres of the finest timber land that I've been achin' to buy, but I'll give up half of it just to have you as a neighbor. We want people like you and your wife in our district."

Father looked the place over. The timber was good—a virgin forest of red and yellow pine, red fir and tamarack. It was only eight miles from a prime market in Moscow. Lee showed him how he could fell house logs right where the building would go up. He pointed out a small clearing of an acre or so grown up to wild strawberries where he could raise a garden.

"Why, man," cried the enthusiastic Lee, "this place is just like a gold mine! When you need a dollar all you got to do is chop a load of your own wood and haul it to town."

To Father, who had chopped many a cord of wood of which the owner of the timber got half, that sounded mighty good.

The real-estate firm of Spotswood & Veach, in Moscow, owned the land. They wanted eight hundred dollars for the eighty Father was to get, but to oblige an old customer—they were the men from whom Father had bought The Forty—they wouldn't require any money down and would give him five years in which to pay.

In his time Father had had many opportunities to make money had he been willing to gamble but he was always afraid of big deals. Yet he had no such terror of debt as obsessed Mother. His trouble seemed to be that he always "saw small."

He made a proposition to the realtors which made even Ira Lee gasp. "I'll take it if you'll let me pay for it in cordwood," he offered. "So many cords delivered in Moscow every year until it's paid for."

The partners looked at each other slyly. "What's wood selling for today?" one of them asked.

"About a dollar and six-bits, but"—

"We can't figure on it staying that high. It might go down to a dollar a cord."

"And it might go up to three dollars," Ira Lee argued.

"It's Mr. Robertson's proposition, not ours," said the partners. "If he will deliver one hundred cords of wood here in Moscow every year for five years the land will be his. That would be approximately a dollar and sixty-six cents a cord."

"I'd rather do that than pay cash," Father said. "Me and my boys can always chop wood, but we can't always lay our hands on a dollar."

They reminded him, of course, that he'd have to haul in a few extra cords every year as interest, and neglected to tell him that if he failed in any payment they could reclaim the land and keep the wood he had delivered. Father agreed. He had made up his mind to have that place. In the end, it was to cost more than double the asking price.

Dread of the impending rumpus was all that impelled Mother to sign the contract. She had hoped for better things for her boys than to have them grow up to be "wood rats," as the men of the timber were contemptuously called in Moscow. She knew that none of the woodsmen made more than a bare living, which was usually helped out by harvest wages in the Palouse country. She couldn't see how we were to live if an extra hundred cords had to be delivered in Moscow each year. Moreover, she saw clearly that each tree that was cut down would decrease the value of the place, there being no market at all for stump land.

When she tried to voice her forebodings he shouted her down. "You never encourage me in anything, you don't want me to have anything! You never recognize me as the head of the house! I should never have come back from Texas!"

"Maybe you're right about that, Will," she retorted. "And maybe I never should have taken you back. But we've got to stick together now, so if you'll only stop your yelling I'll sign your contract."

She signed—but Father didn't stop his yelling. Then, or thenceforth.

Up until now Mother's life had been spent among poor but reasonably peaceful and law-abiding people. Now she was thrown into the society of wild and violent men. Her belief that you could get along with anyone if you did what was right and tried to like them was subjected to a pretty severe test.

Ira Lee was the recognized bull-of-the-woods. A tough fellow but far from illiterate, he could be a charming and engaging talker. He liked to visit with Mother and she enjoyed talking with him, except when he pleaded that if he could have the training of my brother Chauncey for a couple of months he would guarantee that Chauncey could whip anybody of his weight in Latah County. That wasn't exactly what Mother had set her heart on with regard to her oldest son.

In general Ira Lee was a good neighbor, but there were exceptions. It was dangerous to talk about such a man, but Father had never learned to hold his tongue. Once Lee concluded that Father had slandered him, and the only speculation in the district was what form Lee's vengeance would take. Father was frankly scared for he had never been a fighting man and was no physical match for Lee. Father was five feet ten and weighed a hundred and sixty pounds. Lee was only five feet eight, but he weighed a solid two hundred pounds and loved to fight.

He "laid for" Father, knocked him down, and gave him a bad beating. When I came home from school that day and saw Father with both eyes closed and his face bruised and swollen beyond belief I felt sure he was dying. Father hauled Lee into court at Moscow, where the bull-of-the-woods was fined twenty-five dollars and bound over on bail to keep the peace. But Lee held no hard feelings and was soon neighboring with us again.

The next time he got mad at Father his revenge took a different form. He set fire to our timber. Father, Mother and I were paying a Sunday visit to our old neighbors at Tim Bell. On the way home Father saw the smoke from a forest fire, which he quickly decided was on our own place. He whipped the team to a gallop and soon arrived to take charge of the firefighting. Chauncey and Obe, closer to home, had got there first and started a back-fire. To me it was a thrilling sight to see that blazing inferno with the flames leaping from treetop to treetop with the mightiest roar I had ever heard.

Thanks to the back-fire, the flames were soon under control and the blackened trees would still make cordwood. Mother and I stayed up until midnight watching, but Father and the boys didn't go to bed at all. Everybody "knew" that Lee had set the fire, but there was no way to prove it.

Just before we moved onto "the eighty," a feud between Lee and a man named Richardson had come to a head. Richardson had come to Lee's place and taken a shot at Lee while he was working in his field. Lee promptly took refuge behind a stump, and shouted, "Wait till my wife can bring my rifle!" Richardson, a true sportsman, obligingly refrained from firing any more shots until Mrs. Lee arrived with her husband's rifle. Then, from behind their respective stumps the two men blazed away at each other until dark when Richardson went home, his honor satisfied.

Another time Lee made the mistake of trying to bully a man named Hart. As he was coming from Moscow he met Hart with a load of cordwood. Lee got down from his wagon and challenged Hart to fight. "Coming," Hart said and, reaching back for his double-bitted ax, started to climb down. When he reached the ground Lee was back on his wagon and driving on. "Can't you take a joke?" Lee called.

One of the stories Lee loved to tell on himself illustrated his peculiar sense of humor. His wife, Reva, was never seen off her own farm, and the Lees seldom had visitors. Once a vicious bull of the neighborhood came into the yard, and Lee sent his wife out to drive it away. When the bull charged her Lee shouted with great glee, "Run, Reva, run! God Almighty'll take care of you!" Relating the incident, he would then add, "If I'd tried to he'p Reva, He'd likely have he'ped the bull."

Lee and another neighbor, Joe Meeks, carried on a feud for several years; because of it neither was ever without his gun whenever there was a chance of their meeting. Meeks, a tall, raw boned Kentuckian who might well have served as an artist's model for Daniel Boone, was a dead shot with a rifle, and had once given the burly Lee the whipping of his life. I was a witness to the ending of this feud.

Father used to "bank out" cordwood on top of a ridge at the edge of our place. Sometimes there would be ricks containing forty or fifty cords. One time when I had gone up there with Father, Ira Lee suddenly came round one end of the rick, and Joe Meeks round the other. Each man had his rifle cradled in his arm; neither had any idea the other was there until they met, with only a few yards separating them. Joe Meeks was my idol, and I remember hoping he would get in the first shot.

Father admitted later that he was scared, but he greeted each man by name. They spoke to him, but not to each other, though Lee nodded to his enemy.

Joe said, "Will, I've got a sick cow and I wondered if you'd know what to do for her?"

Before Father could speak Lee said, "What's the matter with her, Joe?"

Meeks hesitated a moment, then began to list the cow's symptoms. Father joined in the talk, and presently all three men went to look at the cow. The long-drawn-out feud was over.

Lee's fuss with another neighbor, a man named Walters, came nearer to ending in a murder. Walters, too, a soft-voiced Virginian, had whipped Lee in a fist fight. Then one night in Moscow the two met in a saloon and swore undying friendship. Leaving town with a close friend of Lee's, they started back to the timber, all three riding in the friend's wagon.

A mile from town the quarrel broke out again and they got down to finish the fight. Lee came at Walters with his knife, nearly severing the man's jugular vein with the first swipe, then stabbing him through a lung and laying open his intestines. As he lay helpless on the ground, Lee gave him some more cuts on the arms and legs. So tough were these mountaineers that Walters eventually recovered.

About daybreak the morning after that fight Lee's oldest son came for Father. Father found Lee groaning in bed. He displayed a bruised shoulder where he claimed Walters had hit him with a rack-stake from which he had received internal injuries. As soon as he learned that Walters would recover and that no charges would be pressed, he was sound as a dollar. In the course of time, Walters too became a friend of Lee's.

The fighting wasn't always confined to the men and boys. Two neighbor ladies, one the community termagant, had words about the ownership of a chicken; the other woman scratched her face horribly with the broken end of a shingle.

"Just thought I'd curry the old girl's face down a little," she explained to Mother.

In such a community fighting was one of the main topics of conversation and the younger generation readily adopted the tradition of its elders. Fist fights were frequent and bloody. Both Chauncey and Obe had their full share of battles; at times it seemed to Mother that they had interest in nothing else.

I alone showed a complete lack of warlike temperament. For the most part I wriggled out of overtures to combat—not always with credit to myself. I was fortunate in having as my best friend the oldest son of the redoubtable Ira Lee, who constituted himself my protector; it was soon understood that anyone who licked me had to lick Ike. That wasn't easy to do.

I recall how once his father ordered him to lick a much older boy, an obvious impossibility. Young Ike made a respectable showing, but his father whipped him with a length of barbed wire for having failed. He came to school next day with numerous cuts on his back and legs. Another time, his father threw him into a furrow and plowed him under. Ike, I have heard, became as tough as his father, but I shall always remember him as ambitious, gallant and manly.

One other violent incident remains vivid because I was a spectator. Mother seldom missed a debate, but this particular evening Father and I went without her.

A young man named Pleasant Armstrong lived with a married sister a mile from our house. They were dark-complexioned people, claiming a strong strain of Cherokee blood. I still recall a young unmarried sister of Ples Armstrong as the most beautiful woman I have ever seen.

Ples wasn't often around, but this night it was my luck to have him come in and sit down beside me. Even I knew there was a feud on between him and our neighbor Joe Meeks. There was a sort of unwritten treaty between Meeks and his chief enemy, Ira Lee, that Meeks would stay away from town, and Lee away from the literary and debating society meetings. For this reason Joe Meeks, present this night, was unarmed.

Everyone was uneasy during the exercises, for the violence of Armstrong's temper was well known. Physically he was no match for Meeks, but he always carried the equalizer. Ples didn't even seem to be aware of me crouching beside him. Then, in the customary intermission between the "literary" part of the program and the debate, Meeks came over to our seat and extended his hand.

"How are you, Ples?" he asked courteously.

Armstrong ignored the outstretched hand, and stared straight ahead without speaking.

Rebuffed, Meeks returned to his seat. He appeared to be the most unconcerned person in the room, but his wife sat as if her back was nailed to a board, her face as white as chalk. I glanced at Father and saw that he was licking his lips nervously.

Meeks, one of the evening's debaters, was a great reader and strong in his opinions. I can't remember whether the question that night was whether the cow was a greater boon to mankind than the horse, or if it was resolved that floods had done more damage to the earth than fire; both were favorite subjects for debate. I do know that it must have taken great courage for Joe Meeks to stand there and argue with his usual caustic humor, knowing that within the hour he might be shot to death in the presence of his family. At times he looked straight into the sullen face of his enemy.

The moment the debate was over, Ples left the schoolhouse. The hoodlums in the back seat, including my brother Chauncey, followed him. Meeks waited for his wife to put on the children's wraps. Father said something to him, but Joe shook his head, calling out to his debating partner, "Well, we waxed it to 'em tonight, didn't we?"

Mrs. Meeks's movements were stiff and jerky. Her fingers were so awkward that Joe had to button his four-year-old daughter's coat. He lifted the little girl in his arms and said, "Come on, Rosy, let's go."

It was a quarter of a mile to the big sawdust pile where the roads forked. The Robertsons lived on the ridge, the Meekses in the holler. Father and I walked along about fifty feet behind Meeks and his family. Ordinarily, Father was a fast walker, but this night he sauntered—because the folks ahead of us sauntered. There was none of the usual good-natured bantering back and forth. It was almost as if we were walking in a funeral procession.

Suddenly, Ples Armstrong stepped from behind a bush halfway between us and the little group ahead.

"Joe Meeks, you're a dirty, yellow, lowdown Kentucky son-of-a-bitch, and I'm going to kill you!" he yelled.

Meeks and his family kept on walking.

Ples waved a six-shooter in his hand. "Turn around, you bastard, so I won't have to shoot you in the back!"

Meeks continued his slow, even pace, and Ples got closer and closer as he waved the gun and continued his abuse. To make matters worse young Claude Walters ran past us all and, in sight of Armstrong, stuck a six-shooter in the pocket of Meeks's overcoat.

"You've got a gun now, you coward, turn around and use it," Ples shouted, but Meeks marched straight ahead.

We had to turn off, and so long as we could hear, Ples was still trying to taunt Meeks into turning around.

Mother was still up when we got home. Father was telling her about the trouble, wondering if Joe Meeks was still alive, when there came a knock at the door. Ples Armstrong stood there, pale and wild-eyed. "I'd like a drink of water," he said. He drank two big dipperfuls, muttered, "Good night," and vanished into the darkness.

He hadn't killed Meeks for fear of hitting the little girl in Joe's arms, he said later. He had come back by our house for fear Meeks would get his rifle and ambush him. Meeks told Father later that he had got his rifle and run headlong through the timber to head off his foe before Ples got home. "But I wasn't going to kill him," he maintained. "I was just going to cram that damned sixgun down his throat."

That was the kind of thing that very often broke the monotony of living in the Moscow mountains.

11

The acreage Father had bought was known as "the Norton place." His first act was to clear away the brush and chop a set of house logs. A Swede named Ericksen hewed one side of the logs flat and smooth as boards for the inside, then the neighbors gathered from miles around for an old-fashioned log-raising. The house went up to the square in a single day. But winter set in before Father and the boys could do more than put on the roof and build a lean-to for the horses and the cow. We were lulled to sleep by the mooing of the cow and the stamping of the horses in the next room, so to speak. There was no privy, so all through the long, cold winter each member of the family had to tramp out to his separate thicket beyond the clearing—and snow fell deeply there in the timber.

So much cordwood had to be cut that the older boys could not even think of going to school. They wrapped their feet and legs in split-open gunny-sacks and were busy with crosscut saw, sledges, wedges and axes from daylight till dark. But I was ready for my education. I had long since learned to read. I loved the feel of books and detested anything that soiled my hands.

My debut in school was not propitious. The teacher was a hell-and-brimstone preacher who my parents thought must be a good teacher because he had the reputation of being "strict." I was put into the chart class along with other children and set to learning the alphabet. The teacher wouldn't listen when I tried to tell him I already knew it, seeming to think I was trying to get out of work. Most of the time I sat in my seat, mind and body alike rigid and frozen from fear.

For some time now I had been getting my regular quota of whippings from Father, but I had a morbid dread of the disgrace of being whipped in public. I was sure I would die if I was ever whipped by the schoolteacher, and it was said that no child ever escaped his wrath. No believer in a brimstone hell could have had a greater fear of a horned Satan than I felt for this teacher.

My seatmate the first day was a hulking third-reader lad of about eighteen called Cub, who had loudly announced that his sole purpose in coming to school was to whip the teacher. Cub's bluff was called before his seat was warm. The teacher whipped him with an inch-thick stick as he sat in his seat, and cower though I might I frequently caught the stinging end of the switch. That turned out to be the closest I ever came to getting a whipping in school, though many were the artful and shameful devices I resorted to in order to avoid one.

The school term was only five months, and fortunately for me after a couple of weeks the snows came, and my parents voluntarily retired me from school for the year. I had learned nothing.

In the inevitable debating society Mother had little competition worthy of her steel. The best of the lot was young Warren Matthews—although the Matthews family lived five miles away, they preferred our district to their own. Usually Warren and some other backwoods orator were paired against Mother and her partner. Since Warren took his defeats so hard she often tried to make points for his side and lose the decision herself.

Sometimes a preacher would be brought in, but the ranting style used by frontier clergymen was cut to order for Mother's logical mind and ready wit. Without her realizing it, the overthrow of these preachers did much to help Mother win first the admiration and then the affection of her half-outlaw neighbors.

It was her happy faculty of liking and trusting people which enabled her to get along so well with the local toughs. It was true that she seldom got to see their bad side; even the worst of them acted like gentlemen in her presence. It came as a shock to her when our neighbor, Joe Meeks, who adored his wife and children and always seemed so soft-spoken and kind, impaled another neighbor on a picket fence and beat him within an inch of his life.

Of course, not all the people in the Zeiglar district were of the lawless type. The best of them organized a Sunday School which met in the little one-room schoolhouse. Mother was chosen superintendent. She insisted that it be non-denominational, although most of the members were Campbellites, or Church of the Disciples, as they preferred to be called. Quite often she was able to get some rural preacher to hold services after Sunday School; occasionally, when enough pressure was brought to bear, she preached a sermon herself.

One of Mother's favorite preachers was an enormously fat man called "Uncle Tom," who belonged to the unpopular Dunkard sect. He was quite a sight with his great white beard, shaven upper lip, collarless coat and funny little hat, as he waddled along with a Bible in his hand. Mother felt that he was a good and righteous man, although his preaching left something to be desired. She did not think so much of a long-nosed, foxlike exhorter who beat his breast and preached infant damnation, along with plenty of hellfire and brimstone. But *any kind of a sermon is better than no sermon at all*, she thought.

She was, however, less than enthusiastic when Father announced that as a special treat he was going to take us all into Moscow on a Sunday to hear a very popular pastor preach. The Matthews and the Poes were also going.

Father met her first-instant objection that she had no clothes suitable to wear in a city with a rebuke for her sinful pride. He had his heart set on it, so she said no more. When the day arrived she dressed herself in her best, conscious that it was many years out of style. It didn't help that the countrified pipe-smoking Poes would be just as out of style as the Robertsons, or that Win and Belle would be dressed well enough not to attract attention. Win was used to the city, and Belle always managed to wear good clothes. Chauncey and Obe, of course, flatly refused to go; but I, arrayed in knee pants and clean white waist, had no choice.

Father was never late to any gathering, so the Robertson wood wagon stood at the head of a long line of fancy carriages. Mother looked longingly at what would have been the hoodlum benches at home; but Father, having come so far, was determined to hear every golden word and marched us up to the best seats in front. When the house began to fill an usher informed us that we were sitting in private pews, and we had to move back, Father muttering, "Talk about the House of the Lord!" and Mother suffering shame and agony from what seemed hundreds of curious or hostile eyes fixed upon us.

Once recovered from her confusion, she followed the services closely, partook of the sacrament, and waited eagerly for the pearls of Christian wisdom to flow from the talented, sanctified lips of the minister.

After it was over the pastor came down to the door to shake

hands with the departing congregation. Mother thought he looked a trifle "leery" as we mountaineers approached in a body. Win tried to explain where we were from and why we were here, but instead of being flattered the minister seemed anxious to be rid of us. "Ah, yes," he said. "Splendid! Splendid!" and turned away to shake other hands.

Father was not to be shunted aside so easily. "This is my wife," he said. "She's superintendent of the Sunday School out our way. And sometimes she preaches a sermon herself."

"Indeed?" the minister said. "And has she ever been ordained? Excuse me now, I must go."

As Mother climbed into the wagon she caught Win's eye. He grumbled, "I'd sooner hear old Uncle Tom preach." Mother laughed, and Win joined in with his contagious "Kic, kic, kic" chuckle. Father and Belle were fuming, but Mother and Win had the gift of being able to laugh at themselves.

The hundred cords of wood that had to be delivered every year to pay on the place weighed Father down. The price of cordwood had gone up to three dollars a cord, and he realized what a bad bargain he had made. In desperation he sold off several hundred thousand feet of lumber at a ridiculous price. He took to slashing his timber, picking out the best trees all over the place and spending half his time making roads to them.

The pressure made him quarrelsome, so row followed row after the established pattern. While he hung around the house and jawed Mother, Obe struggled manfully to chop the necessary quota of wood.

These days Chauncey fared better than the other members of the family. To him had fallen the job of hauling the cordwood to town with a four-horse team. He had become an expert teamster who could make the buckskin popper of a fourteen-foot lash sound like a rifle shot, and it was his delight to drive down Main or Third Street in Moscow making as much noise as a small boy with a pocketful of firecrackers.

With that whip he was always killing small birds and ground squirrels along the road, and he could nip a horsefly off the rump of a leader without ruffling a hair.

He associated with the tough, swaggering teamsters with perfect equality and learned to chew tobacco and smoke cigarettes. He would buy a twenty-five cent dinner at a restaurant instead of eating cheese and crackers at the wagon as Father always did. He was always bringing home apples and oranges and other good things to eat, although Father roared that we couldn't afford them.

Flatly disobeyed, at last Father determined to establish his authority once and for all. Trimming himself a gad, he ordered Chauncey to come out and take his licking. Chauncey was a tall, slim lad, quick as a cat, and with muscles of steel. Father lashed out once and then found himself flat on his back while his enraged son pounded his head on the hard ground.

"Ma! Ma! Come pull this boy off of me!" Father yelled.

From that time on Chauncey was his own master, but his emancipation made it doubly hard on Obe. Scarcely fourteen, Obe had long been doing a man's work. He seldom got off the place, except to attend Sunday School and church, and this he stopped doing when he heard Father boast that he *made* him go.

Once Father said in Obe's presence, "I made a mistake with Chauncey, but I'll see to it that Obe never smokes cigarettes before he is twenty-one." Before that Obe had smoked secretly, but now he smoked openly and got whipping after whipping, which he endured silently and kept on smoking.

Once Father happened to stoop just as Obe was striking with a sledgehammer and it caught Father on the head, knocking him down and making a two-inch gash in his scalp. Bleeding profusely, he ran to the house, claiming that Obe had tried to kill him. Mother dismissed the charge as absurd. Later on, he told Win, and got even less satisfaction. "You should learn to keep your head where it belongs," Win said, and chuckled his "Kic, kic, kic!"

The only variety to Father's rows was that sometimes they were more ridiculous than usual. Once when he had gone into his customary sulk and was stretched out in the rocking chair, chin sunk upon breast, lower lip protruding like an angry baby's, he happened to see a bit of dirt on the floor which my near-sighted mother had overlooked in her sweeping.

"If you were any good as a housekeeper," he roused himself to say, "you'd keep the house clean! My mother never would have left anything like that. You could eat off her floor."

"And you probably did," Mother retorted. "I might have seen that dirt if you hadn't had your long legs stretched clear across the room."

Father bounded to his feet. "That's a lie!" he yelled. "I can prove it's a lie! I can prove by Win Matthews that my legs won't reach across this room!"

"Why, Pa—" Mother began in astonishment, but he howled her down.

"You don't ever hesitate to lie if you can put me in the wrong! But this time, Mary Robertson, you've gone too far! I'm going to send for Win and prove to him right before your eyes that you're a liar."

And send for Win he did. When Win arrived Father tried to make him measure the length of his legs and the width of the room. It wasn't the first time Win had been sent for to settle a row, nor would it be the last. Such times were almost as painful to him as they were to Mother. He assured them over and over that they were his best friends, and begged them to bury the hatchet.

They always talked about burying the hatchet. I always wondered when any row would reach the hatchet-burying stage. Sooner or later it always arrived and they generally agreed to bury it, but they always dug it up again.

The family, Father unhesitatingly asserted, was on its way to hell. Chauncey had become a hoodlum and dishonored his parents. Obe would fill a suicide's grave before he was twenty-one—unless cigarettes laid him low first. Mother thought more of the lowest scoundrel in the neighborhood than she did of her lawful husband.

Although I was only eight I did not escape Father's condemnation. I was totally without ambition, and spent all my time out in the woods killing villainous Spaniards. My brothers shared Father's opinion of me. They didn't understand that while I was marching up and down in the woods waving my wooden sword I wasn't really killing anybody. Little did they realize that I was Admiral Robertson, bravely leading my fleet into battle to defend my sorely beleaguered and beloved country, and my sword was only a symbol of my high office as I planned brilliant campaigns against the enemy.

I wasn't always an admiral. Sometimes I was another silver-tongued Bryan crusading against a greedy fat man named Mark Hanna, whose clothes were entirely covered by dollar-marks. Or an Isador Raynor defending a maligned hero, Commodore Schley, before a stiff-necked board of retired admirals who wanted to give the glory to one of their own rank. Or a Bob Fitzsimmons valiantly defending my heavyweight championship of the world against huge bullies like Jim Jeffries.

Even at eight I could read the newspapers with ease. I had followed the course of the Spanish-American War with painstaking anxiety and could give the name and tonnage of every ship in the United States Navy. We had little reading material and what we had I read over and over until it was largely memorized. We had an old *World Almanac* full of facts and figures. If you were to ask me who was the junior senator from Indiana or the Secretary of the Treasury under President James K. Polk, I could give you their names without a moment's hesitation.

Most of my day dreams were strictly autobiographical, though my name was not always Robertson. Sometimes I would adopt a fictitious name—Morgan and Hubbard, for some reason, were two of my favorites—and in the course of an hour I could rise from obscurity and poverty to the highest pinnacle of fame as soldier or statesman. It was simply impossible for me to see myself as the stringy little boy with unkempt hair and bad teeth that I was, except when jerked back to reality by a whipping from Father. I was a man with the physique of a James J. Corbett and the intellect of a Daniel Webster. Such a son, Father was convinced, could never be much of a credit to him and he strove nobly to put such visionary ideas out of my head. Just as he was sure cigarettes would ruin Obe, he was sure that books would be my damnation.

Mother was not willing to accept Father's sweeping condemnation of his family. Their feet might have started on the pathway to hell but she didn't believe they were irrevocably planted there. There might yet be hope for all of them—if only they could get out of the timber.

There seemed little hope of that. Father was always in debt, and even if he eventually got the place paid for, his wasteful practices would make it practically worthless. Chauncey and Obe were following in the footsteps of the toughest characters in the mountains, and she had no reason to assume that I would be any different as I grew older.

Her only hope was that in time God would move in His mysterious way to perform the wonder of saving her family from ruin. The time was closer at hand than she had any idea. It wasn't a mere move or change we were on the verge of, but a complete revolution in our way of living and thinking—and Father was to be the chief beneficiary. It began with the arrival of the first Mormon missionaries in our community.

Mother had just called the Sunday School to order one Sunday when two strangers wearing long black Prince Albert coats and carrying small, oblong leather bags entered the schoolhouse and seated themselves quietly on the hoodlum bench. They looked distinguished. We knew by the cut of their jib that they must be preachers. Their black suits were pretty shiny and rusty, but none of us noticed that.

Mother went back and invited them into a class which she herself taught. During the discussion the older one, a small, wiry-looking man with a sandy mustache, made a few unobtrusive comments. Mother had no idea who they were and, since she never drew the line between sects, she asked them just before the dismissal if they would like to say a few words.

The older man would. They were, he stated quietly, missionaries of the Church of Jesus Christ of Latter-Day Saints, commonly known as Mormons. They had tracts which they would be glad to distribute to anyone who would read them. He thanked Mother for her courtesy and then tactfully added that, like Christ's disciples of old, they traveled without purse or script and were dependent upon the hospitality of the people for food and shelter.

There was a sectarian minister present who was to preach immediately after Sunday School. He was a howling breastbeater, a Come-to-Jesus man from the deep South. He devoted an hour and a half to a bitter attack upon the two emissaries of Satan who, like the serpents they were, would insinuate themselves into the fold and so deceive the very elect. He rebuked Mother for having invited them to speak.

Father had never liked this man, and besides hospitality was his long suit. No sooner was the preaching over than he pressed forward to invite home for dinner the two Mormons, who had sat unperturbed under the onslaught. They accepted readily.

"But I thought you fellers had horns," Father remarked jokingly.

With a grave and sober face the older man, Elder Amos Hatch, replied, "They always dehorn us before they send us out to preach." His eyes twinkled.

Both Father and Mother took to this man at once. His companion, Elder Larsen, whom we never saw again, was a red-faced youth who blushed and stammered every time anyone spoke to him. My parents wondered about him until Elder Hatch explained the Mormon missionary system, which took raw recruits from stores and farms and sent them out into the world to preach the Gospel for two years, which they did entirely at their own expense.

"Both of us," he explained, "are plain farmers, like yourselves. Elder Larsen is just fresh from home and hasn't learned the ropes yet. I live on eighty acres of land and make my living milking a dozen cows and shearing sheep in the spring. My wife is taking care of the farm and keeping me out here. I haven't seen her for a year and a half."

"Did you say, 'wife'?" Mother asked softly.

Elder Hatch grinned. "Everybody is disappointed when I tell 'em I've only got one wife. Elder Larsen here hasn't even got one."

"But your church does practice polygamy?" Mother said.

"Not any more. The Principle was discontinued by the Manifesto of 1890. Of course, those who were in the Principle before wouldn't abandon their families and brand their children as illegitimate. My father-in-law has three wives."

"I call it immoral," Father said righteously.

The elder smiled. "Would you say that Abraham, Jacob and the other Bible patriarchs were immoral characters?" he asked. "They were polygamists."

"But this is today," Father argued.

"Still, in the third chapter of Isaiah, it is predicted: 'In that day seven women shall cleave unto one man, saying, we will eat our own bread, and wear our own apparel. Only let us be called by thy name, to take away our reproach.'"

"Is that right, Mary?"

"It's in the Bible," Mother admitted. "But I thought you Mormons had another Bible, a golden one called the *Book of Mormon*."

Elder Hatch said, "We believe in the Bible as much as you do. We just claim to have other books containing still more truth. You are willing to accept truth, aren't you, Mrs. Robertson?"

"If it is the truth."

"All we ask is an opportunity to prove that what we teach is truth and not in conflict with the Bible," the elder said. So

Mother found herself inveigled into a promise to investigate the new religion.

Before the day was done Father and Elder Hatch had become very chummy. One remark the elder made impressed Father particularly. "We have some very good country, but where I live in southern Idaho it's pretty high, and not very good. We have to irrigate everything; however, a man can always make a living, no matter how poor he is."

Father thought: *A good country for a poor man. I could do all right there.*

He learned that land there was almost as cheap as it was in the timber. A man could get a few cows and chickens and make an easy living. If he wanted to work out, the elder said, there was always a job herding sheep or shearing them.

Mother wanted to talk religion, but the elders shied away from too much argument. "We'd rather leave you some tracts and a *Book of Mormon*. If you will buy them, when we call again I'm sure you will have found that we don't take a thing away from your belief but only add more fullness," Elder Hatch said.

"I've always said there was no reason why God shouldn't reveal Himself to man now as well as two thousand years ago," Father said, when the Mormon doctrine of modern revelation was explained to him.

"But," Mother said acidly, "that doesn't necessarily mean that Joe Smith was the man He would choose to talk to."

Elder Hatch said, "I bear you my testimony, Sister Robertson, that He did. The Prophet Joseph read in the Book of James, 'If any man lacketh wisdom let him ask of God, who giveth to all men liberally, and upbraideth not.' You see, sister, Joseph took God at His word, and he was answered."

At dinner the elders refused coffee. Elder Hatch delivered a little homily on the Mormon Word of Wisdom, a revelation given to Joseph Smith advising against the use of intoxicating liquors, tobacco, tea and coffee. That, too, met with Mother's approbation—even while she wondered if she could ever give up her coffee, or Father his pipe.

She read the Mormon literature faithfully and was amazed to find how absurd some of her ideas about the Mormons had been. She believed the elders when they explained that the Mountain Meadows Massacre, of which she had read, had been done by fanatics in defiance of Brigham Young's orders. When Father questioned her, she replied cautiously that she had found nothing unchristian in their books, and nothing that seemed to contradict the Bible.

Two weeks later Elder Hatch returned with an elder named Miller and asked permission to preach in the schoolhouse. At once there was a public furor. One trustee declared that such heathenish doctrines could not be preached in a public school building. Father, also a trustee, declared they could. The decision was up to that redoubtable sinner, Ira Lee.

"By God," said Lee, "if Mary Robertson wanted the devil himself to preach it would be all right with me—and I'll bet we'd git a goddamned good sermon."

The elders preached, but public feeling against them ran higher and higher. Elder Miller's preaching was so far superior to any other that I had ever heard that he became my temporary idol.

The elders continued to come and go. Scarcely a week passed that some two of them didn't stay all night at our place. Mormonism was the raging topic of the hour. Teamsters stopped in the middle of the road to talk about it, and woodchoppers left their axes buried to the haft while they argued. People asked each other if Mary Robertson had taken leave of her senses.

Said Father proudly: "If we join the Mormons half the neighborhood will join 'em!"

Mother realized that this wasn't too badly exaggerated, and the responsibility sent her to God in prayer more fervently than ever before. But she was still not ready for baptism. She found nothing unreasonable in their idea of a modern prophet.

There was no reason, she claimed, why God's lips should be sealed in a divided and distraught world. She read the *Book of Mormon,* with its alleged history of various civilized races who were supposed to have lived on the American Continent, and found it no more unreasonable than the Old Testament account of Noah's Ark, or the ramblings of the Children of Israel. What impressed her was that nowhere were its moral concepts in conflict with the Bible in which she so strongly believed.

Elder Hatch and his companions still avoided any Scriptural argument with Mother, for she knew her Bible far better than they did. They kept telling her to wait for the arrival of their conference president, an elder named Smurthwaite. When this theological Titan finally arrived, he turned out to be a short, heavy-set, well-educated Englishman who had himself been a convert to Mormonism. He was a powerful preacher and his logic seemed invincible.

It was mid-winter, and elders Hatch and Smurthwaite were to spend the night with us. I suspect that both Mother and Elder Smurthwaite were a bit nervous, each having heard of the other's ability and knowledge of the Scriptures. Elder Smurthwaite was to become still more nervous before he reached the house, but for reasons quite apart from religion.

Whenever we rode to church, as we usually did in the winter, the sleigh was always drawn by a four-horse team. This evening it was piloted by Chauncey. During his sermon Elder Smurthwaite had paused to give vigorous verbal chastisement to the noisy hoodlums on the back bench, of whom Chauncey was one. As soon as we were all loaded in, for the trip back home, Chauncey's whip cracked like a gun and the horses were off at a dead run. It was a crooked road up and down steep hills and bending around trees and stumps.

Elder Hatch, a man used to horses, sat flat on the bottom and grinned. Father, taking his cue from his favorite elder, did likewise. But Elder Smurthwaite was a city man, laden with dignity. He knelt in the bottom of the wagon box gripping each side, momentarily expecting all of us to be dashed to our death. At the approach to every curve he would shout loudly, "'Old on, Brother 'Atch!"

I doubt if anyone else could have taken all those curves as fast as a team could run without tipping the sled bottom side up, but the young devil possessed consummate skill. We arrived safely and Father and Elder Hatch, trying hard to conceal their laughter, solicitously assisted Elder Smurthwaite into the house. He was naturally a little pompous, but thereafter when his self-importance became a little too inflated it was only necessary for one of the other elders to shout, "'Old on, Brother 'Atch," to bring him back to normal.

All that night the Scriptural battle raged. Elder Smurthwaite sat on one side of the table, Mother on the other, each with open Bible at hand. It was an honest inquiry for Truth, and their voices were never raised in heat. Father and Elder Hatch prowled about the room, occasionally getting themselves a sandwich or a glass of milk; neither could have been dragged to bed.

It was dawn when Mother closed her Bible and admitted that she had not been able to stump the elder at any point. She could accept defeat gracefully. "I believe," she said, "that I can accept your Gospel now—even if it included Will's having seven wives. In fact," she added, glancing at Father, "I'm sure I could use the help."

Mormonism opened great new vistas before her. She saw Man not as the product of a chunk of clay, but verily as a child of God. She understood the thunderous voice of God as He asked Job: "Where wast thou when the foundations of the earth were laid, and the stars of the morning shouted together for joy?" The Mormon answer was: In a pre-existent state with all the other sons and daughters of God, waiting to receive a physical body so that they might go on and on in growth and exaltation throughout all eternity.

No gold-paved heaven with a monotony of harp playing and adoration for the righteous—she had never believed in that—

and no damnation or eternal burning in a lake of fire for the sinners. Instead, Mormonism taught that there were varying degrees of glory, shading from the brightest of suns to the dimmest of stars, where each man would receive his reward according to his merits. Here at last Mother could see a place for the Herm Mallorys, the Phil Carlins, and even the Ira Lees of her acquaintance. And they could go on learning and progressing throughout all eternity as they acquired knowledge of God and His righteous ways.

"As man is, God was. As God is, man may become," Joseph Smith had said. To Mother that was tremendous, breathtaking in its scope.

There were many other things that appealed to her. There was a church fully organized in the exact pattern set by Christ, with Twelve Apostles, Seventies, Bishops, Priests, Elders, Teachers and Deacons. All history proved that there had been a great apostasy and it was time for a restored Gospel.

The fact that the Saints practiced the Word of Wisdom and paid one-tenth of their gross income as tithing indicated that they were a righteous, unselfish and God-fearing people. But not yet did she have the testimony without which she would not join the Mormons.

Win Matthews drove over to see Mother and to reason with her. In the midst of their discussion she surprised herself by saying, "Win, I *know* the Gospel is true, and that Joseph Smith was a true prophet." The testimony she had prayed for had come. From that moment on she knew that she was going to be a Mormon.

12

Even with her newly acquired testimony Mother could not bring herself to take the final step immediately. Her roots were deep in the Christian sect which her father had helped to found. It would mean a new life, a change of location and a plunge into the unknown. First she resigned as superintendent of the Sunday School and then, in May, she and Father were baptized by Elder Hatch. Later Win and Belle Matthews and many others followed their example. Father's prediction that half the neighborhood would join the Mormons if they did proved to be correct.

Mother actually pleaded with some of the people not to join

the Mormons. She knew that they were doing so, not because they had a testimony of their own, but because they trusted her, or were impressed by some of the elders. As conditions changed she believed they would fall away and be worse off than if they had never joined. Some of them later did become the worst enemies the Mormons had in that part of the country.

The big thought now in the minds of my parents was to "gather to Zion." No longer did Father's golden voice ring out through the timber, singing old English or cowboy ballads. Now he sang:

> "Oh, Babylon, oh, Babylon,
> We bid thee farewell.
> We're going to the mountains,
> Of Ephraim to dwell."

Mormonism changed all our lives, but Father's most of all. He was in his glory. His home became headquarters for the elders and a rendezvous for converts and investigators.

Mother's little Sunday School was taken over by a bigoted man who let it be known that Mormons were not welcome. We at once organized our own Sunday School, which was held in the long, lean-to kitchen that had housed the animals during that first winter. Father was chosen superintendent because, as Elder Smurthwaite explained, in the church women had their own organizations over which they might preside. Where the sexes were mingled this was the responsibility and privilege of the priesthood; a woman could not hold the priesthood except through her husband.

Father was ordained an elder. He now held the Holy Melchizedek Priesthood, which had been restored to earth by the physical ministrations of Peter, James and John upon the heads of Joseph Smith and Oliver Cowdrey. It gave a man his rightful dignity as the head of his family. Throughout all eternity Father would *rule* over his family and his posterity.

His wife would be *sealed* to him in the temple for time and eternity. He might be sealed to other women in eternity, even though he could have but one wife on earth so long as Mother was alive—but never could she be sealed to another man. His children, too, would be sealed to him and forever and forever they would be jewels in his crown.

Here, then, was a virile, masculine religion where women were duly subjected to the priesthood. The more Father thought about it, the better he liked it. No longer could Mother defy his commands without repudiating the Gospel which she had accepted. It was the duty of the priesthood to determine what was right and what was wrong.

Mother didn't mind in the least. She had never wanted to lead and was pleased to see Father at long last making something of himself. She liked to have the elders at her house. There were as many as six or eight at a time. Secure in their knowledge that they were among friends, they threw off their missionary manners and became human, likable young fellows who loved to have fun. They wrestled and ran races, played jokes on each other. Most of them were farm boys, but even dignified Elder Smurthwaite occasionally became playful. Once I saw a young Danish giant from Sanpete County, Utah, carry him out of the house bodily and deposit him in a snowdrift. Mother went calmly about her work smiling at their antics. They had become her "boys."

There was also a serious side. Fanatics, some of whom had been among our most pious friends, were threatening to tar and feather the elders. When word got round that a towering elder named Talbot had been a professional pugilist, the rumor quickly cooled off the direct-action proponents.

A thorn in Father's flesh was the sinful conduct of his two oldest sons. Even if they remained on the place on Sunday they would not attend services. Instead, with others of their deplorable kind, they stayed out behind the barn smoking cigarettes and telling smutty stories. Here was a situation with which the priesthood couldn't cope. Father's appeal to Mother to "do something about them boys" was to no avail.

Mother lived only for the day when we would reach Zion. In that new and righteous environment there would be fewer temptations, and the boys would have no reason at all not to join the church—something they now steadfastly refused to do.

No one, of course, paid much attention to the impact of Mormonism upon me. I was only nine years old, but to me the friendly, well-dressed elders were demi-gods. The very zenith of achievement, I now felt, would be to grow up and go on a mission. Forgotten now were my political and military aspirations. Instead, armed with a leather thong tied to either end of the discarded goose-neck from the end of a wagon-tongue, in imitation of the grip loaded with literature and clean clothes which every elder carried, I tramped through the timber bringing countless thousands into the fold by the sheer magnetism of my eloquence. I began memorizing songs in the Mormon hymnbook and familiarizing myself with Mormon church history.

I filled missions, wrote learned treatises on church doctrine, became the youngest Apostle in the history of the church, and eventually wound up as Prophet, Seer, and Revelator and Trustee-in-Trust of the Church of Jesus Christ of Latter-Day Saints. However, I had not been baptized—not from lack of conviction, but from a hysterical fear of getting my head completely under water. Chauncey was to blame for this, having once held my head in a bucket of water until I became almost crazed from fear of drowning. Another pastime of his was putting a pillow over my head and sitting on it until I went into a frenzy from fear of smothering.

But young as I was, I was not to escape entirely the attention of the devil. While I loved to watch and listen to the servants of the Lord, Satan also kept tempting me to sneak out behind the barn and listen to dirty stories being told. If discovered by either of my brothers I got a swift kick and was sent back to the house. Maybe in this way, they unwittingly served the Lord.

An event that autumn momentarily threatened to return me to my old gods. A political campaign was on and some candidates on the Republican ticket held a rally at our schoolhouse. Among them were Mother's old and trusted friends, Billy Buchanan and Charley Munsen, seeking re-election as sheriff and state legislator. But the orator of the occasion was a handsome, curly-haired young schoolteacher named Burton L. French. He was only twenty-two and was running for the legislature.

Billy Buchanan, remembering Mother's skill in debate, persuaded her to share the platform with young French. She acquitted herself so well that the young politician insisted upon driving her home in his buggy, pleading with her to make other campaign speeches. Four years later Burton L. French was elected to Congress and, for some years, was known as Uncle Joe Cannon's baby. He had a long and undistinguished career in Congress, but as I remember him he was all fire and persuasiveness and easily became my hero. It was several months before I stopped running for office and returned to the more serious business of saving souls.

One unpleasant duty confronted Mother and she put it off as long as she could; that was to inform her sisters that she had abandoned the faith of her father and become a Mormon. She knew that would be complete proof to them that her ex-cowboy husband had dragged her down to the lowest level of degradation.

It was several months before she heard from any of them. When two of them wrote they refrained from any mention of Mormonism, but a half-sister, mother of several prominent ministers and a successful doctor, wrote a long argumentative letter. She opined that Mary would have affiliated with Adventism, or even "Ingersollism," with equal fervor and abandon had they been called to her attention first. Bitterly would Mary rue the day, she predicted, if she was ever so unfortunate as to find herself among the Mormon people. Mother made an honest and dignified reply, and so impressed were the elders by her defense that both letters were printed in the Church Intelligence section of the *Salt Lake Deseret News,* the official organ of the church.

Father had dug many wells on our place, but had never struck water. There was a spring which flowed until June, but during the summer we had to haul all our water nearly half a mile in barrels, so when Father and the boys went harvesting in the Palouse country, Mother and I moved into the house of a Swedish bachelor some three miles distant who was also away for the summer. There I indefatigably continued my missionary work among Gus Johnson's pigs and chickens.

We were eating supper one evening when a hail came from outside. There sat Chauncey on a fat, sleek little sorrel pony and a new saddle. He wore a new black sateen shirt, new Levis, and cowboy boots.

Realizing that she was looking at the fruits of all Chauncey's wages—money which Father had counted on to get us well along on the road to Zion—Mother could only gasp, "Chauncey, what have you done?"

Father was, of course, furious when he heard about the pony. "That boy ain't twenty-one yet, and I'll sell it," he declared.

"If you do, Chauncey will leave home," Mother warned him.

"You always side against me," he complained. "Joining the church ain't changed you. You *claim* to know the Gospel is true, but if you did you'd honor the priesthood I hold. It's your duty to obey me."

"I do, Pa—whenever I think you are right."

Her answer infuriated him. "You don't understand Mormonism!" he charged. "It teaches obedience; a wife to her husband; children to their parents; church members to the authorities. That's the only way you can have order. But you don't believe in obedience. You never have."

"But I do," Mother protested. "It's just that I don't think anyone can be required to do anything their own conscience tells them is wrong."

"That ain't Mormonism!" Father shouted. "When you say you've got a testimony of the Gospel, you lie!"

Father didn't really believe that—he was often heard to boast about his wife's strong testimony—but he considered the charge to be a clincher in an argument with her.

That was the first of a cycle of quarrels that were to follow the same pattern. From that time on Mother's people were allowed to rest in peace; now every family row centered about religion. It was the strict letter of the law, as interpreted by Father, against Mother's insistence that in the last analysis she must be guided by her own awareness of right and wrong.

One result, however, was to set Father delving into the church books to find doctrine that would confound her. As a consequence, when finally he reached Zion he was better informed on church history and doctrine than most of the elders who had been born and brought up under the Covenant.

Before joining the church Father had said that if he ever did join he would live up to every requirement, including the Word of Wisdom.

"Then," said Nancy Poe, puffing contentedly upon her powerful pipe, "you'll never be a Mormon."

Dramatically, Father walked over to the stove and stuffed pipe and tobacco into the firebox. "I'll never touch tobacco again," he said, and he never did.

Win Matthews gave up smoking at about the same time, but after four or five tormenting years went back to his pipe. Mother, too, gave up coffee, which up to that time had been about the only luxury she had ever allowed herself. Another commandment Father found easy to keep was the Law of Tithing. From the day he joined the church he bestowed upon it one dollar out of every ten he received from any source.

Characteristically, Father had announced that he would get rid of the Zieglar district place if he had to give it away. It was worthless, except for the timber, and the way that had been slashed greatly depreciated the value of what was left. Would-be buyers held off just to see how little he would take.

Father finally traded his land to Gus Johnson for a team of gray horses, one of which was balky. No sooner were the papers signed than Gus sold the place to Joe Meeks, our nearest neighbor, for a neat profit.

Father's plans were made. He and the boys would work through harvest in the Palouse country. We would spend the winter at La Grande, Oregon, where there was a branch of the church, then go on in the spring to Chesterfield, Idaho, where Elder Hatch resided. This was in the southern part of the state, well within Zion.

Here Father could easily make a living and live the Gospel. Here his priesthood would be honored and here would be opportunity for advancement. "The Glory of God is intelligence," the Prophet Joseph had said, and Father would spare no effort to master the complete theory and practice of the Gospel.

He had accepted Mormonism without any reservations or "sectarian" hangovers such as he believed he could still detect in Mother. Whatever the authorities commanded, that would he do. And from those below him in the priesthood he would exact the last full measure of obedience.

Mother's trepidation equaled Father's enthusiasm. She was as eager to reach Zion as he was; she knew the present environment was bad for the boys, yet it was always a wrench to part with friends—even with such bad eggs as Ira Lee and Joe Meeks. They had always remained her staunch defenders in spite of their feuds and fallings-out with Father.

Too, she had come to love the rolling, forest-covered mountains and the tall pines and tamaracks which stood guard round her cabin home. She was no longer young enough to yearn for adventure for its own sake. Above all she wanted peace—and she had no real assurance that Father would hit it off any better with the Saints than he had with the sinners.

There was something irrevocable about this move. She knew in her heart that she would never come back. Most of the old friends who came to see us off she would never see again.

Win Matthews was the last to shake her hand before she climbed into the wagon-seat beside Father. He held her hand a long time and struggled visibly with his emotions.

"Let us know how it is," he begged. "If it's like they say maybe we'll sell out and come."

Joe Meeks waited courteously until we were out of sight round the first bend before he began to tear down the house.

We drove south through a prosperous German settlement of big white houses and bulging red barns. It was too good a country for Father ever to have considered living in. Never did it occur to him that the people living there had once been poor.

Father always did the trading. In Genesee he surprised Mother by placing in her hands a little memorandum book. "Thought you might like to keep a diary of the trip," he explained. Later, had Father read some of the entries in that diary he might have regretted ever having given it to her. This diary, along with Mother's letters, were most useful to me in later years.

Under a simple list of *Provisions purchased,* I found such illuminating entries as this: *Today Pa said he bet Obe would fill a suicide's grave, and I said I bet he would fill an honorable mission for the church.* On another page was this: *Pa prophesied that Frank would be smoking cigarettes before he was fifteen.* So sure was Father on this point, and so contrary am I by nature, that just to prove him wrong I didn't take up cigarette smoking as long as he was alive.

We crossed the Snake River on the ferry at Almoto and drove on to Pomeroy. It had not rained for days and the wagon wheels were hub-deep in dust, which they picked up and poured down like flour. Those choking alkaline clouds at times made it impossible for Father to see his leaders.

Mother sat in tight-lipped silence breathing through her nose, but Father and I were always coughing and spitting out muddy saliva and running our tongues over our sore and swollen lips. Obe, driving the loose horses behind the wagon, was able to stay at the sides of the lane and so escaped much of the dust.

It was impossible even to think of taking a bath. When we climbed down from the wagon we would shake the dust from our clothes and wash our hands and faces in water which turned to mud before our eyes. Cold water on my sore lips was torture. I washed at all only under threat of a whipping while blubbering into the wash rag.

The business district of Pomeroy had just burned down; the ruins were still smoking. A camp ground at the edge of town was full of wagon tramps looking for work, but Father and Obe were lucky and found work with a farmer named Lambie. To reach his place we had to retrace our steps through that awful dust nearly back to the Snake River, where I went straight from hell into heaven.

We pitched our tent in Mr. Lambie's orchard where I had all the fruit I could eat. Often big, juicy plums would strike our table while we were eating. I had to be forced to eat anything other than fruit.

Father drove header-box; he could pitch more headings than any man I have ever known. He was strong and fast. Obe drove derrick for the thresher. He was painstaking and determined to do everything well, and soon became a great favorite with Mr. Lambie and the crew. The men frequently changed jobs with him and he learned, among other things, to become an expert sacksewer, a job which paid two or three times the wages he received. This was actually easier than dragging back a heavy pair of double-trees for fourteen hours a day; but he was still a boy and was paid only two dollars a day and board.

When the heading was over Father hauled wheat down the steep grade to the wharf to be loaded on a boat for Liverpool.

Father's outstanding physical endowment was speed. He and an Irishman named Callahan established a record for loading a wagon with wheat sacks which at that time had never been approached.

At any camp where he worked Father was usually fully dressed while his companions were still groping for their socks. Among the hundreds of teamsters he met not one could harness and hitch up a team as quickly as he. Nobody ever beat him in a hundred yard dash. When he was fifty he could, and did, outrun young fellows of twenty.

It was a wonderful summer for me. Over and over again I rode down to the wharf at Almoto on the wheat sacks. The road was so steep that the men had to rough-lock their wheels so that they would slide instead of roll. Whenever they crossed the creek they would stop and pour water over the tires to cool them. Clouds of hissing steam would arise when the water touched hot metal. They had to replace their burned-out brake-blocks every two days.

Halfway to the river was a large orchard cultivated by a colony of Chinese. I was fascinated by their flopping trousers, bright-colored shirts and long black pigtails hanging down their backs. Each carried a sharp-pointed iron rod—for the purpose of impaling unwary little boys, one of the teamsters warned me—but Obe revealed that they were used to kill the rattlesnakes which infested the country.

One day Father stopped in front of their fruit stand. A withered old man came to the wagon with an armful of peaches and pears which he gave me and explained in broken English that he had a little grandson about my age back in China. For the first time I began to question the justification for the hatred and contempt for foreigners which I had always encountered. The old Oriental's simple "Little boy likee flute?" knocked race prejudice out of my head.

Father and Obe's combined wages when they settled up were in excess of two hundred dollars. We recrossed the river on the ferry and drove to Colfax to cash the check, Father receiving the amount in gold. Obe found work with another threshing outfit, while Father went on a new wheat-hauling job.

A break in the monotony of tent life which promised pleasure, but quickly turned to grief, was the visit of two Mormon elders who were old friends. Father remembered some fancied slighting remark and appealed to the elders to give Mother a suitable rebuke. The elders tried to evade the issue and in some way Father's veracity became involved.

The elders, having committed themselves to stay all night, could not well leave before breakfast. Father's tirade lasted far into the night and was resumed at daybreak. The elders got away, but there was no escape for Mother.

"I'll haul no wheat until this thing is settled," Father declared.

Wherever Mother went he dogged her footsteps. There was not even an outhouse where she could take refuge. It was a week before Father tired of denunciation and went into the injured phase of the quarrel. Each wasted day cost him at least five dollars, but he was not one to count such cost where a matter of principle was involved.

It may be an overstatement to say that Father enjoyed those rows, but surely they were as necessary to him as whisky to an alcoholic. I can recall only one time when he used violence, and that was when I was about six years old. He threw Mother on the bed and shouted for me to bring his razor so he could cut her throat. Of course he was bluffing the whole thing, but I was terrified. He made no real opposition when my brothers dragged him away, and I didn't even get a whipping for not obeying an order.

Up until the day we were to break camp and start we didn't know whether Chauncey would accompany us or not. Then, to Mother's relief and Father's secret chagrin at having a prophecy brought to naught, Chauncey showed up on his sorrel pony with a pocketful of money.

We were on another leg of the long journey to Zion. Once

more people along the road were startled by the sight and sound of a brown-bearded man in a covered wagon, singing strange gospel hymns at the top of his voice as he passed them by.

13

We stopped in Walla Walla, a town of ten thousand, to do our trading and, for once in our lives, went on a spending spree. There were new clothes for everybody. The clerks in the Golden Rule store smiled as the wagon tramps trailed from counter to counter in the proud consciousness that we had enough money to buy anything we wanted.

Father bought himself a new gray suit and to our astonishment went to a barbershop and had his beard shaved off. It made him look years younger, less stern-faced and fanatical. He left his mustache, although eventually that, too, was to go.

For the first time since her marriage Mother found herself

with a brand-new outfit, inside and out, head to toe. All of us boys got new suits; I, my first pair of long pants.

I was more impressed by the huge bunches of green and purple grapes in the grocery department. Never had I tasted anything so luscious. Father bought me a sack of grapes. They were soon gone and Chauncey bought me another sack. When they vanished Obe bought me another. When at last Father settled our bill with nearly a hundred and fifty dollars in gold and the manager said smilingly, "Little boy, would you like a big sack of candy?" I replied solemnly, "Please, can I have a sack of grapes instead?"

The rains began as we started up the steep western slope of the Blue Mountains. It came down in torrents and seemed as if it would never cease. Our progress was pitifully slow. Chauncey and Obe tied their ponies behind the wagon and sought shelter under the wagon cover. The loose horses followed behind like colts.

After several days, quite suddenly, spread out before us was the beautiful Grande Ronde valley. To my parents it was like the open portals to heaven; here they would be among Saints!

Father soon found a small house on the outskirts of La Grande, a town of some three thousand people. For the first time in our lives we had to pay rent, a steady drain on our resources.

The Mormon population would scarcely exceed a hundred—converts and colonizers. Father at once got in touch with the leaders of the branch. The church had just built a sugar factory and was anxious to get members of its own faith to settle the land and raise sugar beets. Father was welcomed with open arms.

Sugar-beet harvest was on and the boys promptly got jobs. Father decided to look around. The brethren implored him to buy land at forty dollars an acre, offering him any terms he wished.

Father was not tempted. He had set out for Zion and to

Zion he would go. Moreover, the forty-dollar-an-acre price was too high and it conflicted with his theory of a poor country for a poor man. Within five years this same land was selling for two hundred dollars an acre.

My parents were entirely unaware that they were caught between the changing tides of Mormon church policy. The old idea of gathering all converts to Utah as swiftly as possible was giving way to a policy of expansion and colonization, to gain a foothold in the strongholds of the "Gentiles." Here in La Grande were Saints going to Zion and other Saints coming from Zion. As usual, the Robertsons were swimming against the main current. Representing the old order were the missionaries warning the people of Ephraimitic blood to come out of Babylon, and on the other hand were Mormon dollars insidiously undermining the foundations of Babylon itself.

Most of the people we met were not city people in the sense of those we had seen in the fashionable church at Moscow. Some worked in the beet-sugar factory or operated farms outside the towns; yet Mother instinctively recognized them, on the whole, as a far more cultivated class of folks than the ones she had lived among since her marriage. Culture, to her, was just a word in the dictionary; but these people had better manners, better speech, and greater consciousness of personal appearance.

She remained quietly self-effacing, not quite sure of herself, watching Father with mingled pride and apprehension. He looked fine in his new gray suit. She was glad that he had shaved off his whiskers, but she wished rather wistfully that he wouldn't talk so much or so loud, and that he wouldn't sing louder than anybody else and keep a bar or two ahead of the chorister. She knew how futile it would be to remonstrate, for Father was completely uninhibited. He could see no reason why a man shouldn't act natural.

At the first Sunday School we met a young couple from Utah, Sam and Polly Storey, who had a pretty little three-year-old daughter. The Storeys couldn't find a place to live, so

Father let them have two of our four rooms. It would cut down considerably on the rent and, besides, Father liked company.

Unfortunately, Polly Storey promptly incurred Father's swift wrath. The walls were so thin that each family could hear practically everything that was said or done by the other. Father, having heard Polly express an unfavorable opinion of him to her husband, immediately ordered Sam to make Polly apologize—something beyond poor Sam's power had he been inclined to do so.

Before the Storeys could find another place Father came down with smallpox and both families were quarantined. Sam was permitted to go to work on condition that there be no fraternizing with the Robertsons. The little girl, however, had been wandering into our part of the house and had to be kept indoors. Polly complained bitterly, her words reaching Father easily through the thin partition, and he shouted back reproof. This verbal warfare continued steadily during the weeks of Father's confinement and there was nothing Mother or Sam could do to stop it.

Just before Father took sick Mother determined to put me in school. While I was precocious in reading, history and geography, I was completely dumb so far as other subjects were concerned. Mr. Starkweather, the principal, was unable to understand Mother's explanation of my lop-sided education. He was used to grade schools and scholars who fitted neatly into their little prescribed niche. He couldn't understand a kid who knew all about John Jay and Henry Clay, yet couldn't name a single part of speech or work the simplest problem in fractions.

"We'll try him in Five-B," he said finally, "but he'll probably have to be put back."

My teacher, Mr. Snyder, proved more understanding and I was not demoted. Nevertheless, it was a relief to me when Father got the smallpox and I had to stay out of school.

Almost from the time we reached La Grande everything

seemed to go wrong. There was the smallpox. While Father was quarantined three of the horses he had put out to pasture ate poisoned weeds and died. Another valuable mare cut off her foot in barbed wire and had to be shot. There remained only faithful old Barney, a sway-backed bay mare, Chauncey's little sorrel pony and a colt.

When the sugar beets were harvested the boys could find no more work; and they couldn't come home. Chauncey finally got a job in a woodyard in Baker City and once more became the sole breadwinner of the family.

Our money was all gone and we were in debt before Father got out of quarantine. There was no prospect of a job for either him or Obe before spring. But just when we had no way to turn Father's aged Aunt Nancy died and bequeathed him two hundred dollars.

Then came the worst blow of all. Father received a telegram from Bishop Baker, Chauncey's employer, telling him Chauncey had met with an accident, and his right leg would have to be amputated. Father took the train to Baker City, and returned three days later. "Yes," he said, "they took his leg off just below the knee," then broke down in tears. He could only thrust a newspaper into Mother's hands while he crumpled into a chair and wept.

The newspaper contained an account of the accident. Tears moistened Mother's cheeks as she read. Chauncey, her eldest, the athlete of the family, he who loved to ride or run and show off his agility and daring—to be a cripple!

Bishop Baker had said that Obe could have Chauncey's job, and Father arranged to move to Baker City. Against the protests of Mother and Obe, Father sold Chauncey's little pony for ten dollars. Father argued that, being a cripple, Chauncey would never again have need for a pony. Again he proved a poor prophet; within a few years Father himself was often to hear Chauncey praised as one of the best bronco-riders, ropers and all-around cowboys in southern Idaho.

Mother went on ahead by train and was taken by Bishop

Baker to see Chauncey. She had never been inside a hospital before.

"Hello, Ma," Chauncey called cheerfully.

"Hello, son," she greeted. They were soon laughing as he told of the antics of a Chinese in the ward who put up a screeching battle every morning when the male nurse tried to bathe him.

Tough times for Chauncey were still ahead. The bruised flesh sloughed away from the end of the bone, and the leg was amputated again. The doctors found it necessary to scrape the bone clear to the hip, and incisions were made every few inches. Each day yards of medicated gauze were thrust into these and removed the next day. It required all Chauncey's stamina to withstand this agony, but he did it without one vocal protest.

Bishop Baker, a fine-looking man with a glossy black beard, was paying the hospital bills. The fault for the accident had been his and he was anxious to avoid a law suit, though he was never in danger of one. My folks distrusted courts of law too much for that. But the bishop did provide us a small house in back of his own in which to live.

Here Mother came up against her first real shock with regard to her new religion. She learned that not all Mormons had accepted in good faith the manifesto prohibiting plural marriage. She found out that the charming "sister-in-law" who lived in Bishop Baker's home and did the bookkeeping for his woodyard, and was called "Miss Mills," was in reality the bishop's second wife.

Once, when passing Bishop Baker's house, I found the door open and got a glimpse of luxury such as I had never known existed. Fine mirrors and paintings on the walls, thick rugs and carpets on the floor, beautifully polished tables, richly upholstered chairs and couches. When I got home and gazed upon the battered old rocker and rawhide-bottomed chairs on the bare floor of our shack I began to wonder for the first time about the inequalities of life.

In a sense, however, life was good to me. It had been decided that since I had missed so much school that winter that I need not start over in Baker City.

Next door to us lived the redoubtable Elder Smurthwaite who had vanquished Mother in that all-night Scriptural discussion. In the mission field he had been a man of great honor and dignity. My parents were astounded to find that at home he was an unobtrusive bookkeeper for the Mormon-owned Oregon Lumber Company.

Elder Smurthwaite had a large family, the oldest child being a lad of about my own age. Jesse was a friendly boy and once prevailed upon me to accompany him and his sister to school.

South Baker, which surrounded the mill, was a Mormon town, but the more populous North Baker where the young Smurthwaites were required to attend school was not. I noticed that my companions became apprehensive as we approached North Baker. Their carefree manner left them, their breathing became more labored, and they walked faster and faster, glancing uneasily from side to side.

Suddenly a dozen or more boys and girls bounded out of an alley, howling like Apaches. "Run!" Jesse cried, and away we went, with the youthful mob in full cry close behind us.

"Mormons! Mormons! Run, you crazy Mormons!" jeered our pursuers.

It was no new thing for the Smurthwaites, who were in perfect condition from these daily workouts, but my wind was short, and I was never too fleet afoot. I was on the verge of collapse when the Smurthwaites made a sudden left turn into the haven of the schoolgrounds and slowed to a saunter. But I didn't stop. To my relief the chase ended there. I went home, and never came that way again. I'd had my first taste of "persecution" for the Gospel's sake—and I wasn't even a Mormon.

We soon moved into a small house in "Stringtown," a narrow strip along the Sumpter Valley Railway where the poorer Mormons lived, and there Mother met the closest woman friend she was ever to know, a gentle old-maid daughter of an elderly

Mormon couple. Josie Stoker had foregone marriage to take care of her aged parents. Like Mother, she had been a schoolteacher, and both had a sense of humor which frequently took unique turns.

A favorite pastime of theirs was a trip to the cemetery on sunshiny afternoons to prowl around among the tombstones. If the epitaphs were not funny enough to suit them they improvised new ones. If, for instance, the name on a stone happened to be Levin, Mother, pretending to read in her nearsighted way, would intone solemnly:

"Here lies the body of Jacob Levin.
He jumped his debts and went to heaven."

And Josie might respond with:

"Here lies the body of old man Squires.
He erred when he said, 'All men are liars.'"

No irreverence was intended. The dead were not injured, and it was something to smile about on the way home. In later years Josie's letters were always bright spots in Mother's life.

Obe's wages of forty dollars a month were hardly enough to support the family and lay aside anything for continuation of the great trek; but each month, despite Obe's protest, Father religiously paid four dollars of the latter's earnings to the church as tithing.

Then, and for the rest of their lives, the church completely dominated Father and Mother. It influenced even the most trifling decision, for the priesthood, which every male Mormon was entitled to hold, hung over them at all times. It was the business of the priesthood to keep the members not only busy but interested and the job was done well. Because of this there was very little time for skepticism or backsliding or trafficking in ideas with the Gentiles.

And yet there was always a difference of interpretation between my parents, with Father certainly holding the more orthodox view. To Mother the living of a good life came first, but to Father the main thing was working for the advancement of the church.

The first Sunday of each month was fast day when the regular sacrament meeting was given over to the Saints in the congregation to bear their testimony. Neither Father nor Mother, burning with the zeal of their newly acquired testimonies, ever neglected these opportunities. Father did so haltingly, for despite his readiness to talk in private life, these were his first attempts to speak in public; Mother, for the most part, with calm sincerity which always held her listeners. Sometimes her emotion was so great that she would break down and be unable to finish.

In spite of her testimony Mother, accompanied by Josie and me, sometimes attended services in other churches in the city. She had investigated Mormonism with an open mind; it seemed only fair to give other churches the same chance. Father shouted angrily, "You're a *sectarian,* and always will be! If you were really converted you wouldn't go to such places."

Mother smiled and went her serene way, but the words she heard from the lips of other preachers did nothing to shake her faith in Mormonism.

Father's restlessness and discontent grew hourly. He had been promised a job in the box factory, but the routine of doing the same thing over and over held no appeal to his energetic nature. He required new activities, new interests for his boundless enthusiasm. Besides, this was not Zion.

He said to Mother, "There's no use wasting any more time. I'm starting for Chesterfield tomorrow."

She was astounded. "But you haven't got enough money to get us there, and Chauncey won't be out of the hospital for a long time."

"You always say the Lord will provide a way," he retorted.

"Me and Frank will go in the wagon and you and the boys can come later by train."

Having spoken, Father got ready for the trip with incredible speed. Mother scarcely had time to iron our clean clothes. We divided the furniture the best we could. Most of it wasn't worth moving anyway. About all we took in the wagon was the cookstove—Father having borrowed one for Mother to use —the trunks, the rocker, several boxes filled with miscellaneous plunder such as our books, Father's tools and extra harness. At that it made a heavy load for old Barney and his mate, a sway-backed mare Father called Juleburg.

Mother didn't mind being left behind. She would have Obe's wages, and a cow bought before Aunt Nancy's legacy was all gone. The price of the cow would go a long way toward paying train fare when the time came.

I had no more choice about making the trip than a chip in the creek. I had never been separated from Mother before and was shy with strangers. Moreover, I knew that someone always had to bear the brunt of Father's temper. Now it would all fall on me.

Mother had never believed in spoiling her children and was never demonstrative with her affection. She never took my part when Father whipped me, at least in my hearing, and made light of my aches and pains. She would dig a splinter out of my finger and gently ridicule me for being a baby if I cried. Never was she unduly fond of my company. She was in every sense of the word an adult, and she got little joy from the prattle of infants. She was kindness itself but, realizing that we were living in a hard world, she did her best to toughen us to it.

I knew she would worry about me. She had worried because the only schooling I'd had in nearly two years was those two or three weeks in La Grande. She also knew and regretted that I wasn't interested in the things which appealed to normal children. She came closest to understanding the daydream life in which I dwelt, but even she did not know how completely I lived in this imaginary world of my own. But I had become something of a stoic and didn't let Father know that I wasn't just as eager as he to make the trek.

Father was happy once he was on the road. Loudly he sang:

> *"Then gather up for Zion,*
> *Ye Saints throughout the land,*
> *And clear the way before you*
> *As God shall give command.*
> *Though wicked men and devils*
> *Exert their pow'r, 'tis vain,*
> *Since He who is eternal*
> *Has said you shall obtain."*

Soon, however, Father had to content himself with humming his songs of praise as our lips became so swollen and sore that we could scarcely speak without cracking them open. Sore lips were always the hardest part of wagon travel for me.

Father was always more sympathetic with physical distress than was Mother and had always been the one who ministered to the croup and chills and fever to which I was subject. Now he did his best to keep me comfortable and happy. He didn't raise his voice in anger when I blundered. For the first time in my life Father and I became pals.

Our money was gone by the time we reached Boise, and four-fifths of our journey lay ahead. Father sold his extra harness and Chauncey's saddle, of necessity at a price far below their value. He sold the cowbell for a quarter. His woodchopper and carpenter tools were next to go; except for the ax, which we had to keep. Little by little we sold off practically everything but the cookstove.

Father's consideration for me shone brightest when one day a stranger on horseback offered us five dollars for my worthless dog, Bryan. My love for that dog was about the only normal instinct of boyhood I possessed. Father turned down the offer.

There are fine highways across the Snake River desert now,

but then there were only a pair of dusty ruts that followed the Oregon Short Line railroad. Every sixteen miles there was a station with a water tank. Sometimes there would be a section crew and sometimes not. The only water along the way was at those stations. Sixteen miles was too short a day's drive, and thirty-two more than we could possibly make. That often forced us to make dry camps. There were days at a time when we didn't see a single person except, perhaps, some lonesome hobo who had been kicked off a freight train.

I was learning a little about human nature. Sometimes farmers along the way would charge us a dollar for fifty cents' worth of hay or grain. Others, seeing our condition, refused pay, and would perhaps bring out milk for our supper or eggs for our breakfast. The dirtiest trick played on us was when a man willfully misdirected us eight or ten miles out of our way along an abominably bad road. Father was so enraged that he picked up the alarm clock and smashed it against a lava rock.

One day while crossing the desert we came to what seemed to be a shallow pond through which the road ran. It had probably been caused by some distant cloudburst in the Sawtooth Mountains. Father drove right in and discovered that it was soft and mucky. He laid on the whip, yelled at the team and got in the middle of it before the wagon settled deep in the mud and stuck there.

I howled, "Pa, we'll *never* git out."

"Keep your shirt on," Pa said. "We'll git out."

Because there was no hay on the desert we had several heavy bales in the wagon. There was nothing for it but to unload everything. Whatever he could lift Father carried to the dry ground on his shoulders. That included practically everything but the stove. But the wagon sank deeper and deeper in the mud and wouldn't budge.

By shifting the stove from one end to the other Father finally got the wagon box off and dragged it to the bank with a log-chain. Even then the team—old Barney, rather, for his mate had little strength left—couldn't budge the running gears.

Father had to uncouple the wagon and pull it out two wheels at a time. It was long after dark before we got the outfit reassembled, but Satan had again met defeat.

After nearly a month the end of our journey was in sight. Old Juleburg had petered out completely. Father had to put a stay-chain on Barney so that the stout-hearted old horse could pull the entire load while the mare merely walked along holding up her end of the neck-yoke. Father often claimed that no heavenly glory could ever be complete for him unless old Barney was there to share it. Certainly he did more than his part in getting us to Zion.

One day we drove out of Portneuf Canyon into a wide valley covered with sagebrush and lava rock, which looked to me exactly like the desert we had just crossed. Father was delighted. On the north he could see a settlement with two small brick buildings, a meeting house and an amusement hall situated majestically upon a hill. This, he knew, was Chesterfield, long the Mecca of his dreams. Despite the efforts of the devil and all his angels, despite his wife's lack of faith, he had gathered himself to Zion. What matter that he had just twenty-five cents left in his pocket?

Beaming, Father turned to me. "Well," he asked, "how do you like it?"

Now and again I return to that valley like a homing pigeon, driving my automobile up the now-paved road. Nothing on earth seems so friendly to me as those green, rolling hills beyond it. But right then I was suddenly overcome by the worst case of homesickness and despair I have ever known. Through my cracked and swollen lips I blurted out, "I hate it."

Father's backhanded slap all but knocked me out of the wagon seat. "I'll *learn* you to like it," he said angrily.

Several hours later, after having to beg a farmer for some hay, we stopped in front of a small brick store. Father got down from the wagon and walked toward an unpainted house a few hundred yards off the road. He was halfway there when a man in a straw hat and many-times-washed overalls and jumper came running to meet him, to shake his hand joyfully and slap him on the back. It took a little time for me to realize that this shabby-looking farmer could be the frock-coated Elder Hatch of my remembrance.

Elder Hatch—thereafter we were to call him simply "Aim"—took Father into the house to meet his wife, Flora. Meanwhile, three barefooted, ragged urchins paraded out to the wagon and squinted up at me. "You a fruit peddler?" the oldest one asked. I shook my head, and the boys marched disappointedly back to the house. I was still in the throes of the devastating homesickness. I wanted my mother and I was on the point of bawling like a baby.

When Father drove into the yard Elder Hatch reached up to shake hands with me, and said, "Flora, this is Frank, the little boy I've told you about who knows so much church history, and knows all the songs in the hymnbook by heart."

I couldn't speak. It required the combined efforts of Aim and Flora and Father's threats to get me into the house to eat. As quickly as I could I crept back and cowered under the wagon cover like a frightened and bewildered coyote pup.

This was Zion—where a man could live the Gospel in peace! For Father it was better than finding a golden pot at the end of the rainbow. It was also the poor kind of country where Father had always believed a poor man would have a chance. He was no whit discouraged when Elder Hatch said earnestly, "If I were you I wouldn't stop here. There's much better country farther south. I'm going to sell out myself as soon as I can and move back to Utah."

I suppose it must have been frustrated ambition that had driven Father from one move to another, never letting him rest. He had always yearned for admiration and adulation, and the belief that his wife unjustifiably overshadowed him had made him disagreeable and quarrelsome.

Here it was going to be different. Here the priesthood controlled everything—and he held the priesthood. He would shirk no duty. He would study and prepare himself. He was still a young man, only forty-eight. As soon as he got a home and his family established he would go on a mission and himself become a hunter and a fisher for the souls of men. When he got back there was no telling to what high office he might be called.

And at the end, after he had performed his temple work for the dead, so that they too might acclaim him as deliverer from their spiritual prison, there would be Celestial Glory, no less. Mother might say that the lower Terrestrial, or even Celestial, glories would satisfy her, since in them most of her friends would surely be found; but that was not for him. He would get his endowments and somehow he would take Mother and us boys along with him, for without us to shine as jewels in his crown his exaltation could not be complete.

In Chesterfield Father at once became "Brother Robertson" and seldom thereafter was he to be called anything else. The first Monday after our arrival he went to work for Bishop Chester Call, president of the High Council of Bannock Stake, founder and namesake of the town of Chesterfield, and father-in-law to Elder Hatch. He was a dignified-looking man with a Van Dyke beard, a penchant for salty, off-color stories, and three wives.

Father rented a two-room log house, moved our goods into it, bought some furniture on credit, and awaited word from Mother that Chauncey was out of the hospital so they could join us. In the meantime we lived with Amos and Flora Hatch. But when Chauncey got out of the hospital he had to return every day to have his leg dressed, the flesh having again sloughed off the end of the bone. He had to have it amputated again, but all his life the end of the bone had no covering except a thin skin which caused him great pain.

Then, just as they were about ready to start, Obe came down with measles. As he began to recover, Chauncey caught the disease, and so the days that Father and I had counted so eagerly dragged out interminably into weeks.

14

Mother had one standard answer when her sons complained about our never-ending poverty. "We've been poor before, and we've never starved to death yet." If it didn't satisfy us, it was at least unanswerable.

From the time she had started teaching school to help support her parents, her mission had been to make life bearable for others. Yet she had never been an aggressive do-gooder. She never professed to bring sweetness and light where there was only darkness and despair. Her goal was to endure, and not waste time kicking against the jabs of adversity. Her children never heard her whine or complain. Subconsciously, we came to feel that any complainer was a coward and a weakling.

I was homesick, but in my short letters to Mother I didn't tell her so; I implied that I was having a wonderful adventure. She wrote back in the same spirit, knowing well that I lied. Sympathy, she sometimes remarked, was like sugar—of which we rarely had enough—to be used sparingly. Understanding was the solid food needed to uplift a sick spirit.

The day came at last when Mother and the boys were to arrive at the railway station at Bancroft, ten miles distant. They were due early in the morning. Mother was afraid that we might not be there to meet them, but she needn't have worried. We'd been waiting for hours.

Peering through the car window, she saw old Barney and his mate hitched to the wagon. Then she caught sight of Father and her ten-year-old youngest on the depot platform, and her thick-lensed glasses momentarily clouded with tears.

Obe, lugging a heavy valise, was the first to reach the platform. Behind him came Chauncey springing along on his crutches. It was the first time we had seen him, except in bed, since his accident. Father's face was working but Chauncey's cheerful grin defied anyone to dare feel sorry for him.

Then came Mother peering at us nearsightedly. She embraced Father briefly, then turned to me. I had determined to be stoical about this reunion but when Mother said softly, "My little son," I broke down and sobbed in her arms.

It was at moments such as these that the sense of family lay strong upon the Robertsons. Poverty will either shatter a family or bind it together with unbreakable chains. Mother felt momentary dismay when she looked around at the dreary expanse of sagebrush and lava rock, so different from the green, rolling hills and fertile fields of the Palouse country. But it was where Father wanted to be, so it was all right.

The house Father took her to was small but the furniture was adequate; the cupboard was well-stocked with groceries and everything was spotless. Father had done the best he possibly could.

That night Mother lay awake and wondered. Would this new and strange Zion be up to Father's expectations? Had he really changed? Was this, indeed, to be the beginning of better and happier times? One thing troubled her. She poked Father in the ribs and woke him up.

"I want to talk to you about Chauncey," she said. "The cords of his leg are drawn up so that he can't straighten his knee. The doctor says that even if he keeps on exercising and massaging it, it will be years before he can hope to wear an artificial limb. I thought maybe he could learn to be a bookkeeper like Harold Staley, but he's twenty years old and hasn't had two years of schooling in his life—Obe even less."

"So you've got to throw it up to me that my life has been a failure and that I ain't educated my kids," Father said harshly.

"Pa, I didn't say you were a failure."

"That's what you meant. I ain't a fool. It's what you've always thought. You've never had any faith in me."

"Oh, pshaw!" He hadn't changed. She turned her back on him, but his harangue went on and on until he fell asleep, to be resumed in the morning. When we got up one of the worst of our family rows was in progress. Chauncey tried to put an end to it by saying, "Damned if I'll ever go to school, or be a bookkeeper for anybody," but it did no good.

Amos Hatch was superintendent of the Sunday School, and after the classes were reassembled he said without warning, "When I was in the mission field I went to a Sunday School and the superintendent graciously gave me permission to bear my testimony. From that opportunity came the best results of my entire mission. Today, I am happy to say, that superintendent is in this audience and I want to return the courtesy. Sister Robertson, will you come forward and speak to us?"

The Mormon audience leaned forward in their seats. A

woman Sunday School superintendent was unheard of, and never before in that ward had a woman been called up to the stand to speak.

I was proud of Mother that day, but all the while she was speaking Father sat with his eyes fixed on the floor, his lower lip protruded in a pout. He had attended meeting every Sunday since his arrival and not once had he been called on to speak, although it was the custom in Mormon meetings to call speakers out of the audience at random.

That very week Mother got a little shock when an elderly, snuff-dipping lady from the South came to see her. "I'm a convert too," the woman said. "I came a long way so I could join the Saints and live the Gospel. The elders told us we should come, but they ain't like they are in the mission field, I can tell you that. Out there they're all sweet talk. You feed 'em and sleep 'em, but here them same elders are ashamed of you and the rest of the people look down on you."

"Well," Mother said somewhat doubtfully, "if they look down on us, it's just up to us to prove that we're worth looking up to."

"You'll find out," the woman said bitterly. "They tell us to pay our tithin' and be blest. We paid tithin' for a while, but my kids can't go to Sunday School because they ain't got no decent clothes, and the other kids laugh at the way they talk."

Mother quickly learned that most of those who had been born under "the new and everlasting covenant" did indeed look down on the Johnny-come-lately converts. She decided to fight back.

Her opportunity came at one of the monthly fast meetings when the sisters as well as the brethren were entitled to stand up in the audience and bear their testimonies. After several brethren had borne rather pompous testimonies, and some of the sisters had timidly told the congregation that they, too, knew the Gospel was true, Mother arose.

"Brothers and sisters," she began, "I, too, want to bear my testimony that God lives and that Joseph Smith was His prophet. I know through the influence of the Holy Spirit that the gospel has been restored to the earth and that the teachings of Mormonism are Christian and moral.

"I am a convert. I did not come among you expecting to find a perfect people, but I did expect to find a people united in their belief and trying to the best of their ability to live their religion. But in the short time I have been here I have been amazed to find back-biting, fault-finding, covetousness and vanity.

"I have heard elders in the field declare that all good Latter-Day Saints kept the Word of Wisdom, but I have already seen returned missionaries with their fingers yellow from cigarette stains. I have heard that some of them get drunk. Now I don't say that this makes them bad men. I have heard other things that I think are worse. I have heard of brethren high in the priesthood who don't pay an honest tithing. I don't say that these things are true but I have heard them. I have heard there are brethren who take advantage of a hard-up neighbor by buying his calves at half their worth. I have heard of brethren who drive their teams with a chain whip, and others who work their animals hard and feed them only straw. I know that I have seen men holding the priesthood whose pride in the positions they hold would be less if they took more thought of the humility of Christ."

If she had mentioned the erring brothers by name it would have been no less clear who she meant. As she pointed out each shortcoming the audience turned and gazed at some deflated brother squirming in his seat. Amos Hatch was hardly able to conceal his pride and delight. The hardened sinners on the back benches—of whom there were some, even in Zion—grinned openly at hearing a verbal castigation, for once, being directed at the other end of the house.

But Mother was not through. She admitted that she had failed in many respects to live up to the principles of the Gospel. She blamed herself that her sons were not members of the church. She told what those principles had meant to her. She had given up home and friends to come where those principles were lived. She had not expected to find hope of future reward greater than she had known, nor ease of living. But she had expected to find truth, justice, and righteousness. She reminded them of the persecutions their own ancestors had gone through for the sake of worshiping as they pleased. Would they now shun the converts to whom the ways of the Gospel were new, or would they set them a shining example?

There was a prolonged silence after she sat down. For anyone else to have borne a testimony after that would have been anti-climactic. All eyes were upon Bishop Call sitting in his accustomed armchair on the stand. Would he denounce this upstart convert woman for her arrogance in chiding the sons of the anointed—or what?

Bishop Call rose slowly. "I endorse and say amen to every single thing Sister Robertson has said," he said. From that moment on Mother's standing in the community was assured. Afterward, one of the riffraff on the back bench said, "Damned if she didn't purt' near make me git up and bear *my* testimony."

Here, as everywhere else she had lived, Mother soon gained the confidence of the disreputables. They understood instinctively that she liked them and was their friend. Many of them would drop in for a chat and stay for dinner or supper, although Mother had never achieved fame as a cook and most Mormon women were wonderful cooks. Mostly she listened; she never lectured them on their shortcomings. The disadvantage for her was that they were always on their good behavior in her presence, so she could never quite believe the wickedness attributed to them.

She soon became a teacher of young Mormon men and women in the Sunday School and in the Mutual Improvement Association, and continued to teach not only Mormonism but tolerance and charity to rising generations of young Mormons for the next twenty years. She became secretary of both the stake and ward Relief Society and was for many years clerk of the Chesterfield school board.

Her closest friends were the two wives of Bishop Chester Call. Both women had been married to the bishop before the manifesto. They lived but a few hundred yards apart and each had a large family. The bishop alternated weekly with his wives, and the arrangement appeared to be perfectly amicable to all concerned. The two good women, Aunt Mary and Aunt Sarah, as they were called, were utterly unlike in temperament, yet they got along like sisters. When Aunt Mary died, precedent was again shattered when Mother was called to the stand to be one of the speakers at the funeral.

It was not often that Mother administered a real rebuke, but when she did it usually carried a sting. One of the things she hated to tolerate was vulgarity, and Bishop Call, much as she liked him, was undeniably vulgar. On one occasion she was attending a sewing bee at the home of Aunt Sarah when the bishop came in and told an off-color story which Mother thought was decidedly unfunny. The other women blushed and giggled, but Mother never smiled, or looked up from her sewing.

"What are you looking so solemn about, Sister Robertson?" the jovial bishop teased.

"You're not the only ass that could talk, Bishop," she retorted. "Balaam had one, too." Thereafter, Bishop Call never told smutty stories in her presence.

Mother didn't travel the Gospel road alone. Father, too, soon became active in the church. He was appointed a teacher in the ward and once a month it was his duty to visit each family in his district, along with a companion, to inquire about the strength of their faith and their material welfare. If any were sick or in need it was the duty of the teachers to assist them or report back to the bishop if it was beyond their resources. If there were disputes or "feelings" between neighbors it was the duty of the teachers to get them settled.

Father loved it. In the many years in which he was a teacher he never missed a visit.

He practiced what he preached. The son of a family on his

beat was fallen upon by a horse. His foot was so badly torn and mangled that it seemed to be hanging only by a few shreds of flesh and sinew. Father was sent for. He put the foot back in place the best he could and bound it up. Then he and another elder anointed the lad with holy, consecrated olive oil, laid their hands upon his head, and by the power of their priesthood commanded the foot to heal.

When the doctor from Soda Springs arrived and announced that the foot would have to be amputated Father made an earnest protest. The boy's father was on a mission in England, and the boy's mother, having heard the promise of the priesthood, refused to consent to the operation. Father had a practical as well as a spiritual reason; he had always believed that Chauncey's leg could have been saved had not the doctors been too anxious to amputate.

After a long argument the doctor said, "Well, Robertson, if I fix up the foot the best I can will you take the boy to your home and assume full responsibility for anything that may happen?"

"I certainly will," Father said.

Father and Mother gave up their bed to the injured boy and Father cared for him two long months. The foot was saved, leaving Eddie Moss with scarcely a limp.

Years later, Dr. Kackley, speaking of this incident, said to me, "I don't believe in Mormonism, but saving that boy's foot was nothing but a goddamned miracle."

That "healing" made a strong impression on the ward and, as a man of great faith, Father was frequently called upon to administer to the sick. Also, he was often called to the stand to speak to the Saints in Sacrament Meeting. He was growing in stature, as he had always known he would grow once given the opportunity.

We wasted no time adjusting ourselves to the life of the community. We got off on the right foot. Father went in debt two hundred dollars for five acres of land with a small log house and a barn. The house had a dirt roof which let the rain through. The three rooms were small but it was our house—or would be when it was paid for.

Father intended to go into the chicken business just as soon as he could build the necessary coops. He was always going into the chicken business, but he never quite made it. "Twenty years a chicken man and never got an egg," Obe told him once with weary sarcasm.

Chauncey, who quickly discarded his crutches for a peg leg in which his knee rested, herded a bunch of dairy cows for a neighbor in the foothills north of town. Obe got a job in a brickyard—and so did I.

My job was to slosh the six-brick molds in a tank of water and then sand them so the wet mud wouldn't stick in the molds. The water chapped my hands and the sand got into the cracks. Glycerine was the only thing that helped. When Mother poured it into the knuckle cracks it burned like liquid fire. She smiled as I danced and howled and, always the logician, told me it would feel better when it stopped hurting.

It was my first job and I was earning fifty cents a day. Unfortunately, the brickmaker became financially involved and, leaving his wife and children behind, eloped with another woman. Neither Obe nor I got a cent of our summer's wages.

That fall Mother finally prevailed on Chauncey to enter the local school. The advanced students attended a one-room log schoolhouse, while the younger ones were housed in the amusement hall. Seventh was the highest grade taught. It was there that Chauncey found himself in a class with other young grownups—and his spindly brother Frank.

I was there because of a rather daring use of chicanery and sophistic reasoning. In La Grande I had been in the fifth grade perhaps three weeks. Since the principal had predicted that I wouldn't be there long I overlooked the fact that he thought I would be set back and assumed that before long I would have gone up to the sixth grade. And at the end of the term I would surely have been promoted again, so I informed Miss Mullins, the Chesterfield teacher, that I was in the seventh grade. It being impossible for her to disprove my claim she, with well-founded misgivings, placed me in the seventh grade along with others from three to ten years my senior.

Chauncey was there for no other reason than to please Mother. The lessons were absurdly easy for him, as lessons had always been, and he derived sadistic pleasure from my desperate efforts to keep up. But he didn't like school. When the musically inclined teacher decided to organize a male quartet with Chauncey as baritone, he refused to remain after school to practice, largely because he didn't like an unctuously pious young tenor of his own age. So he walked out and never went back to school again.

The following spring, the West brothers, big cattlemen from the near-by Portneuf, hired Chauncey to help drive cattle from the Fort Hall Indian reservation back to the summer range. Both Father and Mother hoped the job would be of short duration, for although Father himself had been a cowboy they both felt that it was a life of evil temptation. Moreover, the Wests were of those worst-hated "outsiders," apostate Mormons.

The job lasted more than fifteen years, during which time Chauncey became foreman of the outfit and in true storybook fashion married his employer's daughter.

During the next few years it was mostly Obe's wages that supported the family. He became a sheepherder because the wages were better and sent home every dollar not needed for clothes and tobacco. Obe was always a good rider. Later he worked on the Bar OX outfit with Chauncey long enough to become a first-rate cowhand in his own right.

Father was always busy, but his labor brought scant returns. However, he was careful not to get into debt beyond his depth, and always paid his creditors a little every month from Obe's wages; so he enjoyed excellent credit for his unprofitable ventures. He knew that because Mother and Obe were anxious to get him out of debt, so long as he remained in that condition Obe's wages would continue to roll in.

"If I didn't get it he would only spend it foolishly," he would maintain.

"What Dad wants most people wouldn't give a damn for," Obe said once, "but he wants it so hard that we always give it to him. What he wants he demands, and what he demands he gets. The rest of us demand little and that's exactly what we get."

Father was eternally building, tearing down, and building again. He bought the old log schoolhouse, tore it down and built a henhouse. The hens wouldn't lay so he dug underground coops and kept the birds so fat and lazy they could scarcely waddle around, but they laid him no more than an occasional egg, a task they performed with an air of sheer boredom. Raising his fists to high heaven, Father would shout, "*I'll make 'em lay.*" But the hens were having too easy a life to mind.

He essayed many other money-wasting ventures, always on a small scale, and despite Mother's economy and Obe's hard-earned wages, his debts at the two Chesterfield stores continued to mount.

15

In common with most Chesterfield men, Father went to "the mahoganies" to get part of our winter's supply of fuel. Aim Hatch was usually Father's companion. When I wasn't in school I went along with them. It was so far away that we had to start at dawn of a winter's morning and seldom got home before dark. This was a new kind of timber to Father; it was short, scrubby, brittle and hard as iron. The sharpest ax would make no more than a dent, but even the largest tree could be broken off by a good pulling horse—and old Barney was that horse.

This was a high, cold country. Snow was deep, and forty

below zero was not uncommon. Coming down the mountain on a narrow snow road with a big load was exciting. Nobody bothered to rough-lock, so it was a mad race with the teams at full gallop to escape being run over by their own loads. If a horse happened to fall or a load tipped over it was just too bad for that driver. Nobody could stop to help him.

Father loved all this. His voice could be heard a mile away shouting to the driver ahead to get out of the road. All I could do was freeze onto the binding chain and hang on for dear life. Father never upset a load. As a woodsman and teamster he was far superior to his Mormon neighbors.

Father was far happier than he had ever been before in his married life. Zion had fulfilled most, if not all, of its promises. Above everything, he enjoyed working in the church. He was now assistant superintendent of the Sunday School, and other offices were rapidly coming his way. But there was also a good social life.

Before joining the church Father had been down on dancing as among the most pernicious of sins. At Moscow it had been the cause of many a rift between him and Chauncey; and there they had held only square dances. Now he reversed himself completely and never missed a dance in his own or neighboring wards. His dancing, like his singing, was off in timing. Everybody else was too slow for him. He sounded fine when singing alone but in group singing he always managed to finish a verse about three bars ahead of anybody else. It annoyed him that he was never asked to sing in the choir but, undaunted, he continued to lead the singing from wherever he happened to be. It was the same on the floor, where he was a prancer rather than a dancer. Regardless of the music, he toured the floor at the same rapid trot, dragging his partner along with him at arm's length.

The women sat primly on one side of the house, while the men lolled on the other. When a dance was called there was a wild stampede of agile young bucks to choose the prettiest girls in the hall, but they didn't get ahead of Father, who was always at the head of the stag line. He never danced with the same woman or girl twice until he had danced with them all. Some of the girls giggled with embarrassment and wound up a dance with him flushed and flustered, but not one of them ever dared turn him down. Had they done so they would have been publicly rebuked in no uncertain manner.

All Mormon dances were decorously conducted, opening and closing with prayer. No drinking, profanity or indecency of any sort was tolerated. The first time I bashfully peeked into the dance hall at Chesterfield I had to dodge as a drunken cowboy from the Portneuf was tossed out like a chunk of cordwood by Uncle Heber Loveland, a High Priest and member of the High Council. Two other cowboys followed in the same undignified manner. Uncle Heb said dryly, as he dusted off his hands, "That's the way I believe in casting out devils."

It never occurred to Father that the refusal of his two youngest sons to learn to dance was due to their embarrassment over his peculiar style of dancing—but I doubt that he would have cared. He did at one time, after persuasion had failed, order me to dance or take a whipping. This particular night he had a cold and had to stay home. I tried to screw up my courage to ask some girl to dance, but simply couldn't bring myself to do it.

The next morning Father asked grimly, "Who did you dance with?"

Tremblingly I answered, naming one of the older girls of the ward, "Vinnie Davids."

Retribution overtook me quickly, as that very week we were invited to have New Year's dinner with the Davids family. As we were seated at the table Father said, "Well, Vinnie, what kind of dancer did Frank turn out to be?"

"Why, I don't know," Vinnie said, puzzled. "I never saw him dance."

Father scarcely spoke a word during the rest of our visit. When we got home I expected to be whipped, but Father only ground out, "If there's anything I hate it's a liar." He didn't speak to me for a month. Later, to appease him, I did dance with Vinnie and a few married women, but I was awkward and ashamed and I soon gave it up.

There were times when it seemed that Father was right about certain reservations in Mother's acceptance of the Gospel. Such an occasion arose when a young couple, taken in sin, were compelled publicly to acknowledge their guilt and beg forgiveness. Mother thought she saw expressions on the faces of some of the brethren, her own husband included, when they looked at the weeping young Magdalene, that weren't exactly those of Christian charity. They looked more like speculation.

Most of the women in the house were weeping when the Counsellor-in-charge arose and said, "Everybody in favor of forgiving these erring young people will signify by raising the right hand."

Every right hand in the building, with the exception of Mother's, went high.

After the meeting one of the women protested to Mother, "Why, Sister Robertson, I'm amazed that you of all people wouldn't be willing to forgive them."

"I forgive them freely," Mother said. "But how will they ever be able to forgive us?"

The practice of public confession of sin was quite common in those days. I recall two brethren, fine men and good neighbors, and faithful workers in the church, who were often on the stand to beg forgiveness for getting drunk when they were called for jury duty in Pocatello.

Obe was now Mother's chief worry. Uncomplainingly he had shouldered the burden of supporting the family while still in his teens. He refused, however, even to discuss Mormonism and seemed to have no concern whatever about his own future.

He was away from home for months at a time. In the summer he was up in the mountains near the Wyoming state line, and in winter far down in the deserts of Nevada. For days he might see no one except his camp-mover. Mother heard of blizzards which swept the desert and read of sheepherders found frozen to death in the sagebrush, and there was always the possibility of accident. She knew that Obe was levelheaded and knew how to take care of himself, but still she worried. Often he sent her little poems he had composed, verses illustrated with crude but humorous drawings. He was the wisest of her sons, and she knew that his genius would be unfulfilled.

Only once did Obe kick over the traces. He hoboed back to the Palouse country along with a young Mormon vagabond named Fred Scott; but he returned in the fall bringing money to pay on Father's debts, and, I well remember, for me the first overcoat I had ever owned.

Father still reiterated his dour predictions that Obe would fill a suicide's grave, unless cigarettes got him first, but nothing could shake Mother's faith in her favorite son.

"He'll *never* join the church," Father predicted gloomily.

"Maybe not," Mother conceded, "but I know this: he will always be an honorable man."

Our second summer in Chesterfield was brightened by the arrival of the Matthews family. Cautious, conservative Win had finally got the courage to sell out and gather to Zion. He reached Chesterfield with a team and wagon and a thousand dollars in cash. It was a grand reunion. The Saints in Chesterfield were all right, but none could ever be so close as these old friends who had stood with us through good times and bad.

Win got off to a bad start when he arose in his first fast-day meeting to bear his testimony. His sincerity was always impressive, but here among strangers he was ill at ease. "I know," he stated solemnly, "that the Book of Mormon is true, and that old Joe Smith was a true prophet."

Had he spoken of Christ as "old Chris," he couldn't have shocked the people any more. In Zion one said, the *Prophet Joseph*, and one said it reverently. But from that time on Win bore the stigma of *convert*, and he could never quite gain the acceptance the Robertsons had won. Yet they had to recognize his devotion and ability and as long as he remained in Chesterfield he performed the duties of Ward Clerk.

It was different with his son Rube, who was Obe's age, and knew how to keep the pretty Mormon girls goggle-eyed by a fine display of piety and the pretense that he was on the verge of conversion. Each was sure that it needed only the influence of a good woman to pluck this handsome young redhead from the burning.

The Matthews lived only a block from us. Mother thoroughly enjoyed the renewed association with Win and Belle, but she knew they weren't happy. Notwithstanding her warning letters, they had expected to find a people approaching perfection and now they found the Mormons to be only too human. They talked darkly of going back. She knew that if they went, the old intimacy and understanding which had meant so much to all of them throughout the trying years would be forever ended. And, what worried her most, they would surely drift away from the church if they left the physical foundation of Zion.

Win had been unable to find a farm that suited him. He was afraid of a shortage of water. His savings shrank alarmingly. Rube seemed unable to get or hold a job. Daisy, the oldest unmarried daughter, a lanky, self-conscious girl, began writing letters to a former swain after failing to find any of the young Mormons that suited her.

Worst of all for Mother and Win was the renewal of the old feud between Father and Belle. She had become intimate with the same convert woman who had complained so bitterly to Mother of her treatment by the Mormons. One day the woman told Belle something that Father had said, and she rushed home in high dudgeon, demanding that Win make Father admit that he had lied about her.

"Will," Win demanded, "why did you tell around that Belle once threw a hatchet at you?"

Instantly belligerent, Father replied, "Because she did. She tried to hit me. You were there and saw her do it."

"You're a liar!" Belle screamed. "You're just an old busybody, a troublemaker, and a he-gossip."

"You were hanging a picture and you got mad and threw the hatchet at me."

"I only threw the hatchet away because I was through with it, and it didn't come anywhere near you."

"That's what happened, Will," Win said.

"You know better than that; I had to dodge!" Father retorted.

That was the first time in their lives Father and Win had really quarreled, and they all but came to blows. In the end Win and Belle stormed out of the house. Later, Win laid the matter before the bishop.

Bishop Tolman was a tall, rawboned man who had spent most of his life around logging camps and on the farm. He had very little education, had never even been on a mission and knew very little about the doctrines of his church, but he was a natural leader of men. He couldn't preach, but when there was a job to do, such as getting out wood for the meeting house or putting up a hay crop for a sick brother, he was always the first one there with an ax or pitchfork. He had been known to settle a dispute between brethren by taking them by the napes of their necks and bumping their heads together. He was loved and respected by his people.

Bishop Tolman attacked the problem with plain good sense: "This thing happened more than twenty years ago. None of you can be sure just what occurred. Why don't you just let the whole thing drop?"

But Win, perhaps harried by his wife, who longed to see the mighty fall and was determined that Father should have to get up in church, make acknowledgment and beg forgiveness, would not let it rest.

After several vain attempts to get the bishop to put Father

on trial, Win shouted, "To hell with you! And the church too! I'm going back where I came from."

That was one of the great sorrows of Mother's life. When the time came to say good-by she said to them, "It doesn't really matter where you live, you know the Gospel is true, and you can still live your religion. You two went to the temple last summer and received your endowments, something Will and I haven't got around to yet. If you just do what is right, everything will come out right."

But she knew that things would not be all right for them. Win would go back to the Palouse country, an aging man, broken in spirit and in pocketbook. Bitterness would abide with him. Had it not been for Father's propensity to gossip, things might not have turned out as they had, but he held himself blameless and there was no use to start an argument about it.

Years later, when Father visited them, they had come upon evil days and were living on the bounty of a son-in-law. I have a picture of Win and Father taken together at that time; Father, a spick-and-span Mormon missionary, looking years younger than his age; Win, a broken and shabby old man. No word was spoken of the quarrel that had divided them, but the close companionship could not be re-established. Mother herself never saw them again.

Their departure left her with the feeling that the last link with her old life had been broken. She was happy in her church work and found satisfaction in the way Father was climbing the theological ladder, although his financial ventures were as fantastic as ever.

Long, nerve-wracking rows still whirled about her head, now mostly about religion and the church. Father was still skeptical of her orthodoxy—sectarianism was his word for any independence of mind. As a school trustee, Mother was instrumental in hiring several Gentile teachers, not only because she considered them better qualified, but because she disliked the isolationism of which the Mormons were so proud.

It was common in those days for the elders to refer frequently to the Saints as The Chosen People. Mother didn't like the term because it smacked too much of the pharisaical "We thank God that we are not as other men." But Father could prove by the Doctrine and Covenants, the inspired book of modern revelation, that the Mormons *were* a chosen and select people and was determined to make Mother recant.

Once a High Councilman, bearing his testimony, declared, "We *know* the Gospel is true because we've *always* been taught it." When Mother made some humorous comment about it after they got home, Father took fierce umbrage, not at what she had said but at her manner of saying it. He himself thought the High Councilman was an ignoramus, but he respected his priesthood.

But these disputes were mere zephyrs compared to those where the boys and money were concerned. It was Father's feeling that our refusal to accept the Gospel was a reflection upon himself. He believed Mother could by some spiritual legerdemain bring us into the fold if she wanted to—just as she could always get us to empty our pockets to pay on Father's debts. He was sure that Obe at least could be brought to taw if she would only say the word.

He would shout at Obe, "Do you believe that your mother is *deluded*?" As for me, he decided that I had temporized long enough and settled the matter in his own forthright way. I always went to Sunday School, "Mutual," and Deacons' meetings, and took a part. I understood the doctrines of the church pretty well, for I had read all the church books that were available, yet one baptismal ceremony after another went by with me evading salvation with the cunning of a fox and the slipperiness of an eel. Father believed, quite correctly, that this was largely because of my lingering cowardice about water.

I could not have stayed away from meetings if I had wanted to. I always had to be there, and on time, regardless of how shabby my clothes might be. Yet the fact that neither of my brothers had been baptized gave them a sort of swashbuckling independence that I admired. Also, I enjoyed the distinction of being the only non-Mormon in my classes, especially since I was up on doctrine, proficient in church history and able to answer questions that left the other students blank.

I always took it for granted that some day I would join the church and perform in reality the miracles of conversion I had worked in my imagination. But I was not ready, and I didn't have the "testimony" which had caused my folks to join the church. I was also privately skeptical when on fast day all the other boys and girls in the class would arise and in their thin, piping voices declare, "I know the Gospel is true—name o' Jesus, Amen." I suspected they were pretty fair-to-average little liars.

For another thing I could never bring myself to pray, except once when I lost a favorite pony and believed prayer was my only chance to get him back. Father blamed this on Mother's neglect of duty as much as my own stiff-neckedness.

The business of family prayer was another source of domestic friction. Father wanted to hold family prayer morning and night after reading a chapter in the Bible. Mother objected because it tended to keep the boys, especially Chauncey, away from home. Many times Chauncey brought strange cowboys home with him to spend the night, and their embarrassment when the family formed a circle with the backs of the chairs turned inward and knelt for a long-winded prayer was painful to watch. Mother didn't object to Father's taking one-tenth of his sons' hard-earned wages to pay as tithing to the church—although *they* did—but she did object to their having to go through the mummery of prayer against their wishes.

One beautiful spring morning, while the Matthews family was still in Chesterfield, Father rushed into the house saying, "Mary, get some dry clothes ready for this boy. Rube, and Eva and Bertha Matthews are getting baptized this morning, and so is Frank." It was the first I had heard of it, but Father was very persuasive with a buggy whip, so I became a Latter-Day Saint.

The first four principles of the Gospel are faith, repentance, baptism by immersion for the remission of sins, and the laying on of hands for the reception of the Holy Ghost. This last point was one of the major differences between the Mormon and Christian churches. Over this point of doctrine Mother and Elder Smurthwaite had wrangled for hours. The elder had convinced her that the priesthood did actually have the power to confirm the gift of the Holy Ghost.

Now that I was into the thing I wanted to go the whole hog. While the elders were laying their hands upon my wet head I wondered if I would experience any peculiar sensation when the Holy Ghost entered my body. In the Bible I had read that the Holy Ghost appeared in the form of a dove; while I hardly expected anything so dramatic in my own case, I hoped to experience some pleasantly tingling sensation. But nothing happened. I felt in some vague way that I had been cheated, but I knew definitely that I was stuck. Anyone denying the faith after having received the Gospel committed the unpardonable sin and became automatically a son of perdition, for whom there is no hope, worlds without end.

Father was satisfied, anyway. He had taken out insurance for at least one jewel in his Celestial crown.

I was being brought up the way Father wanted me to be. Whenever I tended to become rebellious a sound thrashing brought me quickly back into line. As always, it was the humiliation of being whipped in public that really hurt, and how could Father show people what a disciplinarian he was if there were no spectators? He felt that at last his theories of child government were being justified.

I was advancing in the church. I now held the Aaronic priesthood, was secretary of the Young Men's Mutual Improvement Association, and taught a class in Sunday School. But I had a quick and violent temper, and when anything went wrong I was likely to blow up and use profane language. I was whipped for this more than for any other reason. When Father had used himself up and had to throw away the gad I would go out behind the barn and repeat over and over under my breath, "You goddamned old son-of-a-bitch!"

16

Father's store bill had mounted to well over five hundred dollars. Nathan Barlow, the proprietor, said to him, "Brother Robertson, we've got a proposition for you. You claim to be a dairyman. We're taking over a herd of thirty cows and are going to build a creamery. You take the cows and we will give you half the milk and half the increase. You and your boys should make a lot of money."

   Father thought the matter over for at least ten minutes, a long period of deliberation for him, and accepted the offer. He already owned a few cows, and one of the unregenerates of the community had offered to sell him eighty acres of land at ten dollars an acre on good terms. A third of it was in hay.

Barlow & Company offered to finance the building of a cow barn on Father's lot in town, and said he could have the job of running a milk route for the creamery. That alone would yield about a hundred dollars a month.

It was a bigger proposition than Father liked to handle, but his rising prestige in the church and his hard-proven good credit had strengthened his self-confidence. However, the primary consideration was that he had felt the older boys were slipping away from him, and by making them partners in the enterprise he would bind them to him.

Chauncey occasionally gave Mother a check, with the injunction that she spend it on herself—which she never did, but promptly turned it over to Father. For the most part Chauncey usually spent his wages a little faster than he made them.

Obe had dropped his habit of sending his wages home every month and sometimes waited until he had accumulated a hundred dollars. Obe's having so much money in his hands at one time always made Father uneasy.

If the boys were going to be brought into the partnership, Mother would have to bring them. Father understood that. He had no influence over them at all. He laid the matter belligerently before her, every intonation of his voice a challenge for her to voice an objection.

Dissent would have brought on a row of titanic proportions. After all, it was the first proposition that had ever come up to promise any return for the money the boys had poured into the family coffers. Professing strict neutrality, she laid the matter before them.

Obe offered no objection; he had long been obsessed with the idea that the family was his responsibility. Father was only a little over fifty and was in superb physical condition, but Obe saw him as a doddering old man no longer able to support himself. Obe didn't want to drag Chauncey into it, and he wanted me to go to school. It never seemed to occur to him that he himself was entitled to a future with some hope. He had no martyr complex; as he looked at it, somebody had to support the folks and he was the logical one to do it.

Chauncey was harder to bring into line. He enjoyed his work and enjoyed spending his own money. This idea of setting aside the major part of his wages every month to go into a partnership that both he and Obe thought was doomed to failure in advance held little appeal. But in deference to Mother, Chauncey came into the firm of Robertson & Sons.

Father was soon receiving an income of around three hundred dollars a month, and it taxed his ingenuity to find new ways of going into debt. He built new and better hen coops, while the dirt roof on the three-room cabin remained as it was.

He and I did the milking, and for the most part I ran the milk route. Although skinny and awkward, I was wiry and strong and could wrestle the ten-gallon milk cans and do most of the farm work while Father "tended to business." He planned that in the summer he would lease more cows and take his herd over the mountain onto the public domain and hire a number of local girls to do the milking, but nothing ever came of it.

Mother's work more than doubled because of the cows. The new Sharples separator was a complicated bit of mechanism that was hard to wash, and there were numerous cans and buckets which had to be sparklingly immaculate. Sometimes when her female trouble was too bad Father would hire a girl to come and help her. In fact, he began to hire help whenever possible—whether he needed it or not.

It was only a small enterprise but Father was at last getting something around him. Occasionally he found time to clerk in Barlow's store, but more often he only loafed there to get in a few good licks for the Gospel. When the manager of the creamery wanted to teach me the trade of butter making, and volunteered to show me how to keep books on the side, Father registered an emphatic veto; I was needed at home.

Nevertheless, I was hired out for a great part of each summer. When I was fourteen Bishop Tolman was paying me man's wages, two dollars a day. The next summer I drove header box with our team for the same good man and headed most of the wheat in the entire valley. Frequently Father hired a boy my own age to take my place while I was away.

At thirteen I had graduated from the eighth grade. Father thought this was enough education for any farm boy. Anyway, I could not have attended a higher school without going away to some city, and that was out of the question.

Almost from the time we had reached Chesterfield I'd been hearing people say I was smart—and I believed them. Offsetting this intellectual vanity, however, was an overawareness of my ungainly personal appearance and the realization that I didn't know how to associate with young people of my own age. At parties everyone else always seemed to have brilliant things to say that kept the girls laughing, but I could only sit in the corner and wish myself dead.

I was tall, skinny, and stoop-shouldered; I had such bad teeth that I dreaded opening my mouth, and seldom laughed or sang when there was anyone near. My hair was nearly always too long and would never stay combed. Because of my peculiar build the local stores never had clothes that would fit me, so I was always conscious of being poorly dressed. I was always being admonished to "straighten them shoulders," and the more I was urged the more I slumped. My stooping was due to my shame at being six feet tall and weighing only a hundred and thirty pounds. Everyone urged me to cure myself of bashfulness, but the more I was reminded of it the more bashful I became.

I was afraid of girls. To me, they were awe-inspiring and of so fine a texture that when I saw them eating I felt that nature had erred in making such a prosaic function necessary for such ethereal creatures. The smutty stories I had heard the hoodlums tell, as well as the scribblings on the inside of the outhouses, made me realize that they had other unethereal functions besides eating and I experienced identifiable urges when one of them chanced to display a more than ordinary length of shapely leg; but my general attitude toward them was one of timorous adoration.

It was not the fault of the boys and girls of my own age that I couldn't loosen up and get my feet off the floor. They were friendly and I usually managed to have a pretty good time with them except at parties and dances. I liked to watch the girls in their pretty dresses, but I didn't often dare to speak to them.

There was one girl for whom I developed an overpowering case of puppy love. Maybe it wasn't just puppy love, for I was still enamored of her long after she was married.

Once when the idol of my dreams dropped a note on my school desk inviting me to be her partner at a ladies' choice dance and social I slid from hell to heaven and back again in the course of an hour. Never had I wanted anything so badly as the courage to accept her offer, but I simply was unable to address her face to face. Though I sat not more than four feet from her, the days passed and I said and did nothing.

The day before the dance another boy told me he was going to take her sister, if he could overcome a minor obstacle that had confronted me—transportation. The girls lived two miles from the schoolhouse and, in the winter time, couldn't be expected to walk. The other boy said we could ride with the girls' folks if we could get out there and back. Old Barney was the answer to that—but did I still have a date?

I screwed up my courage and wrote the girl a note. She wrote back from a distance of four feet that she would still go with me, but she had been hurt by my long delay, and was on the verge of asking another boy.

The next night, silent and ill at ease, I found myself seated in the bottom of a bob-sled alongside my girl with the quilts drawn up over our laps. I had seen Chauncey put his arm around the girls he went out with, and supposed this to be the proper procedure. I put my arm gingerly up over the collar of her coat and let it stay there. I dared not exert the slightest pressure, but once there my arm couldn't be removed. Long before we reached the dance it was cramped and ached unbearably.

Never having learned to dance all I could do was eat supper with my girl, and neither of us seemed able to think of a word to say. It was a blessed relief when I was able to say good night. I remained infatuated with this girl for a good many years. A couple of times I got the courage to ask if I could take her home, but I was turned down cold. She never knew the devotion that was wasted on her.

Another girl persisted in ignoring my bashfulness and many times walked home with me from school, and in every way showed that she was fond of me. I was grateful for her friendship, but it wasn't until she started going steady with a dashing young returned missionary that I awakened to the fact that she would have been my girl if only I'd had the gumption to ask her.

We young fellows used to watch where the rough characters from the Portneuf hid their bottles when they came to a dance, and while they were inside we were having many a hearty swig. Sometimes we would hide the whisky in a snowbank for our future enjoyment, regardless of the threats and curses directed against us.

There was, of course, the usual amount of fight talk among the boys, but nothing like it had been up in the Idaho panhandle. Most of the fights were staged after Deacons' meeting on Saturday nights. The Deacons' quorum was composed of boys from twelve to fourteen, though older teachers and priests often came around after the meeting to watch the fights. There was always supposed to be some member of the higher priesthood to supervise and keep order, but often they didn't show up. Frequently, after the singing of a couple of hymns and a prayer, the meeting would degenerate into the singing of ribald songs and the telling of smutty stories. In any event a couple of boys could usually be found who had difficulties to settle with their fists, which they did out behind the meetinghouse, to the delight of the rest of us.

During these years I read everything I could lay my hands on. Mother ordered a bulky two-volume history of the world from the Sears Roebuck catalog and soon I was conquering the world like Alexander, crossing the Alps with Hannibal, fighting the Persians with Themistocles, and crossing oratorical swords with Cicero. I was preparing myself for the bitternesss of disillusionment when one day I was to find out that the history books I read so eagerly were full of lies; that their heroes were more often than not brutal tyrants and oppressors, and that the wars they glorified were merely downward plunges in the long, slow struggle of the race to justify its existence. Hungry for knowledge, I sucked at the teats of wisdom and imbibed poison.

I was even more familiar with church history. I knew every detail of the life of the Prophet Joseph, I knew the name of every president, every apostle, and every one of the Seven Presidents of Seventies the church had ever had, as well as all the presiding bishops and patriarchs. I had paraded with the Nauvoo Legion, frozen and starved with the Saints at Winter Quarters, and marched with the Mormon Battalion to California. I had stood on the ledges of Echo Canyon along with General Daniel H. Wells, poised to roll rocks down on the hated minions of Johnston's Army when it came to invade Zion. Wherever the Saints had suffered, I had suffered.

Once my parents ordered twenty novels from the catalog. The whole twenty, along with a "handsome bookcase," could be purchased for two dollars and forty cents. Selecting the books was great fun. Father held out for the inclusion of his two favorite authors, Mary J. Holmes and Mrs. E. D. E. N. Southworth. He liked them, he said, because they never insulted his intelligence and were realistic stories of true-to-life people. Mother's choice were books by Thackeray, Dickens, and Sir Walter Scott, and Bulwer-Lytton's *Last Days of Pompeii*.

I had no choice so long as they were books, but when pressed to select at least one I chose one with the intriguing title of *The Girl from the Ranch*. It was far and away the worst book of the lot—even to me. For good measure, and strictly for my benefit, Father ordered a massive copy of *Peck's Bad Boy;* it never occurred to him that nobody could have been more unlike Mr. Peck's mischievous son than I.

When the books arrived I read them all in little over a week. The one I liked best was also Father's favorite, Mrs. Southworth's *Ishmael or In the Depths and Out of the Depths,* a thinly disguised, glamorized biography, so I was told, of Henry Clay, long one of my forensic idols. The book swayed my imagination as nothing ever did before. Some day, I vowed, I too would stir multitudes with my oratory and settle grave public problems with benign wisdom and solid statesmanship. Outside of illegitimacy—and sometimes I almost wished that I had that to further try my mettle—I felt that I had every handicap which beset Ishmael Worth, my hero.

One summer somebody left a traveling library at Barlow's store. Although use of the books was free I was almost the only customer. I read them all. There were a few books of fiction, biographies of men like Benjamin Franklin and Daniel Webster, and others on the technical side. The last volume, which I read faithfully, although I found it a little tough going, was a ponderous tome on American Municipal Administration.

I never failed to read every page of any book that came into my hands. Even before we had left Moscow I had diligently saved up enough Arbuckle coffee coupons to get two books as prizes. I chose Milton's *Paradise Lost* and Charles Reade's *Peg Woffington*. I doubt if many people have struggled through *Paradise Lost* at the age of nine. An old-maid schoolteacher, discovering my love of reading, loaned me copies of such magazines as *Success* and *Cosmopolitan,* and opened before me a whole new world as I learned that there was such a thing as contemporary writing.

It hurt Mother badly to see me miss year after year of schooling. Other boys and girls who had been grades behind me went away to Logan or Pocatello to high school or college. "Next year maybe we can send you to school," she would say hopefully.

"We can't afford to send him to school and you know it." Thus Father would dismiss the subject curtly.

Only to Obe could Mother talk. "Frank hates farming," she would say, "and I'm sure there must be something he could do if he could only get a little education." And Obe would reply wistfully, "I could send him through college if it wasn't for Dad's debts."

But there were always Father's debts, never very big, but carrying us along helplessly like a stream whose banks were too steep to climb. If the money ceased to come in Father's credit would be impaired, and that was a family disgrace which must never be allowed to happen.

Even though Chauncey had pulled out of the firm, we were doing fairly well and Mother had reason to hope that some day Obe would get something back for his years of labor and self-denial. But it was Obe himself who brought about our downfall—Obe the steady, the dependable. He quit his job!

He had herded sheep steadily for several years. Always on foot he had trailed his woolly charges through winter's storm and summer's heat. Only rarely had he taken a short layoff.

He had gone through range lambings where for upwards of a month the herder seldom took off his clothes. Often when he did roll up in his blankets for a few hours they would be soggy from lying out in the rain or snow, or moldy from lack of proper airing. Obe was young and tough and could take it, but those conditions were breeding rheumatism for the future.

Once Obe sent Mother a copy of what he called "The Sheepherder's Commandments," which he had composed.

Twenty-two hours a day shalt thou labor and do all thy work—the other two be up and ready—think not of thy bed.

On sun-dried peaches and apples eat thy fill, but order nothing else upon thy bill.

When thou art worn out, sick and weary, and can no longer stay, call thee on thy foreman and receive thy scanty wages of a dollar and a half a day.

But before thou leavest thy camp, pay thy bills without a frown. Then with thy blankets on thy back thou knowest the way to town.

Obe had given up that pleasant, lucrative employment (as Father saw it) to take a job with Bishop Tolman at ten dollars a month less so that he could be at home during the winter. Father felt that he simply could not go on if he had to put up with this kind of disloyalty. Nothing good could possibly come of it. And Father was proven to be right when, during the first week, Obe lost part of two knuckles and sliced his thumb badly in a sawmill accident. He couldn't work for the rest of the winter.

Father thought, and said, "There's only one thing for me to do—sell out and go some place where I can make a living without being dependent on my boys."

So Obe got the blame for our most disastrous move, though Mother wasn't convinced that it was all his fault. Even before Obe had quit herding sheep Father had been reading in the *Deseret News* some letters from a Mormon bishop far down in southern Utah telling of the advantages there for Saints willing to colonize. The climate was most salubrious. Fruits of an almost tropical nature, such as figs and pomegranates, could be grown with little effort. Water was abundant and land ridiculously cheap.

All this appealed to Father. He had entered into correspondence with the bishop. There were a few disadvantages, he was told, but for a poor man who would be satisfied with an easy living the sand bars along the Fremont River would prove ideal.

Why Father, with his restless energy, believed that he would ever be satisfied with an *easy* living was beyond understanding. As Mother knew, his feet had been itching with wanderlust, and he had seized upon the first excuse to sell out and move.

As usual, when he had anything to sell his sole thought was to get rid of it as quickly as possible without any hemming or hawing. He always accepted the first offer that was made. If it was five dollars for an article he had paid fifty for a month before it made no difference. He took it.

Finally, in the spring of 1906, he loaded his household goods and the old green grub-box into the covered wagon. He had three horses and exactly one hundred and sixteen dollars in cash left.

It was a hard blow for Mother to give up her home, her friends, and above all her hope that some day the boys would get something back for all the money they had paid on Father's debts. But interest in church work had not killed his wanderlust.

He was always involved in a quarrel with some neighbor, and doubtless there were many who were glad to see him go, for he was a perpetual thorn in the flesh of the priesthood over him, though he still professed to be a stickler for obedience. But the people of Chesterfield did the handsome thing by my parents when they left. There was a farewell party in the amusement hall to which practically everybody in the ward, Saint, Gentile, and jack-Mormon, came. Father was given a gold watch and Mother a fine set of silverware.

So now, fifty-six years of age, her brown hair turned to gray, her thin shoulders a little more stooped, a few more of her teeth gone, Mother found herself once more on the seat of that almost extinct relic of the pioneer West, a covered wagon. No tears flowed, but I was old enough to see the agony in her eyes.

But as always when on the move, Father was supremely happy. From his mouth as he drove along the dusty road issued the old defiant marching song of the Mormon pioneers as they were being driven from Nauvoo to the valleys of the mountains:

*"Come, come ye Saints, no toil nor labor fear,
But with joy wend your way.
Though hard to you this journey may appear,
Grace shall be as your day.
'Tis better far for us to strive,
Our useless cares from us to drive.
Do this, and joy your heart will swell—
All is well! All is well!"*

17

Father was, I am sure, sincere in his desire to cut himself adrift from his sons but that did not include me. I still needed a stern and guiding hand.

That spring I had moved sheep camp for a month, and after that worked at a shearing corral where Obe was employed as a wrangler. My job was jamming wool into the deep, swaying woolsacks that would weigh three hundred pounds when I finished with them. It was hard work, hot and dirty, but the thing I really hated was when I had lowered myself into the long sack from which there was no escape until I could tramp my way out on the trodden fleeces and some thrifty sheepman would toss down on my head rotten, maggot-infested fleeces plucked from the carcasses of sheep that had died during the winter. The maggots getting down my neck was bad; the stench was worse. My partner and I took every other sack; no one could have stood it continually. Still, I would rather have tried it than go with Father to Hanksville. Father had spoken, though, and so I had no choice.

I was now sixteen, a lanky six-footer, the same height as my brothers. All of us towered over Father by a couple of inches, but he was much the heavier. Those days I often contemplated having it out with Father as Chauncey had done, but I lacked both my brother's self-confidence and his physical endowments. The thought ran ever-sickeningly through my mind: *Suppose I try to lick him and he licks me?* I would be done for then!

One incident occurred at the shearing corral which showed me that I was not as self-dependent as I thought I was. Obe had given me a little white Indian cayuse called Pompey which I valued almost as much as life itself. For years all the other boys of my age had had their own ponies, but I went on foot or got a lift behind some other boy. Father thought that being without a pony would keep me from "helling around" so much.

When I left the shearing corral Pompey was missing. I tramped the hills for two days but couldn't find him. The men told me that he had probably gone back to the reservation, and that the former Indian owner certainly would not give him up. All other means having apparently failed I resorted to Mother's unfailing remedy, prayer, though without any great faith that my prayers would be answered. However, I decided to search once more and after a couple of hours I came upon Pompey grazing alone on a meadow. There were hobbles on his feet and saddle marks on his back. Some sheepherder had been riding him. I left the hobbles where they fell, got my saddle, and rode home. Next day we left Chesterfield with me riding Pompey behind the covered wagon.

On the way my folks stopped at Logan to get their long-deferred endowments, to be baptized for their dead, and to receive their secret names—Mother, the one Father would use to call her forth on the morning of the resurrection, if he happened to be in the proper mood. They were also married to each other for time and eternity. People often lift an eyebrow when I tell them that while my parents were being married I was pitching hay a few miles out of town.

I couldn't enter the temple to be sealed to my parents for I had failed to get a "recommend" from my bishop. For some time I had sinned by drinking coffee, and so I wasn't eligible. Anyway, I felt that I looked ridiculous enough as I was without donning a long white robe and a green fig-leaf apron for the temple ceremonies. That wouldn't have been necessary but I didn't know it at the time.

I did know that the adults who went through the temple were ever after supposed to wear the "garments"—underwear of the authorized make and length, bearing marks in the shape of holes in breast and legs, which those who had received their endowments were supposed to wear. Arrogant young sinner that I was, I wanted no garments.

When we drove up South Temple Street in Salt Lake City to get our first view of the magnificent temple and tabernacle which meant so much to my parents, I was unable to withstand the stares and the jocular comments of the people whose ancestors had come to the city in just such a rig as ours. I crawled back under the wagon-cover and did my sight-seeing through a slit in the canvas.

We were, I am sure, among the very last of the covered wagons. The difference between us and our predecessors was that they were called sterling pioneers while we were called wagon tramps. In later years those same streets would see many a jalopy filled with transients even seedier than we were. But that would be in a new era, and we were hangovers from the old.

It wasn't all hardship. We were seeing new country in those

pleasant green valleys which snake their way between the high mountains and the desert from one end of Utah to the other. Once that, too, had been desert but Brigham Young had promised his people that they would make it "blossom as the rose," and his prediction had been fulfilled. To the east lay the frowning, craggy peaks of the Wasatch range, and at the mouth of every stream was a settlement of some kind, ranging from cities like Salt, Ogden, and Provo down to tiny little hamlets. Next to their religion the Mormons valued their water supply, for irrigation had been their salvation. Most of the farms were small but looked prosperous.

Utah differs from other Western states in that few people actually live on their farms. Brigham Young had told them to live in the towns for the dual purpose of protection from the Indians and to promote a better social and community life, and his wisdom had been vindicated.

Mormons had been gathered from all over the world. Scandinavians in particular had a tendency to settle by themselves. We found them less hospitable than most. Once, after a long hard drag from one valley to another, we passed through a settlement named Mantua, nicknamed Little Copenhagen. Hay was everywhere but not one farmer would sell us enough to feed our horses and we had to go on to Brigham City before we could camp. It was my job to buy the feed, and twenty times that day I was told, "Aye t'ank Aye not sell any hay."

A worse experience awaited me in a town named after the Book of Mormon character, Lehi. I saw some people sitting in front of their house and went in to ask if they would sell us hay. There was an open cesspool between me and them that was covered with straw; they let me walk into it without a word of warning and I found myself up to the armpits in the loathsome mess. Lehi is only a few miles from my present home and I drive through it many times during the year. No matter how hard it may be snowing I always roll down the window of my car and yell, "To hell with Lehi!" The only time I have ever in my life been stopped by a highway patrolman was in this town. I was in too big a hurry to get through the place.

Father, as always, did most of the cooking on the trip and the evenings around the campfire were pleasant. In the morning Father was up before dawn to build the fire and feed and water the horses. When Mother and I got up breakfast was always ready, and we were on our way by sunup.

One of the reasons that had impelled Father to make this trip was the opportunity to renew acquaintance with many of the former Palouse country missionaries who lived along the way, and we made frequent detours to visit them. Once they had made our house their headquarters and we had given them the best we had to offer. We were treated by some like visiting royalty, while others seemed ashamed of us and sent us on our way as quickly as possible. It was a shock to my folks to find one elder of whom they had been exceptionally fond, who treated us wonderfully, but refused to accompany us to church. He had become an apostate.

Before we reached the promised land Father began to hear disquieting rumors. When still nearly a hundred miles from his destination he arrived at the seat of the county, a little village called Loa. Here he paused to look up the leading ecclesiastical authority, a man named Bastian, who was president of the stake. The man, a prominent sheepman and farmer, rode over to our wagon on a fine horse.

"The country is all that Brother Hanks told you it was," he confirmed, "but you must remember that fruit and vegetables are about all you can raise, and there is very little market for them. But, after all, brother, money isn't everything."

Painfully aware of his own depleted finances, for he would have been stone-broke if he hadn't sold his extra horse, Father asked, "What about work?"

"I'm glad you brought that up," said the president. "My suggestion is that you stop here for a while and work for me. But you must understand that this is a primitive country and you'll have to take most of your pay in produce, such as potatoes and bacon."

Father's uneasiness was increasing by the minute. "How much do you pay?" he inquired.

"I think," said the president, "that I could pay you as much as thirty dollars a month." He paused to run a cold, appraising eye over me. "The boy looks pretty skinny. I think nine dollars a month would be about right for him."

Mother's eyes commanded me to be silent. For a long time I had been drawing a man's wages wherever I worked, and my last job had paid three dollars a day and board.

"We'll think it over," Father said. We drove on as soon as the churchman was out of sight.

That night we camped with a former bishop who was no longer active in the church. After Father had told his story this man said, "Brother, you've been played for a sucker. Everybody down there wants to sell out. When they go to bed at night they can't be sure that the Dirty Devil river won't wash away their little sandbar farms before morning. There's hardly any market. Only a few years ago that country was the stomping ground of Butch Cassidy's Wild Bunch and it's only a few miles from Robbers' Roost. That country was made for people like them, not Godfearing people like yourselves."

"They don't seem to pay very high wages," Father said.

"Wages are higher than what the stake president offered you, even here," the man said. "He sized you up as an ignorant convert and planned to get a little profit. He pays an honest tithing and feels the Lord should bless him with cheap labor."

It was harder for Mother to accept the stark facts than it was for Father. It was always her wish to think well of her fellow man and she honored the priesthood, but this kind of greed was hard for her to stomach. However, she made only one grim comment: "I'd like to get hold of that man with a Bible in my hand."

That evening there was the worst cloudburst any of us had ever seen. It descended so suddenly that despite the efforts of all of us chickens were drowned in the yard and pigs in their pens.

Said our host, "Had this caught you in Capitol Wash, you probably would have lost your team and wagon and been lucky to escape with your lives."

The next morning Father acknowledged defeat and we turned back without laying eyes on the poor man's paradise we had traveled so far to see. If anything could have shaken my parents' faith in Mormonism that long, grinding covered-wagon trip would have done it; but they remained as steadfast in the Gospel as ever.

We were practically broke and we had nowhere to go. Father mentioned writing to Obe for money, but Mother put her foot down.

"If we were back in Chesterfield I wouldn't mind asking him," she said, "but he had nothing to do with this. It's up to us to pay the consequences of our own mistake."

"I'll never go back to Chesterfield and admit that I've been a failure," Father said.

Mother had been getting regular letters from Obe and knew that he was enjoying his freedom. She seldom, if ever, heard from Chauncey; that young cynic had told her when she left that Father would be back in Chesterfield before snow-fly.

On the way down we had passed through a dry-farm area known as the Levan Ridge where the wheat had looked almost as good as it had in the Palouse country. Harvest was coming on and, since it was imperative that we find work soon, Father went back there to a town called Nephi.

He again sought out one of the leading church authorities a man named Grace, who owned one of the larger wheat farms. This man was considerate and helpful. He gave Father a job at the prevailing wage, two dollars a day, but he had to board himself; which meant taking his grub-box out on the ridge Monday mornings and cooking for himself until Saturday nights. Never had he encountered working conditions like these.

I was luckier. Eight miles west of Nephi, where we had rented a small house, was a place called Dog Valley. Here a group of university professors, suddenly turned scientific farmers, had got hold of a large tract of land at a very cheap price which they were just beginning to reclaim. They had six hundred acres of wheat—their first crop—which they were about ready to harvest. I got a job there for thirty-five dollars a month and board.

Most of my fellow employees were rollicking young Mormon students from Brigham Young University. They had little time to waste on a shy and lonesome young wagon tramp. I did, however, find two good friends there. One was a serious young man of about twenty-five named Billy Brooks, who was working his way through college; he was so sympathetic and friendly that I confided to him my own ambition to get a college education some day. The other was a tough old ex-cowpuncher who, like my brother Chauncey, had a wooden leg. He told me he had once served time; rumor had it that he'd been a member of Butch Cassidy's Wild Bunch. He was baldheaded and sported a heavy, fierce-looking red mustache. He was my bed-fellow during the summer. Hank was the waterbuck, hauling all the water we used from springs several miles beyond in the Tintic Mountains. I often rode over to Ferner springs with him where we amused ourselves killing rattlesnakes, which were thick around the tank.

Dog Valley was so named because of the coyotes which abounded there and lived off the more prolific jack rabbits. Later in the fall when I was wind-rowing sagebrush with a brush harrow I made friends with a toothless old coyote who was too stiff to catch rabbits. When I dumped the harrow several field mice usually would run out, and by staying within a few feet of the harrow the old fellow could catch them. Seeing that I meant him no harm he stayed right at my heels.

The manager of the Dog Valley farm was a member of a tidy little band of Mormon aristocrats, descendants of leading pioneer Mormon families. He was the son of one of the Twelve Apostles of the church, bishop of a ward in Salt Lake City, professor of agronomy at the state university, and editor of the state's leading farm magazine. He was a typical go-getting American businessman, the first to teach me that those high in the hierarchy are not always bound by the same rules as apply to the ruck-and-run.

Nourished on the belief that violation of the Word of Wisdom was a cardinal sin—I had been ousted as a Sunday School teacher for drinking coffee—I was amazed when I saw this man puffing on a big cigar.

Teams were scarce and I had been asked to bring old Barney and his mate over to work on a header box. In our country we used four horses to a wagon but here they used only two. It was grueling work for a team and Barney was no longer young. Knowing that the team badly needed a rest, I refused to work them on a Sunday. I received a dressing down from the manager.

"The trouble with you, young man," he declared, "is that you have no ambition. If you had you would be going to high school or college like these other boys, instead of just being a tramp. If you ever get any place in this world you've got to hustle. You can't hide your laziness by pretending sympathy for a pair of worthless old crowbaits."

Crowbait—old Barney—whose stout heart and gallant spirit had almost unaided dragged the Robertson family and all its worldly goods clear from Babylon to Zion?

I stood my ground, and when the big rush was over I was laid off, a more ambitious youngster being hired to take my place.

During the harvest the brother of the manager, who happened to be the superintendent of the Nephi High School, helped out for a few days. He showed an interest in my education. "If you are living in Nephi this winter come over to our school," he told me. "I won't ask you to study books, but we have some excellent manual-training courses such as carpentry. I'm sure we can do *something* for you." After that remark wild horses couldn't have dragged me to his school.

For Mother it was one of the easiest, if not the happiest summers of her life. Six days of the week she lived entirely alone, free from the fear of a family row. She could order what she wanted from the grocery store which would be delivered to our door. She prepared feasts for Father and me when we were home for Sunday dinner. She had acquired two friends, an old lady of eighty who owned the house where we lived, and an old-maid ex-schoolteacher who reminded her of her friend, Josie Stoker. She could enjoy going to church with no duties to perform, and from the bishop down people were universally cordial.

That summer at Dog Valley ended my hopes of ever getting an education. The students' glibness of tongue and their smug talk about a life I had never known filled me with dismay. None of the Mormon college boys took their religion as seriously as I did. They assumed that some day they would go on missions, marry pure Mormon girls and rise to their proper niches in the hierarchy but for the present they just wanted to raise hell. Where going to college had always seemed to me a sobering undertaking these boys took it in stride as their just due which would place them in high circumstance and surround them with the luxuries and finer things of life to which they were entitled.

So college became, for me, something to be forgotten. My folks were as poor as ever, and I knew I would have to help support them for years to come. But renunciation did not come as easily to me as it did to Obe. I felt that Father's constant demands were primarily at fault. Sullen fires of rebellion, of which Father was blissfully unaware, smoldered inside me.

That summer was an interlude, a lost portion of our lives. We had traveled a thousand miles and got nowhere. Father had suffered perhaps the most humiliating defeat of his life.

Mother had done that which she could do best—wait. I, though none of us realized it, had become a man.

I don't think Mother was surprised when one day Father came back from the ridge and, as in days of old, said, "Start packin', Ma. We're going back to Chesterfield."

18

My long-planned declaration of independence came about in a way which neither Father nor I could have anticipated.

Mother had gone back to Chesterfield by train to stay with friends until Father and I arrived with the wagon. The second day we came upon an automobile stuck in the mud. With characteristic neighborliness Father stopped and used our horses to pull it out. The men offered him money. He waved it aside; never in his life had he taken a penny for an accommodation.

It was a raw fall day. One of the men offered a whisky flask. "At least have a drink," he urged.

"I never took a drink of whisky in my life," Father said indignantly. "I'd have left you settin' right there in the mud if I'd known you'd insult me by offering me the stuff."

If he hadn't been cold and irritated by the delay he would have been more courteous. Embarrassed by the onslaught, the man drew back the bottle, then, seeing me, said lamely, "What about you?" I was taller than Father and, bundled up as I was, I probably looked more than my age.

It was an unexpected crisis. Always fearful of making a bad impression on strangers, I didn't want the men to think that I was as fanatical as Father. On the other hand I was reasonably sure that if I took the flask Father would knock it out of my hand and give me a whipping then and there, though it had been more than a year since he had done so.

Well, this was a gamble my pride forced me to take. If Father tried to whip me in front of these men I would fight back. I reached for the flask and let the whisky trickle down my throat. Father's pale blue eyes were fixed upon me with shocked disbelief, but he turned away without a word. More than twenty years passed before he ever mentioned the episode.

I knew then that I had received my last whipping. But later I sometimes carried my newfound independence too far by threatening to whip Father. At such times he would double up his fists, square off and shout, "Hit me. Hit me if you dare." I never accepted the challenge and felt worse beaten than if he had laid on with a club.

It was far from being my first drinking experience. I had often sampled whisky at the Chesterfield dances. But my defection at this time broke Father's heart. He scarcely spoke to me all the way back to Chesterfield. Several times he forgot himself and started to sing, *Come, come, ye Saints*, but would catch himself and relapse into gloomy silence.

He had his revenge. When, that winter, he was back at his old post in the superintendency of the Chesterfield Sunday School, it was proposed to make me a Sunday School teacher again, he knocked the proposal flat. "He isn't fit to teach," he thundered. "He don't keep the Word of Wisdom. He *drinks.*"

No sooner were we back in Chesterfield than Father borrowed a buggy and he and Mother drive out to the sheep camp where Obe was herding. With the hundred dollars which was all that profligate had saved from his summer's wages, Father made a down payment on a two-and-a-half acre lot with a two-room log cabin and started to build a henhouse. We were back in business.

Father became janitor of the church and schoolhouse, but the job only paid twenty dollars a month so it required Obe's wages for us to live. A silly pride made me feel that janitor work was the lowest scale in society to which a human being could fall. Nevertheless, I had to do most of the sweeping and fire-building while Father looked around for new opportunities to go in debt.

Both he and Mother were welcomed eagerly back in the ward and they resumed their old church duties. But Father soon had a serious clash with "authority." As a Sunday School officer he was supposed to attend a Union meeting some forty miles distant. The road was hub-deep in mud and was a horse killer. Father refused to work his horses that hard to attend a two-hour meeting.

Brother Tolman, his superior officer, announced publicly that Brother Robertson was out of harmony with the authorities and must ask forgiveness or resign his position in the Sunday School. He added that horses, like all other animals—he was a notorious horse killer—were put on earth for the use of man, and that if it be required to kill them in the service of the Lord they should be killed.

Father would sacrifice many things in the Lord's service, but not old Barney. He resigned. Cy Tolman had unwittingly snared himself a wildcat. Father had no job, so he had ample time to visit every house in the ward and denounce the treatment he had received. Whenever the hot-stove league gathered in Barlow's store to gossip and shake dice for peanuts there was Father holding out for hours about his wrongs.

Finally Brother Tolman came to see Father. "Brother Robertson," he said, "I know I'm right about the Union meeting because the authorities commanded it, but if I have wronged you in any way or hurt your feelings I'm ready to get down on my knees and ask your forgiveness."

"I suppose," Father cried passionately, "that if the authorities commanded you to kill a man or give up your wife to another man that you'd do it."

"They wouldn't ask me to do anything wrong, but if they should require these things I would obey them," replied the man of great faith.

Obedience to the priesthood was what Father had preached in season and out. Now he swung over to Mother's position that even the priesthood could not expect a man to violate his own conscience. Mother characteristically held that Brother Tolman had done what *his* conscience told him was right and should be forgiven. Brother and Sister Tolman were among her best friends.

"No matter what I do," Father shouted in exasperation, "you always take sides against me!"

Meanwhile, the Sunday School was coming apart at the seams. When Father was in the superintendency he maintained strict order. When children were supposed to march into classes he saw to it that there was no dawdling. It was a custom of some mothers to allow their younger offspring to whoop along the aisles during services. Father put a stop to that and even the youngest toddler would fly to its mother's arms at his frown. A stickler for punctuality, he always started Sunday School on the dot. Once he had "taken up" when only he and Mother were present. He sang the opening hymn himself, had Mother give the opening prayer, and was halfway through the second hymn before anyone else arrived.

He intimidated his officers and teachers so that they dared not be late. If they couldn't make it on time they stayed away.

Thorn in the flesh that he was, even his enemies admitted that he made ours a model Sunday School.

When the smoke finally cleared away Father had replaced Brother Tolman as superintendent. It was the first time in the history of the stake that anyone had rebelled against the priesthood and gotten away with it. A more humble man would have been "dealt with," but Father was a hard man to deal with. It was much easier to placate him, as his family had long since learned.

Having once rebelled successfully against authority, Father was less amenable to discipline than ever before. Although Mother tried to remain neutral in his many stormy fights inside the church she was always accused of siding against him. Once a High Councilman warned Mother that Father was taking the highway to apostasy. This she refused to believe. Mormonism, a "temporal" religion, was his life, as well as his hope for exaltation in the Celestial Kingdom. But a good row was as necessary to him as food and drink.

Once more Father talked about going into the chicken business, and once more he went in debt—just enough to give Mother and Obe a faint hope that some day he might "get on top." A few cows, a few chickens, a team: that, he declared humbly, was all he asked for.

My attitude toward life and toward the church now caused Mother considerable worry. I was sullen and moody. She tried timidly to cheer me with the old half promise, "Maybe next year we can send you away to school," but I yelled at her, "I don't want to go to school; I'm too damned old!"

My interest in church was twisted and, as Mother had good reason to fear, selfish. I went to meetings but would never open or dismiss with prayer as other boys of my age did. Nor would I administer or partake of the Sacrament. I deliberately broke the Word of Wisdom by drinking coffee and taking a drink of whisky whenever I could get it.

I was secretary of the Young Men's Mutual Improvement Association but that meant nothing. Obe had served one term in that office and wasn't a member of the church. I, of course, would not bear my testimony, having none to bear, but I would get up in "conjoint" meetings of the Mutual, which were held once a month, and give a talk on current events.

Mother alone noticed that I had a penchant for giving, not the most important news, but features that would shock my listeners. Because I read a great deal and because most of the people there limited their reading to church literature, I could get away with murder. I wanted to be like other people and didn't know how to do it, so I went to the opposite extreme to show others I could stand by myself.

What I was really after was practice in public speaking. Unfortunately, I thought only of speaking rapidly and without hesitation and never came within miles of being the public speaker that either of my parents was. I suppose my real reason for seizing on every opportunity to speak in public was to atone for my lack of grace as a conversationalist. From the rostrum I had my audience at my mercy. A friend and I organized a debating society, something new for that country, and it gave me greater opportunity. I was using it to try to overcome some of my bashfulness. In the back of my head was the idea that someday I might be able to educate myself.

One Sunday when I was seventeen three or four other boys of my age and I were unexpectedly called into the pulpit to speak in Sacrament meeting. This was considered training for the missions we all expected to fill. There was considerable giggling among the girls over our anticipated embarrassment. The other boys muttered a few unintelligible words, concluding with the inevitable rapidly murmured "blessings humbly pray for, name o' Jesus, Amen."

Here, I felt, was my opportunity to distinguish myself. I could see Mother gazing at me encouragingly and Father staring at the floor in the manner of one ready to be shamed and humiliated before his fellow man. I was sure that he expected, and hoped for, my failure but I was determined to make Mother proud and earn a reputation for myself.

I plunged immediately into the subject of Joseph Smith as a scientist, and for ten eloquent minutes held forth on that topic, and would have spoken longer had not my lips got so dry that I could no longer articulate. I proved conclusively that practically every scientific discovery during the past century had been foretold in one of Joseph Smith's revelations—that strong drinks are not for the belly, but for the washing of the body; that tobacco should be used as an herb for bruises and sick cattle—up to the great principle of the indestructibility of matter—and many other truths not known to science in Joseph's time, all to be found in the Doctrine and Covenants.

It was a good talk and I was sure I held my audience in the palm of my hand; but when it came time to stop I realized suddenly that I simply could not bring myself to utter the customary ". . . blessings I humbly pray for in the name of Jesus, Amen," to which the entire congregation was accustomed to respond with a rousing Amen.

I hadn't asked for any blessings and didn't believe the Lord would grant me any attention if I did. I thought, *I can't go through the blasphemous mockery of a prayer now.* I just shut my mouth and sat down.

Silence bore down like the invisible hand of God. Red in the face from confusion and embarrassment, I stole a glance at Father. The look on his face, it seemed to me, was one of savage triumph. I always wanted his approval but I never got it. It took me years to realize that I was the object of the same bitter jealousy from which Mother had suffered in the early years of their marriage. Now I had disgraced myself, as he had known I would. Mother's eyes were on her hymn book. She was undoubtedly praying silently for me. The faces of the women and girls which a moment before had been beaming with admiration were now stiff with a kind of fixed horror. I had committed a *faux pas* equal to that of Win Matthews when he had referred to the prophet as "old Joe."

That afternoon Mother told me quietly about another lean and bitter young man she had known. He was Win Matthews's oldest son, Warren. Like me, Warren knew a great many things about which his family and the neighbors were not in the least interested. Like me, he was socially awkward, but a fluent speaker. Like me, he was ambitious and hungry for an education, and he, too, often quarreled with his father.

One day while Mother was living in Baker City, after Father and I had left for Idaho, Warren had come to visit her; she told me of the heartache she had felt when he confided that many times while a soldier in the Philippines he had hoped to intercept a bullet. Soon after that visit Warren had tried to interfere in a fight among his in-laws and a bullet intended for one of them had ended his life. Mother felt that he had interfered in that fight with the same rash hope that he might be killed.

Unless I changed my ways, Mother pointed out gently, I was quite likely to live the same kind of a life and meet the same kind of fate that had overtaken Warren Matthews. Frustration in the matter of getting an education was at the bottom of my trouble, just as it had been in Warren's. There was still time, she argued. I was only seventeen. I might still work my way through high school and college if I only would. I would have leaped at the chance when I was fourteen; it should be easier now.

I was not deceived. There were always Father's debts! they would have to be paid, and he would never be able to pay them off himself. He couldn't take time off from his church duties to earn a living, and if compelled to there would be no living with him.

I was not like the other boys. Chauncey was completely normal. He never felt inferior to anybody. He liked to excel in the work he did, and was entirely self-sufficient. Obe, on the other hand, was completely lacking in the vanity that possessed and persecuted me. Already he had developed a philosophy of life very similar to Mother's: *Be calm. Endure. Make others as happy as you can and your own happiness will look after itself.*

As usual when in trouble, Mother consulted Obe. "He had just as well go to school," Obe said. "I can keep Dad going somehow. No matter how much money the old man gets he'll just go in debt a little deeper. But Frank won't do it. If I give Dad a hundred dollars Frank thinks he'll be eternally disgraced if he doesn't kick through with another hundred."

"The difference is that you give it *willingly*."

Obe smiled. "Frank screams to high heaven that he's being robbed, but he'd make you take the money if he had to throw it in your face—just like when we're working together he'll do more than I do if it kills him, even though I like to work and he hates the very thought of it."

Obe had me pegged right, except for one thing. If he would have stopped putting up for Father I would have stopped, but my sense of justice and fair play revolted against one son having to bear all the burden. Obe was too good a man to have to carry it alone.

Mother said, "Chauncey would help if we'd ask him."

"We've got to leave Chauncey out of it," Obe said. "He's done more than his share, and if he starts contributing to the family again Dad will only make it an excuse to go deeper in debt. Besides, Frank won't let anybody help him."

"Then," Mother said resolutely, "there is only one thing to do. We must send him on a mission. Pa won't object to that."

In Mormonland that was the cure-all for recalcitrant Mormon youths. If they were going to the dogs, the thing to do was send them out as ministers of the Gospel. Few of them, if they had been reared in the faith, ever refused the call. Many was the Mormon boy sent out to be reformed while calling the Gentiles to repentance. Always they came back polished men of the world, to bear a powerful testimony; many became fine preachers.

"Two years in the mission field will make a man of Frank," Mother said wistfully and, apologizing to her conscience, added, "He'll make a good missionary too."

Mother took the matter up with Vosco Call, the bishop of the ward.

"Yes," the bishop said, "I believe Frank will be a good missionary. If his father approves I'll recommend that he get a letter from Box B." Box B was the official church address.

The bishop and Mother took the matter up with Father. The proposition startled and dismayed him.

"I don't believe in sending a boy out to reform him," he said. "Frank's worse than a cigarette smoker. He knows Mormonism is true, but he ain't got the spirit of the Gospel. Obedience ain't in him. If it was he'd partake of the Sacrament and pray in church when the authorities ask him. Besides, we can't afford to send him, and he wouldn't go."

"I'll bet he would, and Obe has agreed to send him," Mother said.

Father said nothing, but the way he stared at the floor, Mother knew, was the beginning of a long sulk that would be worse than a row.

"Pa, don't you want Frank to go on a mission?" she asked.

"Of course I do," he replied angrily, "but there's plenty of time for him. What about me? I'll soon be sixty. If Obe can afford to send Frank on a mission he can afford to send me."

From the time he had first joined the church Father's dearest ambition had been to go on a mission. He couldn't be blamed at all for hating to see the opportunity wasted on a young upstart who didn't qualify anyway.

A couple of months later Father was called on a mission to the Central States. Soon after that Obe came down with an eye infection which prevented him from working for nearly two years. I went out herding sheep to keep Father on his mission.

19

Father's farewell was a grand success. The proceeds of the dance and the individual contributions totaled well over a hundred dollars. Even the local atheist contributed five dollars. The rest of Father's expenses we would have to dig up. All the church ever contributed to the missionaries was their return fare home.

So zealous had Father been in prodding the Saints to a performance of their duties that having him away for a season was like vacation to a group of school-weary youngsters. But the laxity that followed his departure made many of them exclaim fervently, "I do wish Brother Robertson was back here to straighten things out."

Soon after Father left, Obe, driving a mowing machine on the ranch of which Chauncey was foreman, nearly lost his sight. He had to hold his team with one hand and dig moss out of the sickle-bar with the other, at considerable risk of losing his fingers. Sweat would roll down his forehead into his eyes and he would wipe it away with his gloved hand. Alkali or something from the moss and weeds caused an infection. Soon he was practically blind. A Salt Lake City specialist performed a delicate operation which didn't help. Finally he came home.

Mother felt as badly as she had when Chauncey lost his leg—only this was worse. Obe was not taking it as Chauncey had. She remembered Father's oft-repeated prediction that Obe would some day commit suicide, and now his attitude frightened her. He was never one to rail against fate, but now he would discuss no plans for his future.

Father had to be kept on his mission. Yet both Mother and Obe were determined to pay Mr. West back for the money he had put up to pay Obe's doctor bills and expenses. My wages for herding sheep constituted our only income and I was getting only forty dollars a month. After long association with non-Mormons, Chauncey considered Father's mission to be sheer folly so Mother couldn't ask him for help; and both Obe and I would have violently opposed her taking his money if it had been volunteered.

Chauncey said, "I'll let you have my last dollar for yourself if you need it, Mother, but not one to support any Mormon missionary."

Mother replied calmly, "We'll make out all right, son."

Even though badly worried about Obe, she enjoyed having him at home, and never were two people more congenial. Our two cows grazed on the vacant lots. In the evening Mother would pound on the milk-bucket and her sleepy old dog, Bounce, would rouse himself and go looking for the cows.

When he drove them in Mother would milk them. She spent much of her time reading to Obe as she had when he was a child and she spared him anything relating to religion.

Father was having a wonderful time. He spent the first few months in Kansas, traveling over sections where in his youth he had roamed as a cowboy. He received a furlough to go to his old home across the river from St. Louis, and visited many distant relatives. After that he was transferred to north Texas, where he visited his two brothers and their families and his step-mother. As always, young people liked him, and he became a great favorite with his nephews and nieces. Only his brother Horton was not favorably impressed by the Mormon missionaries.

His missionary companions were nearly all young men, in some instances mere boys. Only once was he assigned to labor with a man nearly his own age, and he raised a row until he got a younger companion. Young men always admired him. With them he never lost his temper and he was a good raconteur and excellent company. The fact that he was spreading the Gospel here where he had ridden the range as a wild cowboy nearly half a century ago gave him an added glamour.

His public-speaking ability had been gradually improving before he left Chesterfield, but out here, with an opportunity to preach several times a week, he became a really good speaker. His voice had always been good, and he developed a rapid delivery which would have made him a terror to stenographers had one ever tried to take down his remarks. He was never at a loss for a word. His English was bad and he didn't bother to correct it, but his earnestness and evident sincerity made people forget his errors of grammar and pronunciation. He developed persuasiveness along with his ability to preach long doctrinal sermons. He could hold forth for an hour or more with utmost ease.

Always he disarmed criticism by the statement that he was merely a humble, unlettered servant of the Lord, as the Prophet Joseph had been, bearing his testimony that this was the Dispensation of the Fullness of Times; that the angel Moroni, who had delivered the golden plates of the Book of Mormon to Joseph Smith, was indeed that very angel of whom St. John, the Revelator, had written, saying, *"And I saw another angel flying through the midst of heaven having the Everlasting Gospel to preach to every kindred, tongue and people."*

Yes, he truly believed that he was a meek and humble man!

As a house-to-house visitor in the rural districts he was unexcelled. He knew farming as he knew little else, and he always approached the farmer with an intelligent discussion of crops or livestock, related a few anecdotes from his own experience, and would have the man's interest and good will before he ever mentioned Mormonism. Telling them that he traveled without purse or script like the missionaries of old, he rarely had any trouble finding a place to eat or sleep. Still, there was constant need for money for clothes and laundry, and to pay for the tracts which the missionary had to distribute. In winter he had to live in the cities, where he had to pay room and board.

I had got a job as soon as the sheep arrived from the winter range and had to go through the lambing season. We had rain or snow about every other day and since I couldn't afford the slicker and gum boots which the other men wore I suffered some discomfort. I tried to limit my personal expenses to five dollars a month, enabling Mother to send Father the twenty-five or thirty dollars which was the minimum required to keep him going and leave a few dollars extra for her to buy groceries.

When the lambing was over I was assigned a band of ewes and lambs for the summer, which was much easier. I had time to spare, only I could never leave the herd. I didn't mind the loneliness. My great need was for reading material. I often walked for miles to some knoll where I thought sheep might have bedded hoping to find some discarded magazine or newspapers. I've known hunger of various kinds on many occasions but none worse than the hunger for something to read.

It so happened that our sheep outfit, owned by a wealthy and important Mormon family, was constantly feuding for range with the cattle outfit of which Chauncey was foreman. At one time during the lambing season when a band of ewes and lambs had trespassed too far, Chauncey and another rider had driven a bunch of wild horses and mules through them inflicting considerable damage and enraging my employers.

Lambs are born without brains and rarely acquire any in later life. When disturbed they will spring up and follow anything that happens to be moving. The wild mules would run over lambs that happened to be in their way so that many lambs were killed, while others followed them on their spindly legs until lost in the sagebrush. Such events were not conducive to good feeling between the rival outfits.

One day Chauncey appeared at my camp, bringing with him clean clothes which Mother had sent and a sackful of old magazines which he had borrowed from a neighboring ranch.

He was a dashing and picturesque figure on a horse. Even with a pegleg he could, as the rangemen say, ride anything that had hair. As a roper, he was unsurpassed. His knee had finally straightened and now he wore an artificial limb with scarcely a limp. He was addicted to colorful hats, shirts and boots, and always rode a good horse and saddle.

I, with my face covered with a scraggly red beard, long, unkempt hair falling below the collar of my shirt, overalls frayed nearly up to my knees from walking through the sagebrush and liberally splotched with sourdough, was painfully conscious of the contrast between me and this elder brother of mine.

"You tell that foreman of yours that if he don't want his saintly guts sprayed all over the sagebrush he'd better keep his perverted sheep off our range," Chauncey said gaily as he rode away.

Most of the magazines were old Street & Smith pulps. I

read them with the avidity of a starving tramp going after a beefsteak. The stories I liked best were the "Happy Family" cowboy yarns of B. M. Bower in the *Popular* magazine. Chip of the Flying U, Pinky, Weary and the others were not too much unlike Chauncey, Roughy, Bob, Jake, Hi, Jack, and other cowhands I knew personally. I began to realize that there was, or could be, romance in the land in which I lived. I didn't know until years later that B. M. Bower was a woman, and that she had recently spent a summer writing one of her books about some of the men I knew, less than thirty miles from where I was.

But a sackful of magazines couldn't last forever. Once while Father was visiting his old home on the Mississippi, he sent me a copy of the St. Louis *Republic*. I read his letter—he wrote me nearly every week—and tore the wrapper off the newspaper. A big headline stared me in the face:

WILLIAM JENNINGS BRYAN NOMINATED FOR PRESIDENT

That was 1908. My mind went back to the days when the *Republic*, to which Father had subscribed in the Idaho panhandle, had been the source of my knowledge, and Bryan my political ideal whom I hoped to emulate. It seemed a long, long time ago. Then I had been fired by ambition to be another Bryan. Now I was an old man of eighteen without a future; the lowest of the Western breed, a sheepherder. I carried that paper in my hip pocket until I knew even the advertisements by heart, and the print became too dim to read.

The life of a sheepherder is full of ups and downs. He may work from before dawn until after dark and sit up half the night to keep his flock from leaving the bedground, be wet and tired and miss half his meals, or he may live a life of ease that a millionaire might envy.

Except in winter sheep like to leave the bedground at crack

of dawn. The herder must have had his breakfast and be ready to follow them. But in summer they shade up as soon as it gets hot and won't move again until the cool of the evening. Even the coyotes declare a moratorium and the herder may do what he wills. In the mountains there are good fishing streams and he may fish if he likes that sport. He can hunt grouse or he can visit another camp to gossip and have dinner. Or, as I preferred, he can read—if he has anything readable. Before the sheep start to stir he will cook his supper, then sit out on some ridge and watch his charges feed until dark. But if it rains the sheep will trail through the wet brush all day and he dares not leave them.

Most herders I have known were intelligent men who hated crowds. Many were well educated and good company when they chose to talk. Some could play an accordion or a fiddle and invariably they had a sense of humor. Most of them liked liquor, but didn't drink when at camp, though I have known a few who were hell on Worcester sauce and lemon extract. The old regulars liked the girls, and in those days an enterprising madam would set up a tent with from one to four girls and do a thriving business at the range trading posts.

The life of the camp movers was entirely different. They could spend considerable time in town where they went for supplies. Some of them developed an amazing knack of forgetting some essential so that they could go back after it the next day.

I was not a good sheepherder. The good herder would plan his day's activities like a general planning a campaign, but I, not knowing when to leave the herd alone, kept the sheep agitated when they should have been quiet and frequently left them alone when I should have been with them. Bears and coyotes made heavy inroads. Of four herds in our outfit that went to the Caribou mountains, mine was by far the poorest in flesh in the fall.

The sheepherder's boon companion is always his dog. A good dog can save him miles of walking daily. I seldom had one that didn't know more about herding than I did. My dog that first summer was a little part coyote that I called Red. He was a good enough sheep dog but unusually timid and sensitive. If I uttered a harsh word to him he would quit me for the day; and he was afraid of all other dogs and animals.

I shall never forget my first night in the mountains. A bear got into the herd and slaughtered sixteen sheep. I was the only herder in the outfit who didn't have a gun. Before leaving, my camp mover had killed a mutton and hung it up on a tree just outside my tent, assuring me that it was too high for a bear to reach. I kept thinking that if a bear couldn't reach the mutton he might try to reach me. I made my bed inside the tent and slept with my open jackknife in my hand, prepared to slit a hole in the canvas and shinny up a tree if a bear appeared at the door of the tent.

I was awakened by Red who bounded into the tent and burrowed down beside me, whimpering. Soon I could hear loud grunts and, peering outside, I saw a huge black bear on his hind feet making swipes at the mutton. He could barely touch the neck of the mutton and couldn't get his claws into it, but he was batting it to and fro like a shuttlecock. Presently, he mauled over some of the stuff outside the tent and then grumblingly ambled away.

My most disagreeable experience, however, happened on trailing in when I discovered I had lice. I attributed this affliction to an old one-armed sheepherder on the bum whom I had picked up. All our extra clothes had been taken by a roundabout way in the commissary wagon, and when we struck the timber I discovered that lice were fairly dripping from the seams of my underwear. It was a week before I could get relief.

After the lambs had been shipped and winter herds made up I wasn't greatly surprised to hear the foreman say, "Frank, I'm afraid I can't take you to the desert this winter. You can go to Sugar City and feed beet pulp if you want to, but we'll have to cut your wages to thirty dollars a month."

That ten-dollar-a-month cut would put me below an absolute minimum. It would keep Father on his mission, but leave nothing for me and the folks. Besides, my pride was hurt. I drew my wages, walked over to Chauncey's camp, and rode home on a borrowed horse. I had been away from home eight months. Obe was away at the West ranch, but Mother seemed glad to see me and did not reproach me for having lost my job. I felt badly, however, and rode out to Bancroft the next day and got mildly drunk.

Just outside Bancroft I met one of the Hatch boys holding a herd of sheep. We left the sheep long enough to cross the tracks and have a glass of beer. One beer called for another. In a reckless mood, I didn't care what happened. Soon we were wrestling inside a store and, when thrown out, finished our match on the sidewalk.

After wandering from one saloon to the other, we finally remembered the sheep and staggered back across the tracks; but before we could find the herd my friend Pax was taken suddenly sick. I left him there in the sagebrush and rode home.

The next day his employer hired me to herd his sheep. He had fired Pax, his nephew, for getting drunk. Surely the Lord was looking out for Father that day. When snow came we moved into the ranch to feed. I was assigned to an upstairs room in the big brick house and no longer had to do my own cooking.

Meantime, Mother was hunting desperately for additional means to keep Father on his mission. Heretofore, the post office had been in Barlow's store, but now Barlow had been elected county assessor and was moving with his family to Pocatello. He rented Mother his house and she became postmistress of Chesterfield. She and Obe moved in and established the post office in the front room. The pay depended on the cancellation and usually ran about twenty dollars a month. That took up some of the slack, but it still wasn't enough. Obe's medical expenses had put us back, and Dad had been burdened by debts to start with. He was spending the winter in Dallas and his expenses had doubled.

He had written, *I'll ask for my release if you think I should come home.*

Mother prayed, and the more she prayed the more she became convinced that it would be impossible to keep him out any longer. He had been gone a year and a half, long enough to get an honorable release. She believed the Lord would accept this as full performance of duty and wrote Father that he had better come home.

At first he seemed glad to be back. The ward turned out to hear him preach, and he received many a compliment on his improved public speaking. In a few days, however, he expressed disapproval of Mother for having taken the post office. Here there was no opportunity for him to go into the chicken business, and he couldn't keep more than a couple of cows. What did she expect him to do?

Soon a full-sized row was on. Father claimed that Mother could have kept him on his mission had she not been lacking faith in him and in the Gospel. He learned that Chauncey, in spite of threats not to help, had been giving Mother a little money at times. He maintained that she could have got more out of him had she tried.

An incident that happened just before I went away to herd sheep had given Father more ammunition to assail Mother's orthodoxy. An old gentlemen, affectionately known in the community as Uncle Jim, had died quite suddenly. He had come to Utah as a muleskinner with Johnston's Army, married a full-blooded Indian girl who had been raised by a Mormon family, and joined the church. Aunt Ruth, his wife, was the community midwife and loved by everyone. Uncle Jim was a man of sterling character but woefully unlettered, and so was never called to the stand to speak.

There was also in the community a convert who had been educated as a Catholic priest. Brother Scott was a man of many spiritual manifestations. For years he had been developing a mine in the neighborhood in which the Lord had shown him fabulous treasure in a dream. A great deal of stock in this enterprise was sold on the strength of this dream—the average Mormon placing far more faith in dreams than in geological reports—and whenever the treasury became depleted the Lord was always kind enough to vouchsafe another manifestation. At this particular time, however, Brother Scott was digging wells and I was helping him. He was staying with us and, somewhat impressed by my love for learning, decided to teach me Latin.

"Speaking in tongues" had been common in the early days of the church, but the practice had become practically obsolete. So we were all startled when in the midst of Uncle Jim's funeral, Brother Scott arose and spoke in a language nobody could understand. When he sat down there was a dead silence. If the manifestation had been from the Lord some brother would be inspired and translate it into English. When the silence became unbearable a former bishop and highly respected brother arose and stated the translation had come to him. What Brother Scott had said was that Uncle Jim was even now preaching to the spirits in the hereafter, and the particular audience was the Lamanite ancestors of his wife.

While most of the Saints accepted the manifestation as genuine, basing their belief on the well-known integrity of the translator, the idea of illiterate Uncle Jim's being transformed so quickly into a preacher was somewhat fantastic. To Mother and me the "tongue" had sounded suspiciously like the Latin Brother Scott was wont to reel off while he was trying to teach me the language. At the dinner table later Mother put the question to him if it had not been Latin. He admitted that it was, but claimed that he had no knowledge of what he was saying, and how, he asked, could Bishop Tolman have been able to give it meaning if it had not been from the Lord?

Mother had written to Father of the incident in a humorous vein, and he had thought it funny at the time. Now she was taken aback when Father accused her of belittling the Lord's manifestations. The Bible had promised, he reminded her, that signs should follow the believers. She knew that he didn't believe there had been any authentic speaking in tongues any more than she did, and told him so.

Heretofore our family rows had been at least quasi-private but now they were wide open to the delighted ears of the populace. The post office was kept open from morning until bedtime, and since it was actually in our front room it provided a comfortable place for the citizens to foregather. People dropping in to get their mail lingered gleefully to hear Father denounce the willfulness of his family. He always loved an audience and the greater the number the louder he could shout. Chauncey and I were the lucky ones, because we were seldom there.

Father was soon back in the Gospel harness. He now held stake as well as ward offices and was in demand as a speaker throughout the stake, particularly at funerals. His favorite text was from St. Paul: *If in this life only I have hope, then I am of all men most miserable.* He sincerely believed that and must have had great hope, for he was happy most of the time.

He was never too hard-up to buy the latest book on church doctrine. He rose long before daybreak and devoted hours to the study of Mormon doctrine and history. He was no longer jealous of Mother's accomplishments because he had far outstripped her both in popularity as a speaker and in technical knowledge of the Gospel. Her memory was beginning to falter at times, while he never forgot anything he didn't choose to. When he wanted to forget a thing with unpleasant connections, that thing was as though it had never been.

Once, when he was just beginning to forge ahead of Mother as a theologian, he might have entertained some fear that I would become a competitor, but that danger was now removed. I was as backward and awkward as ever, no longer attended church of any kind, and my reading was confined to what he contemptuously dismissed as trash. It enraged him that his boys wouldn't listen to his preachments, but he could dismiss it since he believed Mother was responsible for our lack of reverence.

There were others in the ward who failed to accord him proper respect. As soon as he returned he was installed in his old position as superintendent of the Sunday School and promptly jacked up those who were not diligent. Often some of his women teachers, driven to tears by his fiery reproofs, would resign. It did them little good. He would travel from house to house crying out their rebellion until to keep their names from becoming a hiss and a byword they would acknowledge their error and come creeping back. Others, however, stayed away entirely.

But the one who baffled him completely was his organist, the wife of his most devoted and loyal chum—a young man, of course. Father, a fanatic on punctuality, could not tolerate his organist's habitual tardiness. Neither did her choice of songs always please him. Secure in the knowledge that he could get no other organist, the young woman remained indifferent to his virulent verbal assaults.

He decided to try other tactics. Once, stopping the Sunday School, he went down to the door to demonstrate how the organist entered the building after the school had taken up. He pretended to stop aghast at the realization that the school was already in session. Then, with a great contortion of his hips, much fiddling with his fingers at an imaginary dress, at the same time glancing coyly to right and left, he burlesqued his way to the organ stool. It was a good show and brought a laugh, particularly from the pretty young organist—who continued to be late.

However, when Father tangled for the second time with the authority of the priesthood he finally got his come-uppance. The quarterly stake conference was being held in Bancroft; it was a big event for the Mormons because it was always visited by one of the authorities from Salt Lake. This time it was one of the Twelve Apostles, no less, a man named Richards. Wherever this exalted servant of the Lord moved there was a reverent circle of stake dignitaries surrounding him, for every word that fell from his inspired lips was a pearl of great price to be seized upon and cherished.

As usual, the sisters served lunch cafeteria-style between sessions. Noting that the sisters were waiting and that no one moved to lead off, Father, who never could endure any horsing around when a thing was to be done, picked up a paper plate and passed it up to be filled.

The voice of the stake president rang out: "Hold on there, Brother Robertson, you'll have to wait until Apostle Richards has been served."

Father dropped the plate as though he had been stung by a bee. The apostle and lesser authorities filed past, laughing and talking, but Father indignantly left the building. His feelings had been hurt and he let the world know it. He vowed that unless somebody apologized he would resign all his offices in the church.

He had gone too far. He was told bluntly, "Brother Robertson, if you haven't enough deference for the high authorities of the church to stand aside while an apostle is being served then you are lacking in the spirit of the Gospel and your resignation will be accepted."

Father pulled in his horns, but he never forgot or forgave the affront. From then on he was a little less vociferous in his demands for implicit and instant obedience to the voice of authority. He had been running wild with the Gospel bits in his teeth, and it perhaps surprised him to find that there was still a firm hand on the reins.

20

A mile or so west of Chesterfield a wealthy sheepman named A. J. Knollin had taken over half of the West ranch for the purpose of breeding pure-bred Shropshire sheep. Long sheds were built for winter lambing, which gave employment to many Chesterfield men when work was otherwise hard to get.

I quit my job with my Mormon employer to take one with the Gentile at considerably increased wages. Obe, who by now could see well enough to work—his cure having been brought about by some old wives' remedy, after the doctors had given up—took a job there also.

Lambing, even in sheds, is hard, messy work. Frequently

the ewes have to be helped, and the wet, slimy lambs gotten into the heated pens before they freeze to death. Many times the ewes have to be forced to claim their offspring. If a lamb dies its hide is removed and laced onto some orphan so that the foster mother will think it her own.

The ewes were frequently determined not to assume their maternal obligations, and sometimes the day men would find such directions as these written on the gates of the pens: *Kick hell out of this one every thirty minutes* or *Stomp until head is bloody.*

This treatment, of course, was not approved by the twenty-two-year-old foreman, who had come barefoot out of the Ozarks some six years before, without money and without education, and already owned a substantial interest in the business. Within a few years he was to own it all, and go on to become one of the wealthiest men in that part of the state. His name was Henry L. Finch.

Obe and I always liked working together. That spring we took a job on the range but soon quit to work on a big dam the government was building on the Blackfoot River. Every dollar that we could spare we sent home to the folks to pay on debts.

Here we were meeting a diffcrent class of men, for the most part rounders who did little except follow construction work. When they got a stake they would lay off and go to town. After a few hilarious days in the saloons and red-light districts they would report back to work, broke but happy—unless they had been unlucky enough to pick up a venereal infection.

They were a strong and lusty breed of men. Many were Spanish-American War veterans. Most of them had worked all over the West from Alaska to Mexico. They made much more of an impression on me than they did on Obe, who was older and more experienced. Until now my entire life had been spent in an atmosphere sanctified by religion and the church, but to me that now seemed a thin kind of existence. These men were free and without fear of God, man, or devil.

From infancy I had known the urgency of money. It seemed not to trouble these men at all. What they had they spent, and if they went broke there was always the jungle. Many of them went to California for the winter, got themselves a shack and batched until the jobs opened up in the spring. Most of them were machine men, drillers, or powder monkeys, and so earned twice as much as I got as a common mucker.

How much better is this, I thought, *than the long, grinding, hateful hours of dirty farm work, or the loneliness of herding sheep.* It was the first eight-hour job I had ever had.

Then Chauncey was called to the ranch to take over haying operations, so Obe, who was no slouch as a cowhand, took over Chauncey's riding job, and I was strictly on my own.

Sixty men worked there, but there were few magazines and no books. In their spare time the older men played cards or lay around telling tall tales of their own adventures—largely, if they were veterans, with Filipino women. These, according to report, were far more amorous and sexually satisfying than American women.

The younger men spent much of their time fishing in the Blackfoot River. A lad of my own age and I fished almost every evening, and practically all day Sunday. Neither of us owned waders so we just walked in the river up to our hips in our working clothes. It was harder on shoes than anything else, and I had to cut down on the folks from my customary fifty dollars a month to forty.

This was by far the best job I had ever had—and yet I was dissatisfied. I wanted to experience some of the things which seemed to make the lives of the men around me so rich. I didn't realize that they were all heading up a blind alley and, what was worse, knew it.

One day I rode into the tough little town of Henry with two middle-aged men, and before we left they suggested a visit to a tent place kept by a woman known as Paradise in the cedars just north of town. It was my first experience in a place of that kind, and I was both excited and scared.

Paradise was a youngish woman of decidedly buxom proportions, far more comely than her one girl, Rusty, who was fortyish and plump, with red hair and freckles. Living in the open as she did, Rusty's skin had burned red instead of tanning. But she wore a short red dress which didn't quite reach to her plump knees, and red slippers and stockings, and in those days a man seldom even caught sight of a woman's ankles. She was good-natured and jovial.

One of the men tried to get the madam to accommodate him, but she was content with her fifty-per-cent take from Rusty, and the money she made from the sale of beer. Rusty retired to a small tent with first one and then the other of the men. My turn was coming up. I had bought my round of drinks and I knew it was taken for granted by all that I would go to the tent with Rusty. I would be proven less than a man if I didn't. Both men and the madam assured me that Rusty really knew her business, and that a similar opportunity might not come again for a long, long time. The idea of following two other men was revolting, but I hated to hurt Rusty's feelings by making her think I thought she was unattractive.

Finished with the other customers, Rusty came and climbed on my lap. I tried to beg off, and she wheedled and made good-natured threats. My friends sat and grinned, enjoying my embarrassment hugely, as I blushed and stammered. One of the men was known around Chesterfield, and he was a notorious blabbermouth. Sooner or later the escapade would reach the ears of my folks.

Once Obe had been seen talking to a sporting girl in Soda Springs, a girl he had known back in Baker City before she had "turned out." They had talked as old friends would talk, but I would never forget the demonstration Father had put on. He cried out, "If he had any respect for his mother he wouldn't be seen with such a woman!" Before Father got through Obe was thoroughly branded as a libertine and an immoral character. I didn't want to go through *that*.

In desperation I offered to give Rusty her three dollars without going to the tent. "Keep your money, Slim," she said with sudden coldness. "I don't take charity any more than I give it," and the incident was closed.

In the fall I quit my job and struck out to see something of the world, landing my first job in a stone quarry in the town of Arco, Idaho, now one of the centers of atomic energy. I immediately sent home all the money I had saved, sixty dollars. The job lasted only a few days, but I got another on a ranch on Little Lost River. When the potatoes were dug I was out of work again. With an older man I struck out across the desert for Idaho Falls. A sheepman came along with a wagon and gave us a ride. My friend, who claimed he knew many people in Idaho Falls, and could quickly get us a job, got drunk on our joint wages, and after twenty-four hours in the cooler was fined five dollars and given an hour to raise the fine, on the representation that he had a friend—me—who had the money.

That morning I had received eight dollars by mail from back wages at the stone quarry. I faced a dilemma. My partner was in sad shape, and I hated to turn him down. But if I paid his fine he would try to borrow the other three dollars to get drunk all over again. I told him the money hadn't come. He insisted that I go to the judge with him and promise that I would pay the fine when the money arrived. Idaho Falls was extremely tough on "vags" and I feared the judge would jail me if I told him I was broke, but having failed to tell the truth in the first place I was stuck with my story.

"It lacks about two hours of sundown," the judge told us. "If you boys are out of town by that time we'll forget about the fine. If not, I'll have you both locked up."

We hit the outskirts of Idaho Falls in fifteen minutes. My friend knew of a ranch nine miles out where he had worked before and was sure we could get a job. When we got there we found the potato digging had been contracted to a crew of Japanese. The farmer gave us supper, bed and breakfast, and then hired me as a checker in his potato cellar. He had no job for my friend Charley.

I soon learned to drink *saki* with my Japanese friends, but the job was finished in ten days, and there was no more farm work anywhere. I traveled by train to a mining camp in central Utah where jobs were supposed to be plentiful. It didn't occur to me that my folks might be hurt to learn that I had passed within fifty miles of home without stopping, though I hadn't seen them for more than half a year.

The town of Eureka was overrun with Mormon farmer boys who wanted to earn a little spare cash during the winter months. There were no jobs. Just as my money ran out I got work digging a sewer trench up the main street of the town. The work was hard and the pay small. The boss cursed and threatened to fire us every time we straightened up to ease our aching backs. Curious bystanders were always looking down our necks and offering humorous comments as though we were on a chain gang.

Next to me was a broken-down old gambler who'd had to quit his trade because his hands were crippled from rheumatism. He couldn't dig as fast as the rest of us, and the boss threatened hourly to fire him. Since each of us had a certain yardage to dig, I managed to dig enough of the old man's allotment to save his job. I didn't mind, for I was as tough as whalebone and I had long ago mastered the tools of ignorance. As one old miner said at a friend's funeral, "Tim was only a mucker, but he was a *good* mucker." I was a good mucker.

When this job petered out I bought a ticket to Salt Lake, but somebody picked my pockets of the three or four dollars I had, and the baggage checks for my bedroll and valise, overlooking sixty cents I carried in my vest pocket. I learned from the first newspaper I saw that there were an estimated two thousand unemployed men in the city. My sixty cents was soon spent. I had started out to become a man of the world and had wound up a bum.

I called at the baggage office to try to reclaim my belongings, and got back my bed and my battered old canvas valise after describing the contents. The only things worth pawning were my blankets and razor. I raised two dollars and a half on them. Like all social derelicts I gravitated to the lowest and toughest part of town, which at that time centered around Commercial Street, the red-light district of the city.

Here I found a small Japanese restaurant where I could get a full meal for a dime. It was pretty horrible stuff, and the greasy knives and forks were chained to the table. One meal a day here was all I could stand, but near by was a place called Bond's which catered to workingmen and was clean and respectable. By ordering wisely I could get a fairly good breakfast for fifteen cents. Sometimes for lunch I would buy a couple of doughnuts or even a hamburger. Unless I spent the night in a saloon I would buy a bed in a flophouse, usually paying fifteen cents for a cot in the corridor. A room that was supposed to be free from bedbugs cost fifty cents, the other kind twenty-five, but the fifty-cent houses were only profiteering. Each morning I got a free shave at a Commercial Street barber college. The college must have lost money on me, for I wore a lot of their adhesive tape on my face.

Even with this economy my money dwindled rapidly. Each morning I would make the rounds of the buildings under construction but in front of all of them was the sign, NO HELP WANTED; and there were hundreds of men hanging around on the bare chance that one of them would be called. There was small chance of a green, nineteen-year-old kid from the country finding anything.

I was advised to register my name with the Salvation Army, or the Volunteers of America. I spent much of my time at V. of A. hall in the middle of Commercial Street. Major Mackey and his wife, who were in charge, were kindly people, and because it didn't seem right to accept their hospitality without some return I attended their services.

Twice they got me a job. One time it was unloading a car of pig iron at a local foundry; the other, a carload of onions for a farmer from Lehi, of unhallowed memory. Each time I was sent out with another bum, and each time my companion deserted after he had sized up the job. Each time I unloaded the car alone. At the foundry they paid me the agreed upon two dollars for unloading the car, but the thrifty Mormon farmer pretended to think that I had done only half the work, although it had taken me all day because the onions had to be wheeled far back in the warehouse, and paid me only seventy-five cents for the job. To get even I swiped a couple of onions which I had with my hamburger for supper that night. For two weeks this was my only employment.

Many of the neighborhood girls were street walkers, while others stood in the doorways to attract customers. I walked around there so much that many of them came to know me, and would call out cheerfully, "Hey, Slim, you had anything to eat today?" Being thin anyway, I suppose I had that lean and hungry look.

I didn't have to accept their charity, for I had learned to stretch a dollar till it would last me a couple of days, and I managed to pick up a free meal at the hall once in a while. But I wasn't proud, and if I'd had to panhandle I would have started with the girls. Outside of Major and Mrs. Mackey and a friendly bartender they were the only ones who gave a hang whether I lived or died.

I became quite friendly with one girl in particular. Her name was Goldie and she was quite good-looking, mild-mannered and friendly. She worked the doorway at the foot of a flight of stairs opening on the street. I used to stand just inside and talk to her, and if she snared a customer I pretended to be just coming down the stairs. I found it much easier to talk to these girls than any other women I had ever known. They, too, knew what it was to be up against it, and they talked about sex as frankly as any man. They did far more toward curing my awkward bashfulness than anything that had ever happened to me.

I was a Mormon, and Salt Lake City was the headquarters

of Mormonism, but not once did it occur to me to look up any of the authorities of the church. I knew instinctively that all I would have got was a lecture on thrift.

There was, of course, always a way out, but I would have starved rather than send home for a dollar of the money I had sent there during the summer. The one thing I could not bear was to acknowledge defeat. I wrote Mother that I had decided to spend the winter in Salt Lake, but I didn't tell her I was broke. Father, so Obe has told me, was sure that I was wasting my time in riotous living, perhaps even smoking cigarettes or spending my money on fallen women. "If he was broke he'd send home for money fast enough," Father said.

I got a job at last. Along with half a dozen other men I was told to report Monday morning at the depot of the Salt Lake & Ogden Railway. The pay was to be thirty cents an hour, nine hours a day, and we were to go and come on our own time to the job thirty miles north of town. I was told that I wouldn't get a payday until the next Saturday night. I was down to my last quarter. I got the clerk who hired me to write out a slip of paper stating briefly that I was an employee of the railroad.

Armed with that, I started out early Sunday morning to find a place to stay. I walked from boarding house to boarding house, but I didn't look like a railroad man to the hard-boiled landladies and I was always turned down. Times were hard and they were not risking a week's board and room on a trampish-looking kid who couldn't tell them what he was doing for the railroad. Having had nothing to eat that day I was pretty weary and discouraged by sundown. I was back in the heart of town, and I happened to see a small green house with a sign in the window. With no hope whatever, and expecting a final rebuff I knocked on the door. I wasn't thinking of my mother's ram in the thicket but it was there. The landlady agreed to take a chance on me, provided I would share a room with two other men. She gave me supper, I took a bath, and for the first time in months slept in a decent bed.

Next morning I had a good breakfast, and my landlady fixed me a nice lunch to take to work. But when I returned that evening she met me at the door with a stern and forbidding look. She informed me that she had called the railroad and they said they had no employee of my name. I think that was the absolute low of my life on the road. It was bad enough to lose my job and my boarding house, but to be called a liar and a cheat was even worse.

Fortunately, my landlady's husband arrived just then and urged his wife to give me a trial. The matter was cleared up a little later when we discovered that Mrs. Kinney had called the Denver & Rio Grande instead of the Salt Lake & Ogden.

The job lasted only a couple of weeks, but Mr. Kinney was timekeeper for a construction company that was building an annex to the big Mormon Z.C.M.I. department store, and he got me a job there. We were frequently laid off during the freezing weather, so I made very little; but if the layoff lasted very long my landlord would inquire if I needed any money to tide me over. I have often thought that this would be a pretty good world to live in if people were all as kindly and generous as the Kinneys.

I bought a fairly good second-hand coat and a new pair of corduroys, and when I wasn't working I could go to the Orpheum or Pantages vaudeville theaters, sit far back in "nigger heaven" and be supremely happy. Occasionally I blew myself to a matinee ticket at the Grand where a stock company headed by Willard Mack and his wife, Marjorie Rambeau, was playing. And once I parted with a whole dollar to see Dustin Farnum in *The Virginian* at the Colonial.

At the Salvation Army store I could buy packages of old magazines, six for a nickel. I knew by now what I wanted to read. My favorite magazines were *Hampton's, Everybody's,* and *McClure's.* My favorite writers were such famous muckrakers as Charles Edward Russell, Lincoln Steffens, Ida M. Tarbell, Alfred Henry Lewis, Allan L. Benson, and Ray Stannard Baker. America was then going through a period of unparalleled political and economic corruption which these people were boldly exposing. The "interests" were able to kill most of the magazines eventually, but most of the eloquent muckrakers survived, in spite of the enmity of Teddy Roosevelt, who had given them their name. By this time I was a full-fledged political radical, though it was many years before I heard the saying: "A man of twenty who isn't a socialist has a hard heart; a man of forty who is one has a soft head."

I never tried to break myself of the habit of wandering around Commercial Street, and it was far better to hear the girls' "Come on up and spend a dollar, Slim," than "Slim, could you use a quarter?"

The great majority of the girls were in the age group of twenty-five to forty. Usually, they were rather pretty, and always well-groomed. Many were quite intelligent. Some made a specialty of being ladylike; others of being coarse and vulgar. Some had men who took all their money except what they spent on clothes, while others disdained the pimps.

I am inclined to think there was more sense than poetry in the old jingle:

> *The miners came in '49*
> *The whores in '51.*
> *And when they got together*
> *They produced the native son.*

Many of them played a really constructive part on the frontier. My brother Obe once noticed an inscription on the largest tombstone in the cemetery of a Western ghost town which read: SACRED TO THE MEMORY OF IDAHO MAUDE. He found an old-timer who remembered the woman's funeral as the largest the town had ever known. Scarcely a family there, he recalled, had not been the recipient of the woman's charity and kindness.

They were good to me; I am not going to throw stones at them.

Because I had no money to send home Mother guessed that my situation was not of the best, but she realized that I was going through the mill of my own choice and must make my own decisions. She wrote me cheerful, newsy letters, and said no word about money or about coming home. Nor did she warn me to mind my morals; that, too, she considered to be a matter of my own choice. She believed in man's free agency, and without the usual reservation that it applied only to herself. She sensed that I was in no mood to be preached to. Therein she differed from Father, who believed that a good lecture on someone else's conduct was always in order.

Finally, along toward spring, Mother wrote that I could get a job in the Chesterfield store if I wanted to come home, and I made the discovery that I was homesick. This would allow me to go back with honor. I owed Mr. Kinney seventeen dollars, but he said he would trust me to send him the money. I borrowed ten dollars more, enough to pay five dollars for a good second-hand suit at the Salvation Army store and buy my ticket home.

Even Mother was somewhat puzzled by me. Chauncey she could understand because he was readable as print. Obe never kept anything from her. I talked too much, but seldom disclosed my inner thoughts. I was, naturally, more mature than when I had gone away but I knew that the opinions I held would shock my parents and the community so I kept them to myself. I was at the age of disillusionment when I was convinced that everything I had ever been taught was a lie.

Again the folks talked with the bishop about sending me on a mission, and in due time the call came through from Box B. No youth in Chesterfield had ever disregarded the call, but all my proselytizing zeal seemed to have been expended years ago on Gus Johnson's pigs and chickens. I knew that it would mean putting Obe in bondage for two years, and he owed neither me nor the church any such debt. I would have ignored the letter had not Mother pleaded with me at least to explain to the authorities that I felt financially unable to go at this particular time, but would let them know when the situation changed.

Nothing more was heard of the matter. The authorities were accustomed to instant, explicit obedience; they had no patience for those who temporized or pretended to know more about their own affairs than did the servants of the Lord.

21

To Father's way of thinking, the fact that you *could* go in debt was an indication of good character and credit. Had the rest of the family been able to accept that point of view we might have got along better. To us it seemed that his debts, though petty, were always just beyond his power to pay. He built, tore down, and rebuilt small buildings and fences. He was the best gardener in the community, in which he took great pride; and he always gave away his produce.

He was kind to animals except when angry with them. Cows especially, he always said, must be treated with kindness. But oftentimes sounds of discord could be heard coming from the stable. Above the bellows of a stricken cow would come Father's loud voice. "There"—*whack*—"that'll"—*whack*—"learn you"—*whack*—"to git over"—*whack*—"when I tell you"—*whack*.

He would come into the house exhausted and often suffered a mild heart attack. But within the hour he would have forgotten the incident and would deny that he ever really beat his cows. He merely insisted that they mind him. He talked to them incessantly, and if they failed to understand his every word it was from sheer perversity. He fed them so well that the cost of the feed always exceeded the returns from the milk.

The first summer after returning from his mission Father moved the old two-room log cabin to a central location, added a two-room lean-to, and moved the post office into the front room. He must, he insisted, have a place where he could keep cows and chickens and raise a garden.

The partition in the log house was torn out and the office installed in a corner. Father and Mother had their bed in another corner, the remainder of the room serving as post-office lobby and family living room. Almost everyone who dropped in for the mail remained for a visit. Since there were no closing hours, the family had little privacy.

When I was at home one of the most frequent visitors was a comely young matron whose elderly husband was away herding sheep. I noticed that she always came when Mother was away at Relief Society and we became quite cozy—in a distant sort of way. In spite of my recent familiarity with the vice of Commercial Street, I was young and innocent enough to believe that married women were taboo. I was puzzled when she suddenly began to treat me with good-natured contempt and never saw her alone any more.

The fact that I had failed to send home any money for six months, and was in debt besides, was naturally discouraging to Father. "How can I ever expect to get ahead if I can't depend on the loyalty of my family?" was his constant complaint. He was now road supervisor for the district, but though the job paid several hundred dollars a year his debts continued to climb.

I soon learned that clerking in a store was not for me. Every adult male came to the store to loaf when he had time on his hands, but I could never hold up my end of the talk and was bored by the whole business. I stayed only long enough to pay off Mr. Kinney, then, the wanderlust upon me, I persuaded Obe to go with me out to the new reclamation projects in Snake River's Magic Valley.

Wages were fairly good although most of the work was hard and dirty. Driving a four-horse fresno scraper in the bottom of a twenty-foot cut, with the dust so thick that one could scarcely see or breathe, and with the thermometer hovering around the nineties was no job for the immaculate, and I still hated to get dirty. I soon became a plow-shaker, which was harder work, but cleaner.

During the two or three years in which we followed this kind of work we nearly always managed to send Father his hundred dollars a month, except for the few months in the winter when we went home to live off the folks. We usually managed to pay our way even then by getting out wood or poles from the canyons.

Somehow I seemed to have assumed the lead in our partnership. Anyway, it was I who made the decisions as to what jobs to take and when to quit. Had it been left to Obe he would have stayed with the first job he had until it was finished. But he trailed along. Obe took pride in the neatness of his work and enjoyed camp life. He liked to play sluff with the other men, or occasionally go to the nearest town for a few glasses of beer and a game of pool. He liked everybody and everybody liked him.

Unlike Obe, I was restless and dissatisfied. When not working I preferred to walk long, solitary miles swinging my stick of imagination. When we went to town I stayed away from the saloons and pool halls and walked the sidewalks watching the crowds. I wasn't anti-social—I got along well with the other men—but I preferred the company of my own thoughts at most times. I didn't smoke and seldom took a drink, but I was the champion cusser on most jobs. I permitted no man to outdo me at manual labor, and like Father I took pride in getting dressed faster than other men.

The first year that I was away from home a Kansas family named Hibner moved into Chesterfield and bought one of the big hay ranches. The people of Chesterfield regarded them dubiously when they announced that they were Socialists. The Hibners were considered "queer." The father of the family was a gaunt old man who kept to himself and seldom left the ranch. The mother was a spry, talkative little old lady who went barefoot most of the time and raised turkeys. Two of the three sons were married and had large families. They were all more or less food faddists. It was said of the boys that, with a pocketful of peanuts and raisins, they could take the trail of a wolf and stalk it until it dropped from exhaustion. In winter, dressed in white as camouflage, they would skim around the country on webs or skis, the most successful wolf and coyote hunters in the country.

Lon and Willis Hibner had been minor-league ballplayers. Lon had traveled with a circus as a juggler and ventriloquist. He was also a talented fiddler. George, the youngest, was the intellectual of the family. He was a poet in the Walt Whitman tradition. He had been a close friend of Eugene V. Debs and many other prominent Socialist leaders; had been state secretary of the party in Kansas and had spent many years on the lecture platform.

George Hibner was a true idealist. He cared nothing for money, but injustice could rouse him to lionlike indignation. He was familiar with the classics; on the platform he had the vocabulary of a Wendell Phillips and denounced capitalism with all the fervor of a Mormon Apostle denouncing apostasy.

Father was familiar with that part of Kansas from which the Hibners came, and he was far more tolerant toward outsiders than were born-and-bred-under-the-covenant Mormons. Also he thought he saw a similarity between their brand of socialism and the abandoned or postponed Mormon law of consecration, more commonly known as the United Order, in which all things were to be held in common.

Since the Hibners received a great deal of mail they inevitably became well acquainted with Mother. She was too staunch a Republican to accept socialism, but she recognized that they were idealists and intelligent men and nobody was more welcome to chairs in her front room.

When I returned from Salt Lake with my radical ideas and my conviction that the democracy in which I had so passionately believed had been taken away from the common people by the rich and powerful who owned most of the country's wealth, controlled its press, its schools, churches, and above all its government, I was both surprised and pleased to find people in my own community who believed somewhat as I did. I called myself a Socialist, but I knew nothing of the Socialist party; had scarcely heard of Karl Marx and *Das Kapital*. Now I read numerous pamphlets loaned me by the Hibners, including some that had been written by George himself. He was the first writer I had ever known. Sometimes, while prowling the sagebrush behind a herd of sheep, swishing at the bushes with my stick, I had thought that I would like to write, but the possibility seemed remote and fantastic.

George Hibner's writings were so poetical and involved that I never could understand them, but the books he loaned me fitted my new philosophy of life. Even as a boy my heroes had always been champions of the underdog. One was the great criminal lawyer, Clarence Darrow. I first learned about him during the trial of Big Bill Haywood for the murder of former Governor Steunenberg of Idaho. After the acquittal Darrow succeeded Henry Clay and other dead-and-gone lawyers as my legalistic hero.

I read Darrow's *Resist Not Evil* and other of his writings loaned me by the Hibners. Darrow was not a Socialist but his creed was unorthodox enough to suit my thinking. I saw in the Socialist party the instrument which would some day establish a world in which poverty and war would be no more; one in which selfishness and greed would not be permitted to stifle the ambitions of those who didn't happen to be born with acquisitive instincts.

My acquaintance with the Hibner boys was somehow a connecting link between my daydreams and the world of reality. We organized a Socialist local in Chesterfield; the members were the three Hibner brothers, two Robertsons, a Portuguese sheepherder, and the son of a Mormon bishop. From then on my battered old valise was always crammed with Socialist literature. I went from such easy lessons as Work's *What's So and What Isn't* to Hillquit's *Socialism Summed Up*, and from that to the writings of Marx, Engels, Kautsky, and Bebel. I had the same kind of missionary zeal which caused my father to work so hard for Mormonism, though I would have been shocked had anyone told me so.

Father, who had been the first to take up with the Hibners, now decided that socialism was but another name for atheism when he heard me quote Marx's "religion is the opium of the people." He immediately accused Mother of having brought up her sons to be infidels.

Mother replied, "I think there is a great deal of good in socialism. The Socialists want to end poverty, war and crime. Surely that isn't bad. What they don't realize is that you have to change men's hearts before you can change their institutions. That is why I think the Gospel of Christ, whether you call it Mormonism or not, is still more important than any political movement."

Obe and I hated inequalities and injustice, and we had known very little else. All our lives we had been the poorest of the poor in any community where we lived. We hated poverty and had not the slightest ambition to become rich. We were both workers, and hated the game of making money by taking it from someone else. The industrial gospel as we saw it practiced and preached was grab what you can, and never mind whom it hurts. We believed sincerely in the Socialist proposition that a society in which production was for use, and not for the profit of a fortunate few, would make for a happier and more wholesome world.

It took me many years to learn that the chief cause of the Socialists' failure to bring about a bright new world was that while they preached brotherhood and cooperation they were themselves the most intense of individualists. On the other hand men who believe in capitalism and free enterprise are for the most part organization men. They are bound together by strong ties of self-interest in their civic organizations, lodges, churches, and political parties. Praising individualism, they are frightened by anyone who dares question in any way the standards by which they live.

My friend George Hibner loved his fellow men passionately, but he was always happiest when alone upon a ridge top with a pencil and a notebook jotting down the thunder of his thoughts. And there was I, burning with hatred for sham, injustice, and oppression, putting my trust in "the masses," yet still unable to mingle with people—and the people who lead organizations are the mixers. I envisioned a peaceful revolution in a very few years and wanted to have my small part in it. I found myself running for County Commissioner before I had attained my majority; and two years later, without the slightest knowledge of bookkeeping, I received several thousand votes for State Auditor of Idaho.

Wherever Obe and I went, hot argument on politics was certain to ensue. Such converts as we made succumbed to Obe's quiet and casual comments. Nothing could have inveigled him into speaking in public. I, however, spoke quite frequently before Socialist locals in the various towns we visited. Once Obe betrayed me into conducting a meeting single-handed in a remote settlement in central Idaho. My rural audience stared dumbly while I discoursed learnedly on economic determinism, the materialistic conception of history, and the dictatorship of the proletariat. I had as well have spoken in tongues. Neither they nor I knew what I was talking about.

Meantime, we continued to move from job to job, working with horses wherever possible, both of us being good horsemen. But we took whatever we could get when jobs were scarce, as they usually were. Once we took a contract to grub forty acres of sagebrush on the north side of Snake River. We did it all by hand, driving ourselves unmercifully, spending our rest periods sharpening our grubbing hoes. Together, we cleared ten dollars a day on the job, the biggest pay either of us had ever earned.

Most migratory workers make about enough on one job to get them to another, but we were more closely pressed than most because we had to send our regular quota home to Father and his debts. I don't recall that we were ever broke, but we were down below a dollar in our joint capital many times. We never bought a job but once; I worked at it only half a day, though Obe stuck it out the full day, then we walked away without asking for our pay. We learned that a job that has to be bought isn't worth having.

Obe knew more than I about being on the bum. We were not above taking to the jungles if we got hungry, but Obe would never ask anybody for a meal. I did once. We had fallen in with another transient who argued that the only way to get a job was to visit the farms until we found one. Against Obe's protests we walked far out in the country seeking work. Nobody needed men. By mid-afternoon we were footsore and hungry. Our associate tried several times in vain to beg a meal; then insisted that we take our turn. Obe refused, but I agreed to try the next ranch.

Sure enough, the lady said she would feed us—on one condition. In the yard there was a big pile of Snake River sagebrush, which frequently is as large as a man's leg, and she wanted us to chop it for firewood. She assured us dinner would be ready by the time we finished. I made a bargain to do the chopping; neither Obe nor the other man would turn a hand.

I finished the work in about an hour and we went into the kitchen to eat. The woman had placed on the table some stale bread, cold boiled potatoes and warmed-over coffee. That cured me from bumming handouts.

When we staggered back into town that evening, we were pretty discouraged. I had just struck the sidewalk when a man yelled, "Hey, Frank, do you want a job?" He was a man I had worked with on a construction job a couple of years before and was now running a ranch.

We seldom threw in with anyone else, but one summer we worked with a big kid from Texas, Ben Leslie, with whom we got along fine. When we were out of work I scouted for a job while Obe and Ben played pool. It was a satisfactory arrangement; if there was a job for only one he supported the other two.

On one such occasion we had come to a small Idaho railroad town where there were at least a hundred transients waiting for the haying season to begin. I was lucky enough to get Obe a job irrigating potatoes that kept us in eating and sleeping money. I heard that there might be jobs at a place called Camas Prairie some forty miles north. Having nothing but time on my hands, I walked up there one day to a ranch which was recommended to me. The rancher said he could use three men in about ten days. I assured him we would be there.

The next day I walked back, except for about ten miles when a farmer give me a lift in his wagon. I had started with a blistered heel and had two when I returned to our rooming house. I was sitting with my feet in a basin of hot water when Obe handed me a copy of the local newspaper in which there was an angry editorial about the undesirable hobos who were cluttering up the town and making it unsafe for women and children to be at large. None of these vagrants, wrote the editor, would ever work. They were merely sponging off the good people of the town and would move on when work became abundant.

I realized suddenly that this editor was writing about *me—and Obe and Ben!*

I hollered for pencil and paper and as I sat there with my feet in a washbasin I wrote an indignant rebuttal. We would be only too glad to work if they would give us any work to do, I contended, and I went into the generalities of unemployment and its sociological aspects. Then I put on my shoes and took my article to the editor in person.

His face reddened as he read. He paused to comment that my handwriting was pretty bad, which it was. When he finished he shouted, "I'll print none of that socialist filth in my paper! What you write proves that what I wrote is true. None of you will work."

"Mister," I said, "if you'll go into the field with me with a pitchfork I'll work for nothing if I don't do more work than you, or any other businessman in your lousy town can do." I was a hay-pitching fool and wasn't worried about any white-collar businessman accepting my challenge.

"You take yourself and that trash out of my office, and I warn you to get out of town!" the editor yelled.

I didn't leave town until the Camas Prairie job was open. As long as Obe was working I wasn't a vagrant. But while I was loafing I added some more material to my article, and sent it to the *Inland Echo*, a Socialist weekly published in Lewiston, Idaho. When I got my next copy of the paper there was my article on the front page.

I think Obe and Ben looked down on me a little because I couldn't play pool, but now there was a new respect in their eyes. I was smart enough to get my name in print!

Obe suggested that I try another article for the *Inland Echo*, and when they printed it also I bombarded them with longer and longer articles until I was appearing in the paper nearly every week. Some of the other contributors wrote for such well-known Socialist periodicals as the *Appeal to Reason* and *The Coming Nation*.

My friend George Hibner wrote that he was proud of me,

but suggested tactfully that I ought to learn something about grammar and punctuation. I did buy a Cobden's English Grammar, but it did me little good.

After the Camas Prairie job was finished Obe suggested that I go on to Boise to see if there was any work for the winter, as he had a few weeks' work with a threshing machine. I had less than five dollars in my pocket, so I decided to walk to the railroad. I walked about forty miles the first day through the mountains, when a man came along with a wagon and offered me a ride to Mountain Home, a station on the railroad.

While waiting in the warm depot at Mountain Home for a freight train to come along, I fell asleep. I was jarred rudely awake by a policeman's club across the soles of my feet.

"Come on to the jail with me, 'bo, you can't sleep here," the officer said.

Desperately I said, "I'm just waiting for my train."

"Yeah? Where are you going? Have you got a ticket?"

"I'm going to Nampa," I answered, naming the next town up the line, "and I've the money to buy my ticket."

"Then let's see you buy it," the officer said. "And if you don't get it I'm running you in."

I had barely enough money to buy the ticket, but I rode to Nampa in style, leaving a disappointed officer behind. I got off the train at Nampa and climbed onto the blind baggage of a passenger train which was just leaving for Boise. It was near daybreak and the train was tearing into the teeth of a gale. Had it been a long ride I would surely have frozen to death.

Boise, I had been warned, was tough on hobos, so I jumped just as soon as the train started to slow down. My numbed legs refused to function. Instead of landing on the run with the train, I fell and plowed along for a yard or so on the hard gravel on my hands, knees and face.

Skinned and bleeding and covered with soot, I got out of the railroad yards and entered town just as the saloons were opening. The bartender at the first one I entered poured me a slug of whisky without my asking and showed me where to wash up. I took off the bib overalls and jumper which covered my best clothes, washed and combed my hair, left my bundle with the friendly bartender, and started out to look for work. Before noon I landed a job in a construction camp.

The first night I nearly froze to death. The company was supposed to furnish bedding but there was nothing for me except an old piece of canvas, and it was well along in November. While I shivered there were men near me with quilts and blankets piled so high they could scarcely crawl into their bunks. It was the custom whenever a man quit for the others to divide his bedding whether they needed it or not. When the work shut down a couple weeks later I had a dozen or so quilts in my bunk.

My first day here was the hardest work I had ever done. Three of us had to move heavy iron rollers from the back to the front of a steam shovel as it inched slowly along. My companions were a big, heavy-mustached Bulgarian and an equally heavy-mustached Macedonian, who wasn't so husky. Any moment I expected a minor Balkan war to break out, and I silently vowed that if it did I would grab a club and clobber the big Bulgarian. He was the first man I'd ever met who could make my hardest physical exertion look weak and puny, and I hated him.

My fortunes altered in a sudden and unexpected manner. The boss sent me in to flunky for the cook. There were fifty men in the camp. The cook, an Italian, claimed to have been a noted hotel chef before liquor got him down. I was astonished at the ease with which he cooked for so many men with no helper but me. All I did was wash the dishes in a couple of tin tubs, set the tables, open cans with a hatchet, peel potatoes and wait on table. Such was that cook's genius for organization that it was easy.

After the first meal I started to prepare something for myself from leftovers but the cook stopped me. "We won't eat that slop," he said, and set about preparing a wonderful meal of food such as I had never known existed. I decided he was telling the truth about his culinary past.

My brother Obe and I were two units in the unorganized mobile army of migratory workers without whom the wheat, the fruit, the hops and the hay could not have been harvested. Without our kind the great reclamation projects could not have been built. The phenomenal development of the West would have been impossible; yet the seasonal nature of our work was such that most of us were habitually broke.

Obe and I were fortunate in that we could always go home for the winter and make a little more than expenses by working in the timber. Neither of us drank and I didn't even use tobacco. Our gambling was confined to playing cards for commissary articles such as gloves, socks, and tobacco. For years neither of us owned a suit of clothes good enough for church. In those days I had a weakness for derby hats, such as the Mormon elders wore, but the first time I went into a construction camp with one on my playful fellow-workers used it for target practice.

On our first day at one job a sudden storm came up while we were a mile from camp. It was a brush-grubbing job and one fellow had a hay rake. Obe and I promptly grabbed hold of the rake teeth as the driver put his team to a fast trot. A little more than halfway, I became so winded that I had to let go my hold and walk the rest of the way, but Obe ran the entire distance. The boss didn't know us very well, but he knew that one of us smoked cigarettes and one didn't. Having seen what happened he waited for me to reach the tent, then gave me a long, serious lecture on the Word of Wisdom. If my body hadn't been ruined by tobacco, he stated, I would have been able to run as long and as fast as my brother. You can always trust a Mormon elder to give a good talk on the Word of Wisdom, even if he has a cigarette in his mouth at the time. My employer was somewhat disconcerted later when he learned that the short-winded brother had never smoked, and the long-winded one had used the weed since he was ten years old. But at the time I pretended to be properly chastened and rebuked, while Obe and the other boys held their sides with silent laughter.

On the whole it wasn't a bad life while we were working; it was the between-jobs times that were tough, but we managed to squeeze a little fun even out of those. And we kept Father's debts from becoming too inflated.

I did at this time indulge in one major extravagance. I used eighteen dollars—the price of a good suit of clothes—and bought a small portable typewriter. Its like isn't manufactured any more, for instead of type bars it had a type wheel in the center, and was so small it could almost be put in one's pocket. I learned to type on it with two fingers—the way I still type—and a couple of times a month I wrote an article for the *Inland Echo*.

22

Though we were able to send Father enough money to keep his indebtedness growing satisfactorily, he took a dim view of our prospects and frequently remarked to Mother, "If you really think your prayers will be answered you'd better ask God to do something about them boys. They're going to hell as fast as they know how and you're too stubborn to admit it."

"They might travel slower if you weren't always setting fire to their shirt-tails," Mother would retort.

Father pretended not to understand. "There's no use tryin' to talk serious to you," he said. "You're as light-minded as Obe."

But Mother was serious. The physical hardships we might be going through didn't worry her. What other men could stand, we could stand, but we were getting farther and farther away from the things which she valued most. In my case, in particular, she blamed it on the fancied necessity for using every spare dollar to pay on Father's debts. Where Obe gave willingly and perhaps got a mild thrill out of hearing people say how good the Robertson boys were to their parents, she knew that I resented every dollar of it, but would match Obe dollar for dollar if it killed me.

I swore that I didn't want the money. I denied that I any longer had the slightest desire to get an education. She didn't believe me. If I didn't want to improve myself, she asked, why did I keep on writing for the *Inland Echo*?

Along with being a Socialist I had become an atheist, or so I claimed, though Mother wouldn't believe me. At home we had many arguments when Father wasn't around. My efforts to shock her failed miserably. I would quote Ingersoll and make Jehovah of the Old Testament out to be a cold-blooded monster. I reminded her of such stories as that of the prophet Elisha who was so short-tempered that he had called forth two bears to destroy a group of children whose offense had been that they had said to him, "Go up, thou baldhead." Or of that pious soldier of the Lord who had made a vow to sacrifice the first of his possessions he saw in order to celebrate the victory the Lord had given him, and it turned out to be his own daughter who had come dancing forth in joy over his return whom he had to murder. The Old Testament was full of that kind of ammunition.

I reminded her that I had heard preachers shouting that there would be in hell babies not a span long. I told her how I had heard brethren high in the priesthood of our own church almost come to blows over the matter of Adam's godhood.

Mother felt somewhat handicapped in an argument with me. She could cope with anyone who professed a belief in the Bible, for that was the iron rod of her faith, but it was hard to deal with a conceited young smart aleck who refused to accept the basic premise of religion.

She argued that there was a vast difference between God's word and the faulty history of a wandering, superstitious tribe. She agreed that Ingersoll and others like him had been great men. Ingersoll, especially, she said, had done much to tear down the foolish superstitions which had made religious progress impossible. She insisted that the things foolish men had added to religion in no way affected its original validity. Because religion reaches higher than anything else it can be debased and degraded more by uninformed teachers and preachers, she maintained. That was why she had become a Mormon, she said, because only by the light of modern revelation could the Bible and true religion be understood.

In rebuttal I said that the authorities of the church were too busy raking in the dividends from the many corporations in which the church owned stock to bother about asking the Lord for more revelations. Joseph Smith had received revelations about so trivial a matter as to whether his father should deed him a piece of land, but since Joseph's time there had been pitifully few authentic revelations. Even so important a document as the manifesto abolishing polygamy had begun, not with the majestic *Thus saith the Lord,* but a very earthly *To whom it may concern.*

I, of course, asked her, "Where did God come from? Who created Him?"

"What does it matter so long as He exists?" she reasoned. "The Lord told Job all that he felt it was necessary for man to know: 'I am that I am.'"

Brash as I was, Mother never lost her patience in any of our long discussions; in fact, I think she enjoyed them. But she was getting old now, and tired. She was nearly sixty-five and no longer had the will to give Father even defensive battle.

"Go ahead and jaw, Pa, if it pleases you," she would say, and turn a deaf ear to his exhortations. She was getting hard of hearing and he couldn't be sure whether she couldn't or wouldn't hear him. After lecturing for an hour or so he would take off to someone else's house to tell his troubles.

With old Bishop Chester Call in his grave, Mother had become the unofficial oracle of the community. Gentiles as well as Saints brought their troubles to her door, and they usually went away feeling better. "Sister Robertson says—" was a pretty final judgment. Except, perhaps, with her wayward youngest son. Resentment, she felt sure, was at the root of my trouble. I could not adjust to bondage as Obe could and the only hope for me, she and Obe decided, was to set me free. They conspired to freeze me out.

For years Obe had stood ready to assume the family burden alone and was convinced that my help only served to give Father an excuse to go further into debt. Father was about to enter a new venture from which I was to be pointedly excluded.

Our country was experiencing a dry-farm boom. It was discovered that land long thought to be worthless would produce excellent crops of wheat under proper cultivation. From almost the time of his arrival Father had preached that it could be done and had been laughed at. He had never got a chance to demonstrate his theories.

Now that others had proved that it could be done, all the valley between Chesterfield and Bancroft as well as the foothills was being homesteaded. The land-hungry were on the march. Father still had his homestead right, and now he filed on what was probably the roughest, rockiest, and brushiest quarter section that could be farmed at all.

He had waited too long, but what had really caught his eye was a little flat composed of two or three acres that was sheltered by the hills where water occasionally seeped to the surface. It would be a wonderful place to raise a garden! Having come from one of the best wheat countries in the nation, Father was convinced that he could raise better crops than anyone—and he usually did when he would take time off to do it.

Mother had at first not been in favor of the homestead. They were too old to do any more pioneering. It meant giving up the post office where she had been able to earn a little money for herself as well as associate with friends. The homestead would mean hard work that might be beyond her strength. Father's taunts that it was only her lack of faith in him that held her back left her unmoved. But suddenly she reversed her stand and agreed to move. On one condition.

"That is," she said, "that you take Obe into full partnership with you, give him as much voice in things as you have yourself, and leave Frank entirely out of it."

Father didn't like it. "What does Obe know about farming?" he roared. As for me, if I didn't have some place to put my money I would go to hell across lots. But Mother was adamant, and he had to agree to her terms.

He bought an old log house, tore it down, and moved it onto the homestead. He built a chicken coop and a barn and a granary. He went in debt for more horses and machinery. By the time his elaborate preparations were made it was too late to do anything. He had gone onto a wheat farm. But before starting to raise wheat he had to prepare for the raising of pigs and chickens and for milking a few cows. All this took his time and money.

When Obe went on the homestead, I again hired out as a sheepherder with my old employers, Knollin & Finch. It was an all-the-year-around job and, at fifty dollars a month, I could save more during the year than I could as a migratory worker. Besides, I was coming to appreciate solitude more and more.

Mother and Obe soon found out they couldn't keep the homestead going without my help, so I started to send them forty dollars out of each month's pay—although they insisted that it must come only as a loan.

With Obe home to do the hard work of breaking ground and planting, Father had time to look to his garden. He hired a boy at thirty dollars a month to help him. When not busy gardening they built "improvements" like corrals and pens for the stock. When Father needed more space in the house he just tacked on another room where it might happen to fit. He dug three wells on the flat, a lucky precaution since every summer one or two of them would be filled to the top with debris from the cloudbursts which were common there. It always took a couple of days of hard work to clean them out.

Obe was an efficient workman and a good farmer. The first summer he grubbed and broke up sixteen acres of ground that yielded forty bushels of wheat to the acre, but as against the heavy expenses incurred it went nowhere. The debts now ran into thousands of dollars instead of hundreds. The family had good credit, but the bank charged ten per cent interest and the implement houses, twelve.

Chauncey gave them a big boost when he sold them several horses, harness, and a buggy at practically a giveaway price. They were able to buy hay from Mr. West, who wouldn't sell to other dry farmers for love or money; and if they needed an extra team Obe could always go to the ranch and borrow one. Mr. West, like other stockmen in the West, believed that dry farming meant the ruination of good range.

Obe continued to break up more land and raise good crops, but even with what I could spare from my wages the burden of debt grew greater. The larger the debt, the more time it took Father to "tend to business." Now that he had a buggy he made numerous trips to town to talk to his creditors and to divide my monthly check among them when it came. They always told him not to worry—Will Robertson was known to be good pay.

In spite of Father's petty extravagances, Obe was making a success of dry farming. His third year he raised a record crop of forty-eight bushels per acre. Thanks to his experience in the Palouse country, Obe knew how to handle hilly ground. He was a first-rate header-puncher and he innovated the practice of driving strung-out teams on farm implements instead of the cumbersome local manner of working them abreast that lost time and crippled horses. He was well liked in the community and although he never went to church he was on as friendly a footing with the bishop and high priests of the ward as Mother was with the riffraff.

The homestead was much easier for Mother than she had anticipated. When there was extra help to feed, as when she had headers and threshers, Father always hired some neighbor girl to help out; and, if she was ill, he could step in himself and do the work just as capably as any woman. Now that they had the little black-top buggy they could ride to meeting in style. Mother still missed the people who had formerly dropped in at the post office, but she still had a great deal of company. In the winter Obe spent most of his time getting out logs for the sawmill on the other side of the mountain, and the men he worked with would always drop in for a chat and a cup of coffee on their way back and forth.

Frequently, in the summertime, when the folks returned from church they would find Obe and some of the local disreputables pitching horseshoes. Not so long before, Father would have thrown a fit at the idea of such doings on the Sabbath, but these days he often took off his coat and joined them. Scarcely a week passed that Chauncey didn't drop in. The old animosity between Mormon and Gentile was disappearing, and locally Mother had her full share in promoting the new spirit of tolerance. Chauncey owed much of his personal popularity to the fact that he looked after the cattle of the Mormon ranchers without cost to them.

Because of advancing age Mother had given up most of her offices in the church. Now she had time to look around and survey her Zion. In some ways it had been a disappointment. She had not found the "united people" she had hoped to find. There were constant jangles and discords among them—the people she loved so sincerely, believing their faults were the results of weakness for which they could not be blamed.

There were jealousies over rank in the church. Worse, in

her estimation, was an almost universal feeling that attendance to church duties—going to church, paying tithing, going through the rituals in the temple, and above all being obedient to authority—was guarantee of a safe passage into the Celestial Kingdom. Few of the Saints she knew shared her conviction that these things were only the forms through which the Christian virtues of charity, humility, faith, good works, and love for mankind operated.

Father was the master practitioner of Mormonism and he never shirked a duty. She never doubted the genuineness of his testimony yet she felt that at times he was somewhat lacking in true understanding of its underlying significance.

To know one's self, Mother believed, was as necessary as to know God. The Saints were not quite what they thought themselves to be. It was the asserted mission of the church to save the world, to establish the central stake of Zion at Independence, Jackson County, Missouri—the place where the Garden of Eden had been located, according to modern revelation—as an impregnable fortress against the assaults of the forces of evil—a place where Christ Himself was to reign. With such a destiny Mother felt that the Saints should be filled with a sense of solemn responsibility toward those they were trying to save instead of using the Gospel as a means of self-development and to gain a few points on a heavenly scorecard that would count for individual salvation.

She didn't worry much about salvation—even for her unregenerate sons. There would be a place in the next world for the honorable men of the earth where the spirits of just men would be made perfect; and she considered her boys to be just and honorable men. She herself kept the Word of Wisdom faithfully, but she considered it as guidance for personal health and well-being, and so didn't share the opinion of the modern orthodox Mormon that the breaking of it constituted a moral sin. There were plenty of Saints, she knew, who believed that the smoking of a cigarette or the drinking of a cup of coffee would count heavily against one on the heavenly scorecard.

The older Mormons who had had polygamy to set them apart as a chosen people from the rest of the world hadn't been such sticklers for the Word of Wisdom, and even some of the highest authorities had used not only tea and coffee but even liquor and tobacco.

Notwithstanding the bigotry and intolerance which she couldn't deny existed, Mother believed as firmly as ever that Joseph Smith was a prophet of God, and the Church of Jesus Christ of Latter-Day Saints an inspired religion. She counted the day when Elder Amos Hatch and his companion had walked into her little Sunday School as the most important day of her life. She had never for one moment regretted having come to Zion.

In family matters Obe was, as ever, her staunch ally. They had the same rather negative temperament, preferring to make the best of what they had rather than wearing themselves out striving for the unattainable. They were Fabians, Obe winning adroit victories over me by skillful retreat, just as Mother had often baffled Father by disapproving acquiescence. They never butted their heads against a stone wall.

While Obe and the folks were homesteading and Chauncey was cutting quite a swath as foreman of the Bar OX and boss of the general roundup, I was following what is generally supposed to be the lowest and least adventurous of professions, herding sheep. Popular Western fiction has always had it that a man had to be crazy in the first place to herd sheep, and if he wasn't that way at the beginning the life quickly got him in that condition. He is usually pictured as ignorant, illiterate, filthy, and a dirty range thief besides.

One of the stories Chauncey liked to tell on me was that I met a stranger on the range who said to me, "Where are you from, shep?" "Baa-a-ancroft," I replied. "Well, where are you going now?" My answer was "Baa-a-ck." It's about as close as most sheepherder stories come to the truth.

When I went back to the sheep I didn't know whether I would make a lifetime career of it or not. I could see nothing in sight that looked any more promising. It was better than it had been before, for I could at least afford a slicker and a pair of gum boots and, more important, buy a few books and subscribe to a couple of magazines.

The supposed loneliness of the life bothered me not at all. The longest period I ever went without seeing another human was nine days when my campmover got drunk in town and forgot to come back. I was hardened enough by this time that I could kill a mutton without flinching. It hadn't always been easy. Once my boss, disgusted because I kept ordering ham or bacon on my bill instead of killing a mutton, had handed me an ultimatum to butcher a lamb or lose my job.

Losing my job would have been a major tragedy. I have always hated killing of any kind, but this had to be done. I didn't have a gun, so all I could do was catch a lamb and cut its throat with my pocketknife. I didn't realize what an obstacle the wool on its neck could be. I got the blood coming, but I couldn't find the jugular vein. The lamb struggled and bleated. I couldn't let it go in its wounded condition and I was so sick I nearly vomited. Finally the blood spouted forth and the murder was completed. Skinning and gutting was pretty bad, too; I did a sloppy job. If you let the sheep's wool touch the meat something in it, perhaps lanolin, makes it unfit to eat. My boss almost gagged on the first lamb chop I fried for him and warned me I'd have to do better next time. I did.

We had four herds, with a herder for each band and a campmover for each two herds. Two of the herders were Portuguese boys from the Azores, Tony and Joe Manha. Tony became my best and most loyal friend. Like me, he was a Socialist and an agnostic. Once, a few years later, when I was in financial trouble and Tony was in the East I mentioned in a letter to him that unless I could raise a thousand dollars somewhere we would have to take bankruptcy. I wasn't thinking of a loan, but by return mail came his check for a thousand dollars.

My campmover was a thin, dyspeptic young fellow from the

South who had been a rural schoolteacher and was now saving his money so that he could attend a seminary and become a preacher. The rest of us were acknowledged sinners, so I fear his life among us was not always a happy one. He was notoriously stingy. Most of his clothes had been discarded by others, which he painstakingly washed and mended. The one luxury he allowed himself was a .22 rifle for shooting grouse and sagehens.

Once while he and the foreman were moving my camp round a dangerous sidehill it tipped over and rolled down the mountainside until it came to rest bottomside up against an aspen tree. I was several miles away with the herd, but Mr. Finch came after me. When we got back to the overturned camp the campmover looked up at us mournfully, and said, "Ding it, my gun is in there."

That night I atoned for my laughter. This was our first day out from the ranch and most of the ground was still covered with snow. By the time I got my herd rounded up and back to the wagon on a high, barren ridge it was long after dark and bitterly cold. I hadn't eaten since before daybreak. Instead of the hot meal and warm bed I anticipated I found that my campmover had gone back to the ranch, leaving everything in the wagon just as it was after we had got it back on the road. The stove was loose from its moorings with the stovepipe mashed and twisted almost beyond repair. The bed was piled in the middle of the floor and covered with broken eggs and sourdough.

Only a day or so after the incident of the overturned camp I experienced the worst scare I have ever had. I had a dry band. The only reason we were on the range at all was because it was a late spring and we were short of hay. Only the tops and the south sides of the ridges were bare. I had crossed a two-mile-wide snow basin on the crust early in the morning, while the campmovers put my camp on skids and got it down to the bottom of a canyon where I was left alone for a week.

There was a big bare slope on which to graze the herd, and

after it warmed up a little each day the sheep couldn't cross the drifts on the crust. One day after lunch I left my rifle at camp and started leisurely to climb to the top of the ridge where the sheep were grazing. Suddenly I found myself in the middle of a stampede as the sheep raced madly down the slope, paying no attention to me or my dog. I went on to the top of the ridge and for a moment everything looked all right. Then I heard a faint bleat and walking out on the overhanging comb of a huge drift I saw below me a couple of dozen dead or dying sheep. Some were dragging their entrails over the snow, leaving a bloody trail.

Acting on impulse, I leaped over the edge of the drift to the snow some fifteen or twenty feet below. My feet went through the crust and I was buried up to my armpits. For a moment I was unable to move. I found myself staring into the bloody face of a huge female wolf not four feet from me. She had been engaged in an orgy of slaughter; her lips were drawn back from her fangs in a wicked snarl. She could have torn me to pieces in a minute and was displaying every inclination to do so.

For the moment I was in utter panic. That wolf was about to kill me, and I couldn't do the slightest thing to defend myself. I let out a screech that sounded nothing at all like my own voice. It was enough; the wolf crouched, then whirled about and was soon gone from sight.

More than twenty sheep had been killed. I cut the throats of the hopelessly injured, then beat a trail back through the drift so that I could carry the survivors back to safety. A couple of days later the two campmovers found the wolf's den not more than a hundred yards from where I had faced her; they dug out and destroyed her four pups. The nearest band of ewes and lambs was more than five miles from that den, yet strewn about were the bones of half a dozen lambs the she-wolf had apparently carried that long distance to feed her pups.

I was destined for further adventure that spring, little of

it to my liking. Ours was free range, with no government supervision as there is today. It was open to any outfit strong enough to take and hold it. For several years Knollin & Finch had held the best part of the range, principally because we were able to get there first and keep other sheepmen out.

This year, because of the unusual shortage of feed, several other outfits were determined to make us share it. The only practical way to hold range is by threatening to mix bands. No outfit could afford to mix a band of ewes and lambs with one of rams and yearlings such as I was herding. So since our other three herds were ewes and lambs it was up to me to defend any part of our range that was threatened.

Most of the range-hungry sheepmen were Frenchmen who were strictly nomadic. They shifted about rapidly so that they wouldn't have to pay taxes, and they were skillful range pirates. My first encounter with them came when I saw them crossing Corral Creek, the eastern boundary of our range. I rushed my herd along the ridge until the bucks saw the Frenchmen's herd. Then I let nature take its course.

The moment the amorous bucks saw the ewe band they raced toward it with the playful yearlings galloping behind. Seeing their danger, the Frenchmen hastily bunched their herd against the creek and set their dogs at my runaways. The bucks would be turned back, but when the Frenchmen got them close to where I lurked in the brush I would send my own dogs and turn them back the other way. The excited Frenchmen waved their arms and yelled, but they would have to reform their forces far below to check the stampede.

Eventually they rounded up my rather small band and held the bucks and yearlings in one place, not daring to let their own herd move away from the creek. A couple of them rode close to where I was brushed up waving their rifles and shouting French imprecations. I fired a couple of shots at an imaginary jack rabbit ahead of them and they turned back. I didn't dare go down after my sheep. The stalemate lasted until nearly sundown when the Frenchmen recrossed the creek and my campmover came along and brought back my herd.

Most of the invaders could be bluffed out without much difficulty. One day I ran up against a young herder no older than I and with about the same limited amount of brains.

He said, "I'm going to have this range. My name is Gunplay Maxwell, and nobody had better try to stop me."

It so happened that I had heard about this rather notorious Utah outlaw getting killed some time before, so I replied, "My name is Butch Cassidy, and I'm stopping you."

He looked at me and said, "I guess Maxwell and Cassidy could sue us." We had dinner together, and afterward he moved his sheep back.

Finally an outfit arrived that couldn't be bluffed because they had no other place to go. They had started up the trail late and their ewes were dropping lambs before they got across Bancroft flat. Such lambs, of course, had to be killed. The owners were desperate when they cut through the middle of Knollin & Finch's fine spacious range. I turned my buck herd toward their two bands of ewes and lambs. Our she animals were on the other side of them. Finding themselves in a cul-de-sac, they moved down onto a long peninsula between Corral and Grizzly Creeks. My orders were to keep them from coming back.

My campmover arrived with the disquieting news that the Utah outfit had a killer with one of their herds, a morose German who carried a Luger automatic in a shoulder holster. He was said to have shot at several men coming up the trail. Even his employers were afraid to cross him. I knew that such men were not uncommon on the range. Scarcely a year passed that we didn't hear of one or two murders. I was no hero. I didn't want to shoot anybody, or be shot at. According to my socialist philosophy this German and myself were fellow workers; the real enemy was our employers. Yet when morning came I headed the bucks down a ridge and, when they were feeding nicely, went round to the brink of a big snowdrift that my boss had told me was to be the deadline.

Sure enough, the German was coming up with his herd, and with the determined manner of a man who didn't intend to be stopped. I got a good look at him and was not reassured. He was a heavily built man of about forty with a bristling brown mustache, certainly the kind of German who would later easily get the idea that he belonged to a master race.

When he saw me he placed his hand menacingly on the handle of his Luger. "Get dem sheeps out of my way," he yelled.

I clutched my rifle. I was scared stiff—scared of the German if I tried to stop him, and scared of losing my job if I didn't. I had no thought for brotherly love or comradeship now. I only knew that the range was too long for his pistol, but not for my rifle, and if he came any closer I was going to shoot. If a warning shot didn't stop him, and he shot back, I knew that I would have to kill him. I motioned him to stay back.

The German raged and threatened, but I couldn't back down now. There was a terrible vacancy in the pit of my stomach. My hands were shaking so that to steady myself I dropped on one knee and supported my elbow with the other. To the German it must have seemed an act of cool deliberation, for he turned his sheep back the other way.

I patrolled the drift the remainder of the day in plain sight of the German, but felt no elation. Something was wrong here. We should have been sitting in friendly conversation between our herds and, at dinner time, should have eaten together at one of our camps. That was the law of the range. In all justice the other outfit should have had a larger share of the range, but I was up against a stronger law—that of self-preservation and the survival of the fittest.

When Henry Finch heard what had happened he grinned and said, "I didn't think you had it in you."

Of course nobody would ever believe that anything exciting could happen to a sheepherder.

23

On the whole, the three years I worked for Knollin & Finch were among the easiest and most pleasant of my life. That first summer I was sent from my range to Caribou Mountain to move camp for Tony and Joe Manha. I moved each of their camps about once a week, packing everything on two mules. Neither Tony nor Joe liked my cooking so I escaped that chore. As Finch brought out supplies from Soda Springs, some seventy miles distant, I didn't even have to go to town. I probably worked only ten hours a week.

That fall I was summoned to the Soda Springs ranch and sent to New Mexico with a carload of pure-bred Shropshire rams. Later, I made several fall trips delivering bucks to various parts of the West. Usually I could manage to take a day off on my return to see something of cities like Denver and Cheyenne. As a shipper I was a person of some importance, often entertained by the buyer, and sometimes having checks of a thousand dollars or more in my possession.

Shipping wasn't always easy and I had my battles with some of the train crews. Livestock couldn't be kept in the cars more than thirty-six hours, and I was unloaded in some unlikely places. The worst, I think, was in Wyoming when my car was spotted at a siding a couple of miles from the nearest town. I had to unload alone, and for a while I thought the thirsty bucks would all drown in the Platte River. I had to walk to town and hire a man to haul back a couple of bales of very poor prairie hay. When the car was spotted next day I was given about an hour to get the bucks loaded again. In the big yards you have help, and there are always some trained goats to lead the simple-minded critters into the cars. Here I had to carry a buck into the car, and before I found a piece of barbed wire to tie him up, he would beat me back down the chute. I sweated and cursed, but they wouldn't stay in the car unless they were tied. I had been warned that if the car wasn't loaded the train wouldn't wait for me. I had about half of them in when I heard the train whistle. Then one ram inside decided to let out a bleat; immediately the ones in the chute charged into the car to see what was the matter.

Sometimes when I wasn't shipping to buyers I would pull into some Idaho town with a carload or two of rams where the outfit was to exhibit its fine show flock at a county fair. The show flock was handled by a young Scotsman who was an expert at his craft. This flock was never sold until after the National Livestock show at Chicago. But Henry Finch was always on hand to sell the rams, which I brought in.

I arrived in Idaho Falls one Sunday morning with two carloads of sheep and found no one on hand to help me. To reach the fairgrounds I had to drive my ravenous charges through the heart of town. The lawns were green and soon my bucks were grazing both sides of the street while irate householders yelled at me to get them off their lawns and out of their shrubs. I was threatened with everything from mayhem to a long dismal term in the penitentiary.

I soon attracted a mob of small boys who offered to help for a fee. I would give a couple of the most likely-looking ones a quarter each, only to discover a few minutes later that they had disappeared. Soon all my loose change was gone as were my unreliable helpers. I was on the verge of panic when I finally reached the edge of town and met Finch and Bob Stoddart, the flockmaster, blithely coming in to help me through town.

The last two summers I worked for Henry Finch I had nothing to do except cook my meals. I soon became almost too lazy to do that. I was herding the buck band inside a woven-wire fence along the Blackfoot River. The rams would leave the bedground when they got ready and would come back in the evening of their own accord.

The fall of 1912 was my first opportunity to vote and I hated to miss it. I wasn't much interested in the fact that I was candidate for County Commissioner on the Socialist ticket, but I did want to cast my first vote for Eugene V. Debs. It was twelve miles to town, and I couldn't leave the buck herd long enough to walk that far and back. Then, to my surprise, Finch came along and let me have his private saddle horse to ride in and vote. When I thanked him for helping to cast a Socialist ballot he grinned and said, "I sure wouldn't have let you have a horse to go in and vote for that so-and-so, Woodrow Wilson."

Soon very little of my time was spent in herding sheep. In the fall my headquarters was in the A. J. Knollin barn in Soda Springs. What had once been that millionaire sheepman's office was my bedroom and kitchen. In the winter we always went back to the Chesterfield ranch to feed the sheep. Here my associate, Israel Call—first counsellor to the bishop of

Chesterfield—and I hauled out three small jags of hay a day. I did the cooking while Israel took care of the team. We were drawing fifty dollars a month for this work, while just across the fence a couple of glamorous cowboys were hauling ten or twelve big loads a day and getting only forty dollars a month. That went a long way toward reconciling me to being a sheepherder.

I could go home any evening I wanted to, and if I wanted a few days off Obe was always willing to take my place. Unfortunately, the *Inland Echo* had finally given up. I had been unable to impress any other magazine or paper with my writing, so I put away my little portable typewriter and devoted most of my spare time to reading. I had gone through most of the Socialist and free-thought books and turned to such writers as Darwin, Huxley and Spencer. I read them with no particular purpose except that I thought I should cram my mind with any kind of information that came handy.

I had the annoying habit of taking my books home and strewing them around with Father's books on Mormonism. Once he picked up a philosophical treatise by a French writer entitled *The Right to Be Lazy*, and snorted triumphantly, "There's socialism for you! Laziness!" The way he handled the book reminded me of the time when years before he had found a volume under my pillow called *What a Young Man Ought to Know*. He had hurled it into the fire and threatened me with a sound thrashing for reading obscene literature.

These winters I again became part of the social life of Chesterfield. While I let Father and Obe have all the money I could spare I kept something out for myself. I owned a good suit of clothes and could go to a dance occasionally.

One activity I went in for was acting in the Home Dramatic Club. Every winter our group would put on two or three plays. I was always cast as the villain. Dressed in a Prince Albert coat and tall silk hat rented from a costume house in Salt Lake City and wearing a fierce black mustache, I played my part up to the hilt.

Sometimes we thought we were so good that we would hire a sheep camp and travel around the stake, putting on performances in other towns as much as forty miles away. One night we all had to sleep on the floor of the hall where we performed. Another time the curtain collapsed at a very embarrassing moment. Once some of the girls decided to try a little wine from a jug we boys had bought, and it required strenuous effort by our manager to stop them from giggling long enough to get ready for the show.

One time our wagon tipped over on a high snow road. The stove at the front came loose and the camp caught fire. One of the girls, a slim one, went out through the small window in the back of the camp like a rocket. A heftier girl tried to follow her and got stuck mid-way. She screamed and kicked but we were too busy putting out the fire to render aid. Finally we got the flames extinguished and through united effort pulled her back into the wagon. We righted the outfit, went on our way, and gave a sterling performance that evening.

One church meeting which almost everybody in the ward attended was the Mutual Improvement Association. It was always held in the evenings and after joint exercises the men and women went to separate classes. For several years Father had taught what was called the Senior, or adult, class. Once the Association having been reorganized, Father modestly suggested to the new president that he should get someone else to take the class. It never occurred to him that the suggestion might be adopted. The new president asked me if I would teach the class. "We're studying economics this winter," he said, "which should be right up your alley."

I had seen the manual and accepted, knowing it would give me a chance to get in a few healthy licks for socialism. It was an interesting class with plenty of hot discussions and we had an ever-increasing attendance, but Father was a conspicuous absentee. He didn't attend a single meeting as long as I was teaching the class. These were the only meetings in the ward he had ever been known to miss. When I left he stepped willingly back into the harness.

Father and I were not always at odds. He thought well of me, I'm sure, when I wasn't with him. In fact he encouraged me to quit my job and take up a homestead near his own. I have pleasant memories of riding over the land with him on horseback. At such times he could forget religion and I could then understand why so many young men liked to be with him. No man was more affable when he wanted to be.

My job with the sheep outfit held a lot of variety. It gave me considerable leisure time and I got along well with my boss, but I had been at it more than three years and couldn't see that it held any future. Obe, like the folks, thought I would be better off to take up a homestead. There was only a forty-acre plot available, but there was an illegally held desert claim adjoining which was open to contest. Winning this, I could enlarge my claim to six-hundred-forty acres, although much of it would be on a mountain and relatively worthless.

Mother was most eager for me to make the change as it would be a fulfillment of her old dream in which her boys would get land of their own. She was weary of having me turn in all my extra cash with no prospect of return. If I got a farm of my own, she thought, I might change my attitude toward the church, forget my vain ambitions, and perhaps marry some nice Mormon girl and settle down. Living so close, Father and Obe would be able to help.

I was twenty-five years old and the fiery ambition I had once had should have been dead. Yet I answered dozens of self-improvement advertisements, always hoping to find the shortcut to the education denied me. When I settled with Mr. Finch I had a hundred and twenty dollars. I had already filed on the land. My next step was to invest in a correspondence law course with a Socialist law school at Fort Scott, Kansas. When I rode up to the house with that bulky sixteen-volume law library balanced on the horn of my saddle, Father asked suspiciously, "What's that?"

"Law books," I answered.
"What did you pay for them?"
"Seventy dollars."

Gloom and disappointment spread over his face. The devils inside me had not been cast out! He stormed into the house and I heard him yell at Mother, "That fool boy has blowed in seventy dollars on worthless law books! No good'll ever come of it. What makes him think he could ever be a lawyer?"

It was a good question and I certainly couldn't have answered it. Mother did as well as anyone could. "Study never hurt anyone," I heard her defend me. But she, too, must have been disappointed. Those books could only add to the flames of my discontent.

About all I could do with them was to run my hands lovingly over their leather covers and put them away for the time being. I had a homestead on my hands. Actually, all I had was a promise from the government that if I lived on the land for three years and did certain things it would give me a patent to it.

Father gave me a small tar-paper shack which we moved onto my forty. Chauncey loaned me a team and gave me a little bay saddle horse called Shorty, and I went in debt for three unbroken colts and four or five hundred dollars' worth of machinery.

I helped Obe put in his crop; then the two of us started grubbing brush and breaking sod on my land. We had always worked together and money in the pocket of one was money in the pocket of the other; it was ridiculous for us to try to keep our accounts separate. So we went into partnership, taking Father in as half owner of the entire enterprise. Robertson & Sons rode again!

Mother was the only one skeptical of the venture. She foresaw trouble. I was completely lacking in the tolerance which made it possible for Obe to get along with Father, and I had a temper that could match Dad's in explosiveness. In spite of my socialistic philosophy I was the rankest kind of individualist and rebellious against discipline of any kind. I was indeed cooling off quite definitely on the Socialist party with its dogmatic beliefs and insistence on party discipline. It seemed completely absorbed in doctrine and theory and had lost sight of its declared mission to liberate the oppressed.

The correspondence school had promised that I could finish the law course in three years if I worked hard, but I soon found that I couldn't live the hard life of a farmer and find much time to study. I could do fairly well in the winter by putting most of the work on Obe, but there was no time at all to study in the summer. By fall I had forgotten most of the rules I was required to memorize, and by the time I had made the necessary reviews it would be almost time to start spring plowing.

Nevertheless, I did send in over two thousand written opinions on the legal cases I was asked to judge. The school used the case method of instruction. It did help to increase my vocabulary. I was not being at all hypocritical when I published an article in the school magazine called *Salvaging Self-respect*. The course had done that for me; it had kept something alive which would otherwise have died.

If I could have studied law uninterruptedly during the wintertime I think I might ultimately have passed the bar examination, but there were too many things to do. Wheat had to be hauled to the railroad and wood from the canyons. Cattle and horses had to be fed, colts broken to work or to ride, and harness and machinery repaired. Farming is never a part-time job.

As always, Obe stood ready to assume the major burden, but being hell-bent to hold up my end, I wouldn't often let him. This tried his patience sorely sometimes. "Why must you always act like a damned martyr?" he would demand angrily.

Father was never in accord with us about the payment of debts. Whenever there was any money, no matter how small the amount, he wanted to divide it up among all our creditors. We, on the other hand, liked to clean up our smaller debts and depend on the bank for credit. We shrank from the complete exposition of our financial status which Father always insisted on making whenever he paid anything on account. In addition, it was this kind of "business" which kept him on the road in his buggy so much of the time, when a little assistance with the farm work would have been welcomed.

Father had not been wrong about his little flat being ideal for gardening. Each summer he hired a boy to help him and raised the finest garden in the country. When the vegetables came on he would load them in the back of the buggy and distribute them free of charge to his friends. This was a sore spot with me for I thought that in view of our straitened finances, paying a boy thirty-five dollars a month to distribute largess was carrying charity a bit too far. Mother and Obe pointed out, however, that the gratification of this little philanthropic whim was a small price to pay for the peace of mind we all enjoyed when Father was happy.

He was handy with tools and did keep up many of the loose ends about the place; whatever might be charged against him, lack of energy was not one of them. His devotion to church duty at whatever cost was the thing I resented most, and it was this which led to the final rupture between him and me which Mother had so greatly feared at the beginning of our partnership. One of the duties he never neglected was making his monthly visit as a ward teacher. Sometimes he and young Roscoe Loveland, who was his best friend and constant companion, would take off, leaving us so short-handed that the whole outfit would be practically stalled.

My resentment over this came to a head one day in a late, cold, backward spring when we were far behind with our farm work. Roscoe was changing work with us for a few days, and he and Father and I were fanning seed wheat in the granary.

In the middle of the forenoon Father said unexpectedly, "Me and Roscoe have got to quit now and go teaching."

I stared at them in disbelief. I couldn't fan grain alone, and they hadn't said a word about quitting me when I had turned my four-horse team out on the foothills for a rest that morning. Had they warned me earlier, I at least could have made my own labor count for something.

"With all this work to do?" I protested bitterly.

"Yes, 'with all this work to do,'" Father mimicked. "We're goin' teachin', so shut up about it."

Through the years I had built up quite a vocabulary, much of it profane, and I called upon it now for all the blistering sarcasm I could command. Resentment had been preying on me too long, and I lost all control.

"Get out of this granary!" Father shouted when I ran out of breath.

"All right, you old son-of-a-bitch," I yelled at him, "and I won't come back!"

Father was as mad as I was, but he could still dramatize. "You hear that, Roscoe?" he demanded. "He called my mother a bitch. I'll have you know my mother was just as good a woman as yours is."

The rift was too deep for even Obe, the peacemaker, to patch up. Father had but one song to sing: "Buy me out." Obe realized that Father had long been weary of the partnership. What he wanted was to get a place of his own and demonstrate that he was a better farmer than his boys and could raise better crops. We would never flatter him. We knew that what little we possessed had come from our sweat, and while we didn't reproach him we couldn't bring ourselves to pretend that it was all the result of his genius. Roscoe and his other young friends could. They thought he was a wonder and he gloried in it. His piety and good fellowship didn't impress us at all.

"How much do you want?" Obe asked.

For the first time in his life Father asked more for a thing than it was worth. "Six thousand dollars," he said. Free from encumbrances the whole place was worth about that much, but he had mortgaged his homestead for three thousand dollars which had been paid on debts, and we had other obligations.

"We'll take it," Obe said.

I took no part in the negotiations. Whatever Obe did was all right with me, although I felt that Obe was being made to pay for something he already owned and I couldn't see where we were going to raise six thousand dollars.

There had been things going on of which I knew nothing. For one thing, Father and Roscoe had already arranged to lease the farm of a young Mormon who was on a mission. For another, Obe and Mother had their heads together, and it was Mother who really administered what Father thought was a stab in the back.

She said to him, "Will, the boys can't afford to pay six thousand dollars and you know it. But half of what you've got belongs to me, and maybe they can raise the other three thousand."

"You mean you ain't comin' with me?" he thundered.

"No, Will," she replied quietly, "I'm too old to follow you around any longer. The boys will take care of me. I'm staying with them." It was a crisis she had long dreaded, but even now her sense of humor didn't desert her. "That three thousand dollars will pay my board for a long time," she smiled.

"I always knew you'd leave me some time," he said, almost triumphantly.

"It's you who are leaving me," she pointed out. "You're just as welcome to stay here as I am."

"And live off their charity?" Father trumpeted. "I've never taken charity and I never will! I'll show you who's the real farmer around here!"

"I wish you well, Will," Mother said, "but now that you are leaving I hope you'll have the manhood not to come back on the boys for help."

"Never fear," he said. "I'd die first!"

We borrowed two thousand dollars in cash to pay Father and gave him another thousand in horses and equipment, and we assumed all liabilities of the partnership. Father was, for once in his life free from debt and with more ready money than he had ever possessed. I didn't believe we would ever be able to pay out but Obe was optimistic. World War I was on and wheat was bringing $1.65 a bushel at Bancroft. If the price held and we didn't have a crop failure we had an even chance.

Father and his inexperienced but loyal young partner at once went on a buying spree. Father's first purchase was a brand-new sheep camp which cost him two hundred dollars. He installed it temporarily alongside the granary. Here he ate and slept within speaking distance of the house he had moved out of. As always, the prospect of change made him happy, and it was only a few days until relations between him and me were more cordial than they had been for years.

Father and Roscoe bought the lessor's machinery and cattle at an inflated price. They bought new equipment as though they had a ten-year instead of a two-year lease, and as though it comprised a section instead of a mere quarter section. Obe tried to caution Father but got no hearing. He was going to show us what a real farmer could do.

So my parents were to all intents and purpose separated after having put up with each other over so many stormy years, even though they saw each other at church every Sunday and often during the week. Mother would be seventy her next birthday and no longer able to climb in and out of a wagon or "git up and go" whenever Father ordered her to start packing. She felt that he no longer had any need for her, but wherever Obe was, there would be her home also. With Obe she would have the peace she had always craved.

That fall I was called up for the draft, having waived my claim for exemption long before. I was sent along with a small contingent from Pocatello to Camp Fremont, near Palo Alto, California. Our reception was far from cordial. "This camp is already overcrowded; why do those stupid draft boards keep sending us more men?" said the officer to whom we reported.

But we passed our physical examination, were issued uniforms, and set to drilling.

After about ten days another farmer and myself were summoned to headquarters for questioning about our farms. "Take another physical examination and report back here," we were told.

The examination was brief. The doctor discovered that I had pyorrhea and a deviated septum and my friend had thin scar tissue over an old appendectomy, so we were considered unfit for military service.

I got home in time to help harvest the crop and to prove up on my six-hundred-forty-acre homestead by producing witnesses who were willing to swear that I had lived on it the required time and cultivated the proper number of acres.

This matter of living on the homestead was a hit-and-miss business, but I complied with the law as well or better than most. I slept in my tar-paper shack along with a colony of mice which used to play hide-and-seek over my bed. In the morning I would saddle my horse and high-tail it to the ranch for breakfast. The only time I lived there consistently was when we happened to be working near by, or in the winter when I had little to do, and found the shack an ideal place to study my law course. I didn't mind the mice, but I never cared for the pack rats and skunks who also thought they were homesteading.

Following the end of the war, the price of wheat tumbled. Worse, for the farmers around Chesterfield, there were several years of drouth. Instead of the forty bushels per acre we had been getting our yield dropped to twelve or fifteen.

Father and his partner fared even worse. One year they harvested only about six bushels to the acre. It was harder for Father to endure the knowledge that he hadn't out-produced us than it was to know that his two thousand dollars was all gone; but he hadn't given up easily. Although everything seemed to be against him—once he had to thresh his grain in two feet of snow—he stayed out and worked as he had never worked before. Many times we saw him out driving a six-horse team on a gang plow or tandem disc harrow, perhaps with a cold northwester nearly freezing his hands and feet and filling his eyes with dust. The long day over, he would take care of his horses and cook his own supper.

The second year was almost as bad. They seemed to owe everybody and had nothing to pay. To make matters worse the missionary-lessor returned and accused them of shiftlessness, neglect, and dishonesty, even threatening to sue them for grain which they had never raised.

Whenever it was possible Obe and our hired man would take their teams and implements over to help out Father and Roscoe. In the end we assumed the obligations Father had incurred during his great experiment. New ones had the habit of popping up unexpectedly even years after we had thought we had them paid off. The biggest surprise of all was when Roscoe, whom we had thought we were helping almost as much as Father, dunned us for a couple of hundred dollars he claimed Father owed him. Anyway, we paid it.

When it was all over, Father moved his sheep camp back to the ranch, but presently he was eating and sleeping in the house. He voluntarily took over the chores and the necessary running around, and was far more help on the place than he had ever been as a so-called partner. It wasn't in him to be a humble or contrite man, and none of us wanted him to be that way; but he was more agreeable to live with than he had ever been. At times he acted as if he thought the best friends he had were right in his own family!

He hadn't lost any of his religious fire. He was still superintendent of the Sunday School, and he spared not the mightiest when he thought a tongue-lashing was in order. One of his favorite targets was Chris Call, young bishop of the ward, who was by way of being a financial genius and was by far the wealthiest man in our end of the valley.

"If you'd quit chasin' the almighty dollar you'd be a better bishop and be able to live the Gospel better," Father would tell him.

"Well," the bishop would say with a sly grin, "maybe if I had a couple of boys—" But Father by that time would probably be giving the bishop's wife, whom everyone called Annie Chris, the dickens for breaking the Word of Wisdom. She was a woman of notoriously good heart who gave most of her own time, and more of her husband's substance than he liked, to aid the sick and needy of the ward. But she had a weakness for coffee and Father found this most unseemly in the wife of a bishop.

Although he was nearly seventy, his hair was still coal-black and only slightly thinned. He was as erect in posture as the Indian ancestors he boasted of were supposed to be, and he never missed a dance. His rapid prance had lost none of its vigor.

24

The next year had Obe and me down to bedrock. The drouth continued and a nationwide depression had set in. Farmers everywhere with over-extended credit were going broke. I had got a patent on my land and we mortgaged all our holdings for seven thousand dollars which cleared up the mortgage on Father's homestead and some of our other obligations; but things were rapidly getting worse.

We owed a couple hundred dollars on a plow bought from an implement company largely owned and controlled by the Mormon church, and it was always less lenient than other companies. We raised what money we could, some forty dollars, and paid it to a special collector who assured us we would be given more time on the rest. But the next day the company reclaimed the plow and said they would sue us for a deficiency judgment.

We drove into Bancroft and told our banker friend that we had decided to take voluntary bankruptcy. He said, "I can't let you do it. The bank can't lend you any more, but I can get you a five-hundred-dollar personal loan from the bank president."

We signed the note. I was too stiff-necked to pay the balance to the Mormon outfit and get the plow back. Instead, we bought a new plow, losing a hundred dollars or so in the process but saving our pride to some extent. We were not sued although we got quite a few threats.

When we got into financial difficulty the next fall, my friend Tony Manha came unasked to our rescue and we remained solvent. I hated the very sight of the farm, but I was morbidly determined not to go broke.

"What if we do go broke?" Mother used to say. "We've been poor before."

"My God, when have we ever been anything *but* poor?" I would rave.

Not half our land was under cultivation, though we had bought an additional quarter section of brush land. Getting off the brush and breaking the sod was always a slow and expensive process. It took a lot of horses and we had to buy feed. A minor expense was wages for a girl to help Mother.

We were considered good men to work for and never had any trouble getting help, but Roscoe summed us up pretty accurately when he said, "If Obe ever starts to swear, or Frank ever stops cussing you want to look out."

Our house was partly logs and partly frame, with no modern conveniences. The closest we came to that was gasoline lamps; also Father had a phonograph and a collection of records. Since we didn't go to church or dances our chief recreation was riding the range whenever we could get time off. We had a few cattle and were raising a special breed of horses bred up from a tough little Indian cayuse mare and a Hambletonian stallion. The colts made good saddle horses and were ideal for the kind of light work horse we needed on our foothill ranch. Our difficulty was that having broken them they became pets and we didn't have the heart to sell them, so we had more good saddle horses than one needed on a wheat farm.

I had lost interest in socialism. When the war came on I followed Charles Edward Russell and other pro-war Socialists out of the party. Though I had written nothing for a long while, I wrote an impassioned defense of Russell which, to my great surprise, was printed in the national organ of the party.

I no longer renewed my red card in the party, although on one occasion it had served me well as I was taking a carload of sheep through southeastern Colorado during one of our more violent strikes. The militia had been called out against the striking miners, who were dispossessed from their homes in Ludlow, Walsenburg, and Trinidad and were living in tent colonies. At some of these places the militia had fired into the tents killing men, women and children. When I passed through, the militia had their cannon trained on the tents of the strikers.

Whenever the train stopped union pickets were on hand to see that no scabs got off. I had only to show my red card to go and come freely. A Fort Worth horse buyer was not allowed to leave the caboose. I didn't tell him what I used for credentials. I'm sure he thought I was a union spy.

Orthodoxy in politics had become as obnoxious to me as it was in religion. I was better able to understand a saying of my preacher grandfather: "Orthodoxy is my doxy; heterodoxy is your doxy." The most orthodox people in the world today are the Communists. Where there is no heresy there is no liberty.

As a migratory worker in the Northwest I had often come in contact with the Industrial Workers of the World, the much maligned and hated IWW. I used to enjoy their street meetings because of the zest they put into them and because there was something fascinating about the angry looks on the faces of people who stopped to listen. The "Wobblies" knew they were hated and returned the hatred with interest. They were probably the only truly militant labor organization this country has ever seen, yet they were far from being the anarchist devils they were portrayed.

The "Wobblies" had ribald parodies on all the popular songs and hymns of the day which they sang with gusto at their street meetings. The most popular was Joe Hill's famous *Pie in the Sky* song, the chorus of which went:

> *Work and pray, live on hay,*
> *You'll get pie in the sky, when you die.*
> *(That's a lie!)*

The last three words would come from some deep-voiced Wob planted in the audience. The others sang it deadpan.

As for me, I had long since given up reading economics, sociology, philosophy and religion, and had abandoned my law course after virtually completing the required amount of study. I had no background to be a lawyer, no money to put out my shingle if I could pass the bar examination, and I had learned that many states required a college education before one was permitted to take the examination. I was reconciled to being a farmer the rest of my life—if I could keep from going broke. It seemed that I had finally learned what my parents had always tried to teach me—to be content with the station in life to which I had been born.

Obe and I were fundamentally different in temperament; I was a sentimentalist, Obe a realist. Like Mother he could laugh at a child's pain—and soon have the child laughing with him, but he was never one to inflict pain. I was like my father. I seldom saw a picture show or read a novel that did not bring tears; but I was subject to outbursts of rage in which I was capable of almost any kind of violence.

Nevertheless, our partnership was ideal. One bank account was always ample for us, and neither ever asked the other for an explanation of what he had done. In a sense Obe was a brake for me and I a spur to him.

With my thirties crowding me hard I had overcome some of my bashfulness, but none of my restlessness. I occasionally went out with girls and often thought of marriage, but I couldn't bring myself to go wife hunting in the businesslike way of the average young Mormon farmer. First, he got himself a team and buggy—presently it would be an automomile—and went after the girl of his choice with the determined purpose of a young bull breaking into a cow pasture. The girl knew that he had marriage in mind, and that if he couldn't get her he would pursue the next girl with just as much ardor. It didn't leave much room for romance, but it always worked. I didn't have a buggy, and anyway I was too much of a prude to use such straightforward methods.

Among the girls who came to work for Mother was the eldest daughter of a man who had just moved on to the adjoining dry farm. Her name was Winnie Bowman. Her father belonged to the lost tribe of American frontiersmen. Like Will Robertson, Archie Bowman followed the retreating frontier all his life, but unlike my father Archie didn't care much whether he had people around him or not. He was a loyal friend to a few but, in general, liked horses better.

Archie had taken his young bride out to a temporary logging camp in Wyoming and there Winnie was born without benefit of a doctor or birth certificate. He then moved to the high, grassy valley over the mountain from Chesterfield in the middle of the sheep and cattle range. A few families had tried farming there but all had given up except Archie Bowman and one other man.

Here Winnie had lived until she was eight. She saw more Indians, cowboys and sheepherders than she did *white* people. Finally, to keep Winnie and her brother and younger sisters from growing up in complete ignorance, Archie moved his wife and children to Chesterfield for the winter so the kids could go to school.

Once when I was passing out mail while Mother had the post office at Chesterfield, a timid voice inquired, "Is there any mail for Bowman?" When she got it she scurried out like a frightened rabbit. Such shyness was most unusual among the kids, and from the memory of my own timidity I felt a pang of sympathy for the bashful little girl.

Winnie was most happy at the isolated ranch where she served as her father's right-hand man. While most girls of her age were playing with dolls she was mowing and raking hay, tramping it in the rack when her father pitched it on. She also drove the derrick and dragged back a pair of double-trees which weighed nearly as much as she did. She milked cows, rode horseback, and accompanied her father to the canyons on trips for firewood. If she had any spare time she went fishing. Once I went across the mountain to help Archie put up his hay, but Winnie, dismayed by the prospect of having a strange man around the house, rode her horse into Chesterfield to visit with an aunt until I went home.

When Archie finally bought the dry farm adjoining ours and came there to live we hired Winnie to help Mother. She hated housework, but could get a great deal done. She was shy as an antelope; it was plain, common humanity to try to put her at her ease. We never really "went together," as it was called, but after she had been with us some six months she and I drove down to Pocatello in our first automobile, a 1917 Overland, and were married. Neither of us had got further than the eighth grade in school, but we both liked to read. We liked animals and didn't care much for social life. On the whole we are fairly compatible.

Mine was not the first marriage in the family. A couple of years before, Chauncey had married Myrtle West, eldest daughter of the cowman he had worked for so many years, and now they were living on a ranch of their own on the Lemhi river, several hundred miles to the north.

Mother's greatest disappointment with her daughters-in-law was that neither had the slightest interest in religion. Although Winnie had been baptized a Mormon, and her mother was a devout church worker, her father had never gone into the church—and she took after him. Mother soon accommodated herself to the radical differences in the girls' temperaments and got along with both. Where Winnie was quiet, Myrtle bristled with arguments. Winnie's ears would prick up when the conversation turned on people or animals, but Myrtle was serious-minded, well educated, and interested in abstract problems, questions of high finance, and world events.

Father usually liked to be with Myrtle. He got along fairly well with both—although seldom with both at the same time—and he would expatiate longer on their faults than on their virtues. Where Myrtle never hesitated to give him battle, Winnie blandly refused even to argue; the one thing he could never stand was to be ignored.

My marriage should have set the stamp of finality on the grave of my ambition, and in truth I had intended it to do just that. It had been seventeen years since I had graduated from the eighth grade, and certainly it was high time to forget about those imaginary careers and come down to earth. A farmer with a family to support has no time to indulge in foolish fancies.

Ten years earlier I had been steeped in the best books I could find. I read Tolstoi, Hugo, Voltaire, along with the then big four of British literature, Shaw, Wells, Bennett, and Galsworthy. Now I was happy when I could read the magazine serials of writers like Jack London, Rex Beach, David Graham Phillips, and Oliver Curwood. I read for entertainment only. I didn't want to think.

Three dry years and the agricultural depression had us in debt so deeply that we couldn't see our way out; and few people could have hated debt as badly as we did. We could only hope for a few big crop years and a good price to pull us through. Naturally, Obe was sure that would happen and I was equally sure it never would.

One day I picked up the old copy of the law-school magazine containing my article on *Salvaging Self-respect,* and it struck me that I had betrayed myself. For years I had been searching desperately for something, and failing to find it. I had all but given up hope when I had decided to make a final gamble with the law course. It had come to nothing, of course, and yet while I was studying I had more hope than at any time since leaving school. But I had given up any ambition to be anything except a farmer, something I had always known I was unfitted for. Farming, for me, would always be a downhill road and if I didn't at least keep trying for something else I would lose what little self-esteem I had managed to retain. The only thing I had to build on was some small skill in putting words together.

There was a young fellow down in Arkansas named Hapsburg Liebe whose stories I saw in many magazines. Somewhere I had got hold of a bunch of old magazines called *The Editor.* In one of them I had read an article by Liebe telling of his struggles and ending with the sage advice to the beginner to write only about things he knew. Knowing nothing of any state except Arkansas, Liebe had made a success of writing about Arkansas hillbillies.

In the same magazine was another article which seemed to make the whole thing clear and quite simple. There were, it said, just seven steps in the writing of a short story: inciting incident, conflict, complication, further complications, crisis, climax, denouement.

With this guide, and with Liebe's advice in mind, I cast about for material for a short story. There didn't seem to be a story in anyone I knew. I thought back to my sheepherding days. I had never formed any great affection or admiration for sheepmen as such. Obe, looking up from the Bible one day, remarked, "The reason Jehovah loved sheepmen so much was because in His infinite mercy and compassion he realized that nobody else could possibly love them." I was inclined to agree.

Part of my job had been to frustrate the depredations of predatory animals, and I had always had a sneaking sympathy for them, especially the coyotes, who had outwitted me so many times that I had to respect their cunning. These gray marauders have a keen sense of humor. I have walked miles and have seen other men do the same, to hang out red lanterns at night to frighten away the coyotes. However, I have often found the carcass of a lamb under the lantern the next morning, as though the coyote had dragged his victim there as a practical joke.

If I carried a rifle I seldom saw a coyote. If I left it at camp I would often see one grinning at me from less than a hundred yards distant. The explanation, of course, is that coyotes learn to associate the powder smell with danger, and they seem to know that a man without a gun is helpless. I have known them to lure a camp or ranch dog far away from base by pretending to be scared, then double back suddenly on the astonished dog and nip it in the rear with every jump until it was chased home.

I have seen a coyote, when chased by dogs, dive headlong into a snowbank, leaving them baffled and humiliated. I have seen them work singly or in pairs, but never in a pack of more than four. I am infuriated now when I see them being hunted down by airplanes and with other means which give them no chance.

The coyote was far more of a sportsman than his hunters. The real coyote hunters respected him, and even when they resorted to poison they knew few coyotes would succumb to it. It took a smart trapper indeed to conceal a trap where a wily coyote couldn't dig it up and spring it with no harm to himself. Give a coyote an even break and nine times out of ten he will survive. Almost any other animal, hunted as the coyote has been, would have been extinct long ago.

With this background of knowledge, and sedulously following the seven steps, I wrote a story about an old three-legged coyote battling for his existence against the odds of starvation, men, dogs, guns, traps, and poison.

The story material and the technique were easy, but even as a schoolboy I had been baffled by the intricacies of grammar. I had never memorized the rules, and if I had I wouldn't have known how to apply them. I knew even less about punctuation. When in doubt, I laboriously searched the pages of a book or magazine until I came to a sentence which seemed to be similar in construction to mine, and punctuated accordingly. But sometimes this led me astray, as once finding the word *but* followed by a semi-colon, I jumped to the conclusion that it was always so, and for many years any *but* of mine was trailed by a semi-colon as faithfully as a mare by a sucking colt.

I was sure that I would be the laughingstock of the community if my crude attempts to write fiction were to become known, and that meant that it must be kept from Father. My little coterie of backers, however—Mother, Obe, and Winnie—were close-mouthed and the shameful secret was well kept.

When the story was finished I sent it to a Street & Smith pulp magazine. After three weeks of anxious waiting I received a thin, blue envelope instead of the self-addressed one I had enclosed. There was a brief note from Mr. McLean, the editor. It read: *Your story,* THREE-FOOT'S LITTLE GAME, *is not acceptable to* POPULAR MAGAZINE, *but we are taking the liberty of sending it down to* TOP-NOTCH *for their consideration.*

There ensued more weeks during which, when Dad wasn't around, we talked of little except *Three-foot's* chances. Winnie and Obe professed themselves certain that the story would sell. Mother's more logical advice was, "Wait and see." I wondered why they didn't send it back immediately instead of punishing me with false hopes.

One morning as Obe and I were on our way to haul a load of hay we passed our mailbox, a mile from the house, and there was another small blue envelope. Inside was a two-line note of acceptance and a check for thirty-five dollars. I'll never experience a greater thrill. Obe looked at me as if seeing me for the first time.

"My God," he said in awe, "you're a writer!"

25

One story doesn't make a writer any more than one swallow makes a summer, but it was nice to think that it would. Obe and I went on to get our load of hay, pausing after every forkful to talk about how wonderful it was; forgetful that Mother and Winnie would be almost as excited about it as we were.

The next day we took the check to Bancroft to deposit in the bank. Henry Van Slooten, the banker, was our long-time friend. Often he had loaned us up to three thousand dollars when our visible assets wouldn't have justified a hundred dollar loan.

He asked, "What have you been doing—selling magazine subscriptions?"

I nodded. In case I couldn't repeat my success, and I was by no means sure that I could, it would be just as well if no one knew that I had sold one.

I wrote two more stories about the same coyote, and each came back with a curt rejection slip. I burned one of the stories, and sent the other to an outdoor magazine called *Sports Afield,* which bought it as an article, and sent me ten dollars' worth of books in payment. I wrote a couple more articles, one of which brought us five dollars; the other, an article on how to drive a four-horse team, sold to a farm magazine for three dollars and a half.

That was the extent of my earnings for the winter, and before I knew it the spring break-up had come and I had to forget about writing and get busy putting in a crop.

Our normal working day was around fourteen hours, and I had no idea of doing any more writing before snowfall, but one day as Obe, my father-in-law and I were fanning seed wheat in the granary I conceived a humorous story about a tenderfoot, a bear, and buried treasure consisting of a wagon-load of whisky which legend had it had been buried many years before only a few miles from where we lived. I rushed into the house for notebook and pencil and while standing in wheat up to my knees, and pausing every few minutes to fill the hopper with a scoop-shovel I dashed off a thirty-five-hundred-word story.

That evening I typed it, sitting up until midnight to do so, and next morning mailed it to a magazine called *Cartoons & Wayside Tales.* A week later I received another thirty-five dollar check.

I did a little figuring. The highest wage I had ever received was five dollars a day, and here, without losing so much as an hour of work, I had made thirty-five dollars! The check bore the imprint of the well known *Popular Mechanics* magazine, and my slightly suspicious banker friend asked if I had sold them an article. Again I nodded; that was better than having him think I had been wasting my time writing *fiction*.

No more story ideas came, and the farm work had to be done. It was late in the fall before I could again sit down at my second-hand typewriter. The stories I had hoped would flow through my fingers were not there.

We had had another below-average year and were a little deeper in debt. Obe was logging at the sawmill over the mountain, and as I could feed the stock in three or four hours a day I had time to do some writing. Unfortunately, no full-blown story entered my mind. I realized finally that I couldn't depend on inspiration, and if I was going to accomplish anything I would have to manufacture the story as I went along. It occurred to me that it would be just as easy to plan a novel as a short story, so I decided to try my hand at a Western novel.

My brother Chauncey was the most dashing, colorful man I knew, so I used him as the model for my hero. He read that story later, but it never occurred to him that he had anything in common with Steve Malty, the hero of the yarn. Actually, they didn't turn out to be much alike, but some of Chauncey's characteristics started the fictional ball to rolling.

I finished the story in about a month, and sent it off to *Adventure*, a magazine to which we had subscribed for several years. I knew the story was crudely written, and I had no real hope for acceptance, but in a couple of weeks I received one of those long brown envelopes so familiar to writers in the early twenties. The first thing I saw was a check for eight hundred and fifty dollars! It had taken me seventeen long hard months to make that much herding sheep, and this represented only half-time work for a month. If I could keep that up I might soon be making ten thousand dollars a year!

Then I read the accompanying letter and my rosy dream of a moment before became a black cloud of disillusionment. It read in part:

We like the novelty and fast action of your story, THE

HOLE IN THE ROCK, *and to avoid delay we are vouchering it herewith. There are, however, a great many things in it which do not seem altogether clear, and, as you know, the readers of* ADVENTURE *are sticklers for accuracy. On separate pages we are listing the things which we consider doubtful or confused, giving page, line and paragraph for your convenience. Please correct them from your carbon copy and return to us as soon as possible.*

Sincerely yours,
Arthur Sullivant Hoffman.

Carbon copy! I had never seen a sheet of carbon paper in my life. The only copy of the story was the one I had sent to the magazine.

On three sheets of single-spaced pages were references to no fewer than sixty pages of the manuscript. They wouldn't want the story without the corrections, and I couldn't make them. That check would save the farm for another year, and I couldn't cash it.

I lay awake all that night, and in the morning I wrote a frank statement to Mr. Hoffman, and with it I sent about twenty pages in which I tried to answer the objections as best I could. If this was not enough I would rewrite the story if they would send it back.

By return mail Mr. Hoffman told me to go ahead and cash the check; that the story could be fixed up in the office. I don't believe I have known any other editor who would have done that, though some of them have had to do a lot of fixing up of my yarns.

Frantically, I wrote more stories. I sold another novel, a novelette, and a short story to *Adventure* and got my word rate raised. Meanwhile, *The Hole in the Rock* had been published, and the nice things Mr. Hoffman said in introducing me to the magazine's Campfire Department convinced me that I was an arrived writer.

Then, suddenly, my stories all started coming back, and I

was confused and bewildered. Again it was Hoffman who straightened me out. He wrote me a long letter. The essence of it was in one paragraph. *Like a lot of young writers,* he wrote, *you are getting too magaziney. We liked your stories at first because of their freshness and originality of approach. Now they sound just like many of the stories we are publishing every month.*

To Hoffman, being "magaziney" was the complete and utter damnation of a writer. But I had only been following the advice of the "experts" to study the magazines and get their slant, the best way in the world to become an imitator. Hoffman was the deadly enemy of the formula story, soon to become so popular. He believed it was the business of the writer to create an illusion of reality in the reader's mind, and anything that destroyed that illusion was bad. Thanks to Hoffman I learned early not to depend on the textbooks. His own book, *Fundamentals of Fiction Writing*, by its very heresy started many a young writer on the right path.

Fortunately for me, whenever Hoffman rejected one of my stories he took the time to analyze its faults. Each rejection was an invaluable lesson, worth more to me in the long run than if I had received checks and no criticism.

But now it was time to start farming again. We were not getting ahead, and except for my earnings would probably have had to quit, but so long as we had the damned thing we had to serve and support it. I couldn't work on the farm and write, so I stopped writing.

After *The Hole in the Rock* was published my shameful secret could no longer be kept. While Father could not conceal his chagrin at having so worthless a son, quite a number of housewives and others in the community got busy writing short stories on the logical assumption that if Frank Robertson could do it anybody could.

In the fall I sloughed more and more of the work off on Obe, and soon was selling practically everything I wrote. I had a lot of things yet to learn. In *The Hole in the Rock* my secondary hero was a Mexican. *Adventure* had fewer taboos than most magazines, its most important one being a pious aversion to profanity in any form. Even such harmless words as "hell," or "damn" were represented by a dash. My Mexican had all but run away with the story. At that time it was customary to depict our neighbors to the south, especially in Western fiction, as black-hearted villains. The magazines tended to maintain the old Texas idea that one American could whip ten Mexicans, and one Texan could whip ten Americans. But I received a great many letters praising me for my courage in treating a Mexican as a decent human being.

I had always hated race prejudice of any kind, and some of my best and most loyal friends had been Portuguese and Mexican sheepherders. Encouraged by those letters, I wrote a Western novel which had a Mexican as the hero. *Adventure* wouldn't touch it, so I sent it to the magazine's chief competitor, *Short Stories,* at that time edited by Harry Maule.

Mr. Maule wrote, *We will pay you a thousand dollars for the story if you will change your hero to an American. Our readers would never tolerate the idea of a Mexican getting the better of an American.*

I needed that thousand dollars badly, and it took me only two days to change the complexion of my hero. I suppose that then and there I sold my soul and became a literary prostitute.

Taboos, I was learning, were as sacred to American editors as they were to the witch doctors of Africa. They had to be for their business was to sell magazines to the great American public, and they couldn't afford to go counter to that public's prejudices. Religion, race, politics, free enterprise—these were the most holy of holies, and not to be profaned by any mere fiction writer.

There were a thousand minor taboos. In action stories the greatest taboo was sex. A prostitute must never be called a whore, but a dance-hall girl. The wickedest of badmen might kidnap the heroine, but the only thing on his mind was ransom, or marriage—never such an ugly thing as rape.

Once I got these little things straight in my mind, it was easier, but writing wasn't the sinecure I had once thought it might be. I had to sweat blood even to write for the pulps. There is nothing quite like the agony of feeling that you have written yourself out, which is an experience I believe most writers at some time undergo. Several times each year I know positively that I have written my last story. It's a nasty feeling to have—especially when you have to have a check not later than day after tomorrow. There are times when story characters march like joyful children in a parade, and other times when they hang back with the obstinacy of a dog tied under a wagon.

I was making more money than I had ever expected to make, but it didn't improve our standard of living, for it was all going to pay debts and to support the farm. When Obe was short-handed, which was most of the summer, I would put away the typewriter and pick up a pitchfork. I was still the stacker for the header outfit and took pride in pitching more headings into a threshing-machine than anyone else on the crew.

Only our banker friend knew how badly off we were financially. At public auction our assets would not have paid half our debts, but we were climbing out. That was the main thing. And then our good luck suddenly played out. We had endured various kinds of misfortune through the years, but in general we had all enjoyed good health. Without warning, sickness, accident, and tragedy befell us.

Mother was the first victim. During the winter we had noticed her occasionally put her hand to her breast with a flicker of pain on her face. "It's nothing," she would deny when we questioned her. "Just a passing pain." But one day in the early spring she said quietly, "Boys, I think you should take me to Soda Springs to see Dr. Kackley. I believe I have a cancer."

"Why in God's name didn't you tell us before?" Obe asked.

She smiled apologetically. "I wanted to wait until the roads got better. You couldn't have taken me in the car."

The doctor was an old friend, the one Father had thwarted when he wanted to amputate a boy's leg.

"Your mother is old," he told us, "and she never has been very rugged. The operation will probably kill her, but it'll be better than letting her suffer. We won't tell her what she has, but you'd better send for Chauncey."

He didn't know Mother like we did. Obe said, "No, we'll tell her now. Whatever it is she can take it."

It was, of course, no surprise to her. "When can you operate, Doctor?" she asked.

"I thought next Monday."

"But this is only Wednesday," Mother protested. "Can't you do it tomorrow?"

The doctor looked at her. "All right, Mary," he said, "if that's the way you want it we'll operate tomorrow."

She went under the anesthetic with a smile on her face and came out urging them to give her more ether because she was still conscious.

"Whichever way it goes," she had told Father and us boys calmly, "it will be all right." And she meant every word of it.

Ten days after the operation, she returned home cheerful enough, only to find Obe in bed with a badly broken leg and twisted knee. He had roped a jug-headed colt which we had donated toward the building of an annex to the amusement hall, and was taking it to the auction along a muddy road. The colt bolted and Obe's horse slipped and fell. His leg was broken in the fall and when his foot caught in the stirrup he was dragged some distance. His leg was an inch or so shorter than the other when it finally healed, and the knee was to cause him distress as long as he lived.

The pride and joy of the Robertson ranch was our little daughter Nellie. She was a pretty, sweet-dispositioned child with the intelligent blue-gray eyes and quizzical smile of her grandmother. She was just learning to talk, pronouncing her words slowly but distinctly, when she was stricken with convulsions.

The only doctor immediately available was a young man just starting to practice in Bancroft. After a couple of days he admitted that the case was beyond him and we took her to our old friend Kackley.

"It's a form of meningitis—probably what we used to call brain fever," he told us. "Better get her to a specialist in Salt Lake City."

My wife was pregnant. I carried the little girl in my arms all the way on the train. Dr. Kackley had given me a bottle of chloral for use if the convulsions became too violent. I have asked myself many times if I gave her too much. The convulsions were halted at last, but they kept recurring at intervals, sometimes as many as a hundred in a twenty-four hour period.

We watched in agony as she forgot one word after another of her small vocabulary until she no longer had the power of speech. Lights had always held a fascination for her, and for a long time she would say the word, "lamp" when one was lighted; then it too disappeared as the darkness closed in over her mind. Only her sunny smile and sweet disposition remained.

We went hopelessly from doctor to doctor, trying them all through the years from high-priced specialists to chiropractors, but none could do her any good. Once, when we returned to Chesterfield, Mother reminded me that there was a time up in the Idaho panhandle when she and everyone else thought I was going to die of scarlet fever. The Mormon elders had administered to me and I had got well. She asked me to let her call in the elders for Nellie.

Father, who had a reputation as a healer, himself administered to Nellie. He prayed for Nellie as he probably had never prayed before. But she got no better. The doctors told us the brain cells had been destroyed and could never be replaced.

For years as I saw my little daughter suffering torment, I was ridden night and day by the thought that I should free her from it once and for all. Many times I drove around the country looking for some cliff or dugway over which I could drive my automobile and make sure that death came to both of us instantaneously. There were surer ways, of course, but it was in my mind that it must be made to look like an accident. After all, I had some obligations to the other members of my family, as Mother was constantly pointing out. She had long ago divined the direction of my thoughts. Sometimes in the evening when we were alone and the room was dark, she would take my hand and talk to me about my obligations to my wife and my son.

Eventually a doctor friend of ours in Salt Lake City said firmly, "Frank, for the sake of your wife and the little girl herself you must put her in an institution."

He was right. Dr. Frank Root went with Obe and me when we took her away. I felt like a cowardly traitor when I kissed my little girl good-by.

Dr. Root remained with us all that day, and when I offered to pay him for his time and the use of his automobile he said gruffly, "I don't take pay for that."

Nellie lived until her early twenties, largely under the affectionate care of another inmate whom my wife and I have made our special ward as much as possible. I was in Albuquerque during World War II when I got a message that Nellie was sinking. I arrived an hour or so before she died. She looked up at me with her grandmother's smile which I remembered so well. I think that for just a moment she remembered me.

I was thankful as I stood beside her that my dark, desperate plans had never been carried out. After all, she had not been conscious that she was different from other people, and all her life, when not in the grip of the convulsions—and new medicines had lessened them to a tremendous extent—she always had a happy little unintelligible song on her lips. But above all her smile told me that despite the ravages of disease she had retained the one great heritage her grandmother had been able to give her—the capacity to endure.

For some time Obe had been grumbling about taking money which he hadn't helped earn. We had been partners ever since I had been big enough to earn a dollar, and we knew each other's inmost thoughts. I wanted it to continue that way. Again it was Mother who solved that problem.

While Obe was convalescing from his accident she persuaded him to try his hand at writing a story. He hadn't had more than a year of actual schooling in his life, and he was now nearly forty. But he had always been a raconteur, able to keep a group interested for hours with his yarn-spinning.

I read his first story. It was crudely written and rode roughshod over the taboos, but it had interest, spiced with Obe's own particular brand of humor and philosophy. And it was unique, as were his subsequent stories, in that his heroes solved their problems with their brains instead of their guns and fists. I knew instantly that I could work it over into a salable story. There was nothing now to destroy our partnership.

With writing, as in everything else we had ever done together, I was a much faster worker than Obe, but he was far more thorough.

26

My wife and I had been spending so much time in Salt Lake City that we decided to move there. Father's former partner, Roscoe Loveland, was willing to move onto the ranch and work for Obe, allowing Father and Mother to move back into the little log house in Chesterfield, *sans* the post office. There was more privacy than in the old days, but their front room was still a lobby for friends dropping in for a visit.

Father was still restless. Our family was getting along well, except that Father was sure that my success as a writer was transient and evanescent. He couldn't believe that writing stories was a respectable way to earn a living. Usually he greeted me with a sarcastic "Well, have you sold any more stories?" He treated each sale as if it were an accident which could not possibly be repeated and would sooner have suffered snakebite than to read one.

He wanted to go on another mission for the church. We saw no reason why he shouldn't, knowing that this time he wouldn't have to come home for lack of funds. He had always wanted to go back to the Northwest and it was there he was called. It would give him a chance to visit Moscow and see the Matthewses and other old friends, and show them once and for all that joining the Mormons and gathering to Zion had been no mistake.

I think the rest of us got just as much satisfaction from this as Father did. Now a well-dressed Mormon missionary, they would see in him little resemblance to the be-whiskered, quarrelsome, poverty-stricken woodchopper they had known. Surely, the Mormon Gospel had saved Father, and through him the family felt justified.

Mother moved to Salt Lake with us, where Obe would join us as soon as the ranch could be sold. It saddened us to think that now we could give her some of the things she had missed all her life and that she was almost too old to enjoy them. The one thing she wanted most for me to do I couldn't do. That was to become active again in the church. Perhaps I am somewhat like Stephen Dedalus in James Joyce's *Ulysses:* "*You have the cursed jesuit strain in you, only it's injected the wrong way.*"

Outside of that Mother was contented. At last she had time to read some of the books she had always wanted to read, and she took little slow, exploratory walks around the city. She was cautious in traffic, but never afraid. She loved to do new things on her own initiative. Once she wandered into the largest cafeteria in the city. Winnie and I still lacked the courage to visit such a place for fear we would do the wrong thing, but Mother came home in pleased excitement, telling us what a fine meal she'd had.

"But how did you know what to do?" we asked.

"Oh, I just stood there until a nice gentleman came up and asked if he could help me. He helped me pick out my lunch and we ate together and had a wonderful time."

Winnie and I ceased to worry about her.

Those days I wrote desperately, trying to pay off our debts and meet the constantly rising expenses due to doctor bills and Father's mission. I had reason to be thankful now that I had a wife with quiet, undemanding tastes and no social ambitions. The only extra money Winnie ever asked was to take a course in a Salt Lake business college so that she could serve as my part-time secretary. Winnie, Obe, and I had a joint checking account and no one of us ever asked another to explain why he had written any certain check.

I was soon earning more than ten thousand dollars a year, a sum that not long previously I would have thought fabulous; yet we were not saving any money nor were we living in the style of most people with half our income.

There were other demands on me which I could have avoided had I been made of sterner stuff. Some of our friends and relatives thought we were rolling in affluence. Desperate appeals for financial assistance came in, many hard to ignore.

Those were the days of the Fabulous Twenties, when everybody was supposed to have been prosperous and happy. The myth can't hurt anyone now, but I knew plenty of people who were neither. I had gained my place on the tread-mill and become a fiction factory. Now I had an agent, and was selling practically everything I wrote. I wasn't a big money man, but I have written a short story in a single day for which I got as much as two hundred and fifty dollars, but my style was too crude for me to hit the big, high-paying slick magazines.

Once I locked myself up in a cheap hotel in Los Angeles and did a seventy-thousand-word novel in ten days, and I estimate that I have made, book royalties and all, nearly five hundred dollars a day for those ten days. But those were the exceptions.

My earnings never did reach much over ten or twelve thousand dollars a year.

The first of my novels to be published in book form was called *Owyhee*, after a county in Idaho. It was rather a mild book, and I patterned my hero, Owyhee, after my brother Obe. No pulp magazine would touch it. Arthur Sullivant Hoffman wrote, *It's a whale of a story in some ways, but you have tried to write a Western story without any of the usual props, and in my opinion it can't be done.*

I valued Mr. Hoffman's opinion highly, but I still had faith in Owyhee.

Eventually, the story sold to a slick-paper magazine with a wide circulation throughout the middle West. Shortly thereafter it was brought out in book form and had a sale of around twenty thousand copies—not bad for a Western. In England the book went through more than twenty editions, the last, a paperback, being the first of a series called *Blackout Novels*, published at the height of the German blitz. The book has been translated into half a dozen languages, transcribed into Braille, and was widely syndicated in American newspapers. Once it even sold to an American movie company, which went broke before the book could be filmed, and my agent and I gave back the money because a Hollywood agent had got caught in the middle.

The lesson I learned from *Owyhee*, which was published in book form under the title, *The Foreman of the Forty Bar*, is that the experts are not always infallible, and it sometimes pays to have faith in one's own judgment.

All this time I was aware that I should take time out to master the English language if I was ever to do the work of which I felt myself capable, but I could never find the time. There was always need of an immediate check. I was a young man in a hurry, going nowhere, and I couldn't stop.

I had been writing more than ten years before I went to New York and met my first editor. The ones I had broken in with were gone, and the ones who had taken their place told me frankly that I knew too much about the West. In the eyes of most readers the synthetic West of the horse operas of that day was the real thing, and the West I knew was a dull and drab place where people didn't even know enough to say, "He went thataway."

Commenting on that trip, Ham Park, a Salt Lake City columnist wrote, *The Robertson brothers have recently returned from New York, where they went in search of material for Western stories.*

There were a few concessions which Obe and I would not make. We would not let our heroes be violent-minded morons who spent their time looking for a fight, nor would we allow our heroines to be complete little imbeciles whose mission in life seemed to be to get the strong, silent men who reverenced them into trouble through their stupidity or obstinacy, which seemed to be the average editor's idea of what Western women were like. I knew too much about Western women to portray them as helpless little idiots, but even I never dared to have one of them defiled.

The truly colorful words of the old West were first used around the corral and the campfire, and the synthetic ones were given birth to by a typewriter, and so we tried to avoid the popular magazine jargon such as using "ankled" for walked, and "hair-pinning" for mounting.

Chauncey had gained a reputation as a reckless rider, especially when chasing wild horses on the Fort Hall Indian reservation along with the wild young Bannack and Shoshoni bucks who rode with him. He had hundreds of spills when his horse stepped in badger holes, or slipped on ice, but he never killed a horse, and the only time he ever broke a leg was when his horse fell in sight of his employer's house, and he writhed in agony while his fellow-workers carried him tenderly into the house, where he burst into laughter as he explained that it was his *artificial* leg that was broken.

Both Obe and I had our share of spills while running horses or cattle at full speed, with no worse consequences to ourselves or our horse than a little shaking up. But in the Western stories of those days—and in many of them now—whenever a horse falls it has to be shot. We knew, too, that horses don't "scream" every time they get hurt. I have seen horses literally cut to pieces in barbed wire, and have had to shoot several to get them out of their misery, but never have I heard one make more than a slight groan, and seldom that. In fiction horses are always "screaming."

Most irksome to us was to read how the handsome hero was always galloping off somewhere on a noble stallion. Practically no Western hero, it seemed, ever rode anything except a magnificent studhorse. In reality, a man who rode a stallion into a cow camp would be sent home before his mount split up the cavvy and ruined some good geldings. Nowadays many writers are overworking the word "gelding" when plain old horse would be a lot better.

It seems odd that those little things of which we had personal knowledge should be a handicap to us as writers, but they were.

About five years after I had sold my first story my biographical sketch appeared in *Who's Who in America*. At the time it was still easier for me to think of myself as a sheepherder than as a writer. When, with considerable pride, I showed the volume to Mother she glanced through it casually, then remarked dryly, "My, there's a lot of other people in there, isn't there?" No one could shrink hatbands more deftly.

Some years later I achieved another ambition in a backhanded way. I got inside an institution of learning. Professor Harrison R. Merrill, head of the Department of Journalism at Brigham Young University, invited me to address a group of students and professors at College Hall. When I had given up my dream of ever going to college I certainly did not anticipate that my first trip to a university should be to deliver a lecture.

After I had concluded my remarks a group of us gathered around a table to view some paintings by a prominent young artist named Glen Potter, who hailed from my part of Idaho. Presently, he showed us a picture of an old dirt-roofed log cabin sitting lonely on the prairie, miles from any other house.

"Maybe you'll remember this, Mr. Robertson," he said. "It's the cow camp on Corral Creek."

"And I remember it," I answered, "as the place where my wife spent the first sixteen years of her life." I remembered, also, that I had been in sight of that cabin the day I thought I was going to have to shoot the German sheepherder. I remembered it when it was a far wilder country, when my brother Chauncey had been roundup boss, and even a log cabin would have been considered luxury.

I don't go back to Chesterfield, my old home, very often. There is little except a ghost town to go back to. It has been the victim of what we call progress. When I first saw the place it had a population of three hundred people, two stores and a post office. There were a church, a schoolhouse and an amusement hall. Now there are less than fifty people, the stores and post office are gone, and the public buildings stand unused and forlorn. Once a man with a hundred and sixty acres of land and a dozen cows could make a good living. Now it takes at least a thousand acres, and thousands of dollars' worth of machinery. The young fellows with nothing but muscles and ambition have had to go elsewhere to make a living; the land belongs to a few men. When I go back, except for a dozen or so old friends, I find myself among strangers. The town means nothing to my future, but what a lot it meant to my past!

The 1930's brought us our share of troubles, though compared to what most people had to suffer it was nothing. Chauncey was in difficulty with his ranch on the Lemhi, so we tried to help him out by buying a ranch in Teton Basin just before the big crash of 1929. It was the worst possible time to buy, and Chauncey's old nemesis, drouth, still pursued him. Asked one day to state his idea of heaven he replied disgustedly, "For me, it would be a hundred tons of hay and one cow."

The upshot of the whole business was that we all went broke, losing not only the Teton ranch and the cattle, but even our home in Salt Lake. The bank in which we had our spare cash folded, and when we had dug up for the outstanding checks we had, as I remember, some twenty dollars in cash. And magazines were folding up about as rapidly as were the banks.

One magazine that survived, though it was once reduced to the extremity of issuing promissory notes to its writers, was *Ranch Romances*. For many years this magazine was edited by Miss Fanny Ellsworth, and during the depression it was the Robertsons' meal ticket. When the first number was printed I led off with the first installment of a serial. When the magazine celebrated its twenty-fifth anniversary I again had the first story in the book, a short complete novel. Between those dates I sold the magazine literally millions of words.

Fanny Ellsworth was the first person to say to me, "Frank, why don't you write your autobiography?"

She and her husband, Jack Davis, and I had our feet on the rail of a New York bar one night after attending a party, and as people will under the circumstances, we got to talking—or maybe it was only me. Anyway, I had been telling them something about my childhood when Fanny Ellsworth planted the seed that eventually resulted in this book.

27

Father filled several short-term missions to the Northwest, and did so very successfully. There were quite a few elderly men on missions out there, but Father disdained them as traveling companions. He placed them all in one sweeping category: *old fogies!*

Young men pulled wires to get to travel with him. He would stand up to the conference president to defend them, if necessary. His ability to talk on any subject stood him in good stead. He had become widely read, and much reading had improved his diction. He was still a fluent speaker.

Hearing him preach, one would scarcely suppose that he

had once been a Texas cowboy, or a wagon tramp whose chief interest in life lay in goading his wife into a quarrel. He still enjoyed a good row occasionally but he had learned to conduct it with dignity, and sometimes with a patience that would drive his adversary to distraction far more than his former shoutings and fist-shakings.

He wore the best of clothes now and never was he caught unshaven or with his shoes not shined. Between missions he and Mother went to church together, but she had grown hard of hearing and derived little pleasure from it; while Father, still as spry and vigorous as a man of middle age, found it hard to accommodate his rapid pace to her faltering gait. He was soon on the go again.

When not on a mission he liked to visit among the old neighbors in Chesterfield, or out around Boise where many of them had moved. He was welcomed wherever he went. Even those he had chastised most severely seemed to hold no grudge. If he had hurt their feelings sometimes, he had helped them out of difficulties at others. He helped the men with their chores and the women with their housework, and kept them stimulated by frankly pointing out some of their faults. He stood for something in the lives of every one of them that they liked to look back on. He had become more than Brother Robertson to them; he was almost an institution.

Once I had resented bitterly the time and money it had taken for Father to raise the garden truck he distributed among the neighbors. However, when some of the poorer people in his teaching block told me with tears in their eyes that they didn't know what they would have done if it hadn't been for Brother Robertson, that in poverty or sickness he had never failed them, I felt that I had been short-sighted and mean.

How he had mellowed was shown when Obe visited him on his final mission. While Obe and Father's young missionary companion played a few games of pool, Father stayed outside on guard to warn his companion if some other elder or convert should happen to come along. Even young elders, he declared, were entitled to some recreation. He spent considerable time with Chauncey, and with us. He began to keep a diary, and in it he expressed great charity for our shortcomings.

Near the end of his last mission he wrote that he would like to remain in the city of Tacoma, Washington. He admitted freely the mistakes in his past life, and begged Mother to come out so they could spend their declining years together. He wanted Obe to come along, too. He assured them that he would gladly do all the housework.

Obe took his time driving out to the Coast. Physically frail though she was, Mother could ride all day without tiring, and she enjoyed going over the old trails which she had once traveled in a covered wagon. With remarkable memory, she recalled the location of practically every old campground.

Father was ready for them. For some time he and his young companion and two young lady missionaries had been together in Tacoma. The girls had a deep affection for him, and he would smile benignly if they wanted to play hooky from a street meeting and take in a picture show once in a while. They turned in and had the apartment spick and span against the time of Mother's arrival. Father was excited and happy and everyone was determined to see that all was made pleasant and comfortable for Sister Robertson.

Mother had always wanted to see the sea and the ships. Obe would take her out on the shore of Puget Sound, and there she would sit contentedly for hours watching the waves and the shipping. At home, Father waited on her hand and foot.

One day she lay down to take a nap without removing her glasses. She smiled a refusal when Obe offered to take them from her. When Father went in to call her to supper the same kindly smile was on her face, but she was dead. The death she had never feared had come in her sleep.

When I received Obe's telegram I felt a great sense of loneliness, and pity for Father and for Obe who would be most lost without her.

Winnie and I met the rest of the family at Chesterfield where Bishop Chris Call and Annie Chris threw open their home to us and our friends. There were no relatives outside the immediate family, but friends came from hundreds of miles around. At the funeral roughnecks who hadn't been inside a church for years sat quietly in the back seats. They knew to a man that Mother had been their friend.

After seventy-seven years of poverty and hardship she had achieved success. Her greatest victory was that she lived to see Father, man of turbulent moods and violent temper, become loved and respected, even by all three of his sons. But Mother had always been a success, because she had never let life get the better of her, had never conceded defeat except in honestly admitting her own mistakes. She had never whimpered, never whined. She had never lived in a place where she hadn't been able to rise above her poverty.

With Mother gone, Father lost all desire to return to the Coast. He wanted, he said, to be near his boys. He still did considerable traveling, visiting with Chauncey's family and other friends, but most of the time he spent in Salt Lake City, where he and Obe had their own apartment. He loved to cook and keep house, and we no longer asked him to worry about money. He wouldn't have done it anyway. He came to our house nearly every day, and even read some of my stories with mild approval.

Most of the time he worked in the Salt Lake temple, performing the ordinances for the dead that were a fundamental part of his religion. His sight and hearing remained unimpaired, his mind and memory keen, and his body erect. He still retained his liking for young people, and they for him. Not all the fire had gone out of him, for occasionally he blew up in a rage. Most often it was when some lonely elderly widow working with him in the temple would make overtures toward marriage.

"The old fool," he would yell, "what does she think I would want with her?"

Once he went to the rescue of the proprietress of a house of prostitution. Her pet dog, which she was walking, was set upon by several mongrels and she was helpless. Father, who never had any fear of dogs, drove the mongrels away and walked up the street with the woman to the door of her house, talking about dogs. He knew who and what she was, but when she turned in he courteously raised his hat and bade her good day. He thoroughly enjoyed his role as a kindly old gentleman—and so did his sons.

Father outlived Mother by four years. On his deathbed, which lasted five cruel days, he was grimly determined to wait on himself, even while under influence of the morphine given him to ease his pain.

He remained steadfast in his adopted religion. He said to me, "Frank, I have not been mistaken all these years. No matter how I may have acted at times I have always had the testimony that the Gospel is true."

He died on his seventy-ninth birthday, October 6th, 1931. The chief speaker at the funeral was a garbage inspector from Salt Lake City, Mathias F. Cowley. He was the same Mormon Apostle who had thrilled my parents and me at Baker City, Oregon. Then he had been the pride of the Mormon church. Later, he had been dropped, along with another apostle, from the Quorum of the Twelve, because he had refused to go along with the man-made manifesto against polygamy. Not only had he married other wives himself, but he had performed plural marriage for others in Canada and Mexico.

Cowley was a poor man. My father and Obe rented an apartment in his house, and they were living there at the time of Father's death. Although Cowley at that time was not permitted to speak in L.D.S. churches we asked him to accompany us to Chesterfield and speak at Father's funeral. We knew it was Father's wish, and we knew that Bishop Call would not deny him the right to use the pulpit on that occasion.

I doubt if the good man ever preached a more powerful sermon. It did me good to see many of the elderly sisters who had known him when he was the darling of the church come up and throw their arms around him and kiss him, much to his embarrassment. Cowley may have been wrong in clinging to his belief that polygamy was a God-commanded practice, but there is always something admirable about a man who will suffer ruin rather than give up a principle in which he believes.

Some of the Mormon elders we had known in the Palouse country attended Father's funeral. These gray-headed men had made our house their headquarters a third of a century before and I could see the wonder in their faces as they listened to the tributes to a man they had known as a "wood rat" in a half-outlaw community in the Moscow mountains. This was Father's last farewell party and, as with Mother, friends came for hundreds of miles to see him off on his last journey.

It is a strange feeling to see the last of a generation pass. Somehow, until my father's death I seemed to be living in his generation, and now it was all in the past, its hopes buried, its mistakes and bitterness forgiven and forgotten. Mother's part in molding my life was easy to estimate. She had steadied me when I was as uncertain as a web-footed bird on a tree limb, and as surly with the world as a wasp in a glass bottle.

It was not so easy to appraise what Father had meant to me. For years I had considered him the stump in the highway of my ambition. He would never acknowledge the gifts I thought I had, or scorned them as useless if he did, but I surely worked a lot harder to prove that he was wrong than I would have if he had given me flattery.

I thought many times that I hated him, though I doubt that I really ever did; for even in his worst tantrums I found myself making excuses for him. So did everybody else. In time I came to share the affectionate, protective feeling for him which Mother and Obe had always seemed to have.

Soon after Father's death we moved to Springville, Utah, so that we could be near our daughter Nellie. Perhaps it was because as a child I never got enough fruit to eat that we bought a rundown orchard with a dilapidated old brick house in a place called Mapleton, five miles out of Springville, at the very foot of a beautiful mountain called Sierra Bonita, which towers ten thousand feet above us.

We modernized the house, and began to build up the orchard. At first we considered it a hobby, but it presently grew into a business. I have been lucky in having others do the work for me. First, it was Obe who handled the orchard. But Obe, that kind and good man who would endure any hurt himself before he would hurt another, finally fell victim to the cigarette habit, as for more than thirty years Father had stoutly predicted he would. In 1944 Obe died from cancer of the lungs. We brought him home after an unsuccessful operation and I was with him sixty days and nights because he wanted me at his side at all times.

At the time cigarettes were rationed and hard to get, and in his semi-delirium Obe insisted that he must have a pack on the table at each side of his bed. He would light one, doze off and let it slip from his fingers, and we had to be on the alert to keep the bedclothes from getting on fire. Not once did he complain of the pain in his lungs, but he suffered untold agonies from the sciatica that had bothered him for years.

I had to lift him in and out of bed, but once on his feet he insisted on walking to his chair or to the bathroom. The cancer ate into his vocal cords so that he could scarcely whisper. On his last day he motioned me from the chair where he was sitting and whispered, "Get me back to bed." He died in my arms as I laid him on the bed. So passed the best and most loyal friend I have ever had; the man who asked nothing for himself, except to be helpful to those he loved.

Before Obe's death Chauncey had moved down from the Lemhi to our fruit farm, and with the wonderful gift for adaptability he had always enjoyed he changed from a cowman to a fruitgrower, and threw himself into the new line of work as zestfully as he had ridden bucking broncos in his youth. He could do anything he turned his hand to; from butchering a beef to building a house, from patching up an injured animal to repairing a tractor.

Like Father, Chauncey remained young and gay. Like Obe, he remained straight as an arrow, and never carried an ounce of surplus flesh. The kids who worked in our orchard adored him, as they had Obe. One morning, five years after Obe's death, I looked across the road and saw Chauncey on a tractor. Two hours later I was told that he was dead of a heart attack.

One of the largest floral pieces at his funeral was bought by the girls who had worked for him in the orchard, and there were two rows of them, dressed all in white, just back of the bench where the family sat. There could be no better proof than this of Chauncey Robertson's genius for making and holding friends.

For a number of years I used to move ladders during the cherry harvest; a job that requires a strong back and considerable tact. Most of our pickers are young girls, and as we try to treat them well most of them come back year after year until they get married, or get steady jobs elsewhere. We are proud of our kids, and believe they pick more cherries per person per day than any other crew in the county. Of the hundreds who have passed through our orchard I don't know of one who became a juvenile delinquent.

The kids treat me as I like to be treated. I recall an instance when a new girl was nearly hooted out of the orchard when she called out, "Mr. Robertson, will you please come and move my ladder?" Another girl put her right. "Around here we say, 'Frank, come and move my ladder.'"

I finally had to give up moving ladders to become a mere errand boy during the rush season. I get up around four a.m.

to pick up in my car the kids who live too far out for the trucks to reach, and I take them home, sweaty and dirty, in the early afternoon and listen placidly to their gripes about what a lousy place it is to work—knowing well they wouldn't work any place else.

In the evenings after the crew has gone home I sweep out the packing shed, against the protests of my family, for now my battle is to keep from being treated as a revered patriarch. I, alas, am the last of my family generation.

Chauncey's three sons, Russell, Cecil—whom everyone knows as Kelly—and Jack have been almost as close to me as my own son Glen. Tragedy struck when Jack, the youngest, was killed in an automobile accident. He was twenty-two, as handsome and capable as his father had been. They were much alike; quick in mind and in body efficient, hot-tempered at times, disdainful of opposition, and completely fearless.

Russell lived with us a number of years while getting his education, and now lives with his own family near Chicago. Kelly leases my farm, and is the man I lean upon; not only as manager of the farm, but as critic of my stories. I see in him many of the best qualities of my two brothers. He sees through my little pretenses as keenly as Obe ever did, and is just as patient with my idiosyncrasies. Every burden that he can he takes from my shoulders.

I am proud of the generation that will succeed me. I think I can see something of my mother in every one of them. Her qualities are most pronounced, I believe, in my son Glen. He has the same kindly tolerance, the same gentle humor. After several years as a newspaperman Glen became a teacher, and now teaches English in a college in California. Naturally, in view of my own thwarted efforts to gain a college education, this is most gratifying to me.

Like Kelly, Glen sees through me as if I were transparent. During the war years I started writing a Sunday newspaper column called, *The Chopping Block*. I dislike wearing any man's brand, which makes me, I suppose, a political and religious maverick. If I ever adopt a cause my readers may be sure that it will be an unpopular one. I hate do-gooders and conformity, so I shun the worthy causes and crusades, for much the same reason that if I have largess to bestow I seek out the undeserving poor, because somebody will always help the deserving. When I want to get grandiloquent about my attitude I claim that I try to be a voice for the inarticulate.

Glen once wrote about me perhaps more accurately: "There is a typicalness in his reactions to events in the news. A regular reader of *The Chopping Block* can soon predict with accuracy the Robertson line on any given happening. If a bum is arrested by a policeman, and an incident results, many would side (without knowing the facts) with the policeman. Robertson (also without knowing the facts) would side with the bum, because of the well-known Robertson sympathy for the underdog. His fairness may be questioned because he has a pronounced dislike for all groups holding the upper hand. He will go to great lengths to keep from being identified with society's elite, yet constantly rubs shoulders with them, and is always amazed to find himself liking them. He distrusts 'the herd' even more, and likes to picture himself as a lone wolf roaming the social world alone. . . . There are those who support or oppose his views fanatically, but there are few who would question the integrity of his opinions, or believe that any amount of money could buy one of them."

Thus I am seen by my son, and I will let it go at that. I occasionally receive letters addressed simply to, "The Sage of Mapleton," and frequently politicians beat a trail to my door. I think perhaps I am a more or less useful member of society.

One member of my family I cannot overlook is my daughter-in-law, Vera. She is a Czech girl whom Glen met and married in Rio de Janeiro, and the story of her adventures is more fascinating than fiction.

When Hitler invaded her homeland, Vera, a young girl still in college, joined the underground fighters for freedom. Her group was finally betrayed, and she spent two years in the infamous Rawensbrueck prison for women, where she suffered incredible hardships and barely escaped with her life. For a time after liberation, being unable to get home, she wandered between the German and Russian lines, finally to be taken prisoner by the Russians and sent to Poland.

Escaping from there, Vera made her way to Berlin and finally back to Prague only to find that her mother had been killed during the American bombing, and that she had no home or family.

For a time she served as secretary and translator for the American War Claims team, and when the Americans left Czechoslovakia and the Communists took over she was suspected of being an American spy. Warned that a fifteen-year sentence to a slave-labor camp in Siberia impended, Vera made another break for freedom and got across the border, finally winding up in a displaced-persons camp near Munich. She eventually was sent to Brazil by a Dutch firm for which she worked, and after a year or so there came to the United States as a member of the Robertson family.

The only bitterness I have ever heard Vera show was when she told of the brutal S.S. *Oberaufsherin* who asked her to intercede with the Americans in her behalf just before the liberation. Vera says she told the woman, "The only thing I'll be able to remember about you is your boots in my face." The woman had once beaten Vera unconscious for having put her hands in her pockets one bitter winter morning while she was standing at attention.

The rest of the family tell me that Vera is the only person from whom I will take orders, and I suppose they are right. The example they most like to point to is my lawn, which I delighted in letting go wild until the grass was knee-high. I maintained that I had not moved into the country to become a slave to a lawn mower, and besides, I enjoyed having my neat Mormon neighbors shake their heads over my lack of civic pride. But when Vera said, "Fadder, get yourself a power lawn mower and keep the grass cut," I dutifully complied.

She is in considerable demand as a speaker, and when she laces into American club women for not properly appreciating the liberties of their own country, I can imagine they feel much as I did when she was shaming me for the deplorable condition of my lawn.

Most of my neighbors are Mormons, and I know of no other neighbors for whom I would exchange them. Today I hear more criticism of the church from its own liberal members than from outsiders. Some of them complain that the church has become more of a business organization than it is a spiritual institution. They secretly resent the church dictum that: *When the authorities speak the thinking has been done.*

One former High Councilman once remarked to me with considerable pride, "If any church can serve God and Mammon we can do it."

Utah, I have long maintained, is a Western state only by geographical accident. Its culture, its passion for blue laws and for making money, hails straight from New England, which never produced a more astute leader, or a sharper trader than Vermont-born Brigham Young—and his hand is still sticking out of the grave directing his people.

In Utah you will seldom see big hats and high-heeled boots, or hear Western or country music, and if I want to buy one of my own Western novels I must send away to another state to get it.

Some of the older Mormons see a threat to Zion in the influx of Gentiles since the war, but that is not the popular view. The state is changing. One lady put it rather neatly when she said, "We Mormons like to think of ourselves as a peculiar people, but we don't like others to think that we are *too damned* peculiar."

I owe the Mormon church a debt of gratitude for what it meant to my parents, who never wavered in their testimony once they accepted its tenets. Most of my best friends are Mormons. My wife charges me with being a self-appointed Mormon missionary when I am away from Zion and the Mormon Kingdom, though I give them hell when at home. I have never claimed to be consistent.

My parents were always people of the frontier. The conditions under which they lived were always hard. Their kind and their era are gone forever. They were pioneers if ever people were, yet they never thought of themselves as such, any more than it ever occurred to them that they were helping to create a great American tradition—the Old West.

I Called him Frank
FRANK C. ROBERTSON AND HIS FAMILY

*A Personal Memoir and Retrospective
by his Son Glen*

Others may call him "Robertson." I can't do that. My problem is what to call Frank C. Robertson after the first mention of him by that name. Being his son, I find that calling him "Robertson" suggests a kind of clinical detachment I don't have. In *A Ram in the Thicke*t, I am quoted by my father as referring to him as "Robertson," not once but several times. Although it sounds unlikely to me, if he said I did, then I did. I was callow at twenty—and fifty and seventy. That is not to say that, at age seventy-two, I might not now have ripened into wisdom.

I always called my father by his first name. I was always "Glen"; he was always "Frank." My mother, naturally, was always "Winnie." After Frank's death in 1969, I came to realize that I had options—like "my father" or "father"—that I would have been driven to had my father been named, as he easily might have been, for his maternal grandfather, Tunstal Quarles. Confronted with that name, I think I would have said, "Tunstal Quarles, would you mind if I called you 'Father'?" But Frank I was able to live with. I've always thought it simply a good name.

Frank was a bit sensitive—even thin skinned—about what he was called. One woman writer friend, taking her chances, called him "Pappy." This didn't bother Frank as much as it bothered Winnie. My mother thought "Pappy" was pushing it. There were lots of ways others referred to Frank. I have heard him called "Frank Robinson," "Frank Robson," or just plain "Robason," as in "Hey, there, Robason, how's tricks?" which is how one farmer neighbor regularly greeted him. This ranked in Frank's estimation with being hailed on the streets of New York City as "Tex." That really shook him, and he modified his dress thereafter to a basic business suit topped by the most discrete Stetson he could find. He feared little in life except ridicule.

Frank's feelings were really very close to the surface. He wept easily, not from pain but from empathy. Animal and human suffering moved him to tears. Being a Scot, he was never allowed to show his own pain, and he was very good at concealing it. He could carve slivers out of his palm without a grimace. Of course, the source of his pain, if it were an inanimate object that had it in for him, could be in for a hard time as Frank exacted his revenge. He was capable of completely dismantling a chair he had barked his shins on.

Frank never said it in so many words, but he gave the impression that Scots were the pluckiest and most intelligent people on earth and that Robertsons were first among Scots and he among Robertsons. My father aspired to be the perfect Scot and even beyond that to be the perfect man. To him the perfect man was a man cast in the mold of Robert G. Ingersoll, the famous agnostic and orator. Frank was an idealistic agnostic who believed ardently in socialism. He believed in a great democracy of races and genders, quite modern thinking. How he sought to reconcile the equality of everyone with his conviction that Scots were superior and that he was a superior Scot led to great tension in his life and no easy resolution. It was quite a struggle.

Frank's theories of family relationships and child rearing largely came from reading, but his practices—though he surely would have hated to admit it—came from his father. Although he tried in every way he knew to avoid being like his father, nevertheless he was his father's son. The son pledged to Ingersoll and the father to the Bible, but each wrestled with some doubts and were hot-tempered Scots first before they were atheists or Christians. Will quoted the Bible and Frank quoted Ingersoll, but both men *tried* to be true to their faiths.

It must have been Ingersoll who persuaded Frank to put everybody in the family on a first-name basis as a symbol of equality. If Winnie and I accepted as gospel the proposition that we were all equal within the family, in retrospect it appears that we were taken in. Certainly I felt betrayed by his first (and last) use of physical force against me. It was a pair of rubbers that set him off.

What happened is that a girl named Dorothy had left school early wearing my rubbers. If I wanted to come home from school at all, it had to be without my rubbers. I told my mother this matter-of-factly. She listened stony-faced and then left the room. The next thing I knew, a raging giant I hardly recognized was rushing at me with a razor strop. But where was the dialogue? There was none. So one of the first vivid memories of my life is of my father coming at me with the seeming intent to kill me. I was unprepared to receive the beating of my life for what seemed to me an event over which I had no control. This incident defined our relationship for me: He was big; I was small; and that was all. I was also disappointed in my mother, who, instead of defending me, apparently played the role of Lady Macbeth in urging my father to perform the man's part.

It was not difficult to fire up my father. He was pretty much self-igniting, and, as he once wrote to me, his temper just "explodes." It exploded that day because he had worked hard for the money to buy those rubbers, and he hated to "waste" money. Never mind the furniture he demolished in his sudden rages. And forget about the time when, pressed for a house payment, he told the mortgage holder, "Take the goddamned house!"

It is easier for me to forgive my father than Dorothy, who had caused all my trouble, and I have carried a life-long grudge against her. Her mother showed up at our house the next day with the rubbers and an apology. She had found my name and address plainly inked inside the rubbers. One of these days, I may forgive Dorothy, but it won't be soon.

Actually, if it hadn't been Dorothy and the rubbers, it would have been something else. I have no complaints. In the long run there is little doubt that I came out a winner. There was no word of apology from my parents, but actions speak louder than words. From that day forward, neither one of them touched me in any way. Not that they shouldn't have. I was extremely wary for many years, wondering when an unexpected storm would come down on my head.

There were some very good times in the years following the Dorothy incident. More than a half-century later, I learned that my father had been so remorseful that he adopted a think-before-acting policy. My mother told me that once—unbeknownst to me—I was accused

315

of pushing a boy in front of an oncoming car. The injured boy's parents acrimoniously demanded that my father do something about me. Frank heard them out and then went up and down the street calling on dozens of people and interviewing children. I certainly hadn't pushed anyone, and I hadn't even been in the vicinity of the injured boy, who had blurted out my name because I had irked him recently. My father then called on the complaining neighbors. I am glad that they, not I, took the brunt of my father's wrath.

On another occasion, my father received a note from school that I was at the bottom of my class in my studies. This could have been a disaster for me had my father accepted the note at face value. Instead, he went to the school to investigate. My father discovered that my record had accidentally been switched with that of the class's poorest reader, Dorothy most likely, and I once again escaped chastizing.

I may be too hard on Dorothy to think of her as my nemesis. It may be that I owe her a great debt of gratitude. It was after the rubbers' episode that I discovered that my father's wrath miraculously was falling all around but never directly on me. Even at the dinner table, I discovered that I could with impunity break one of my father's cardinal rules: waste no food! I had a phobia about my father's favorite part of a steak—fat. I now found that if I could endure my father's glaring at me and other signs of gathering fury, I could trim away the fat. And I did hate fat! Little by little, I discovered that it was safe to carve out even the tiniest speck of fat. If my arteries are not clogged today, I think it is because of Dorothy and the guilt she inspired in my father.

In retrospect, it seems to me that my father regretted giving me that godawful beating so much that he adopted a whole new approach to me, much more in accordance with Ingersollian respect for human dignity and equal rights. In the pre-Dorothy era, wherever my father chose to take me, there I went. Chiefly, we went to baseball games, vaudeville shows, and wrestling matches, and so early to them that I was paralyzed by boredom. Frank could no more abide being late then he could abide being ridiculed. At any rate, when my father suddenly offered me the option of not going with him, I was profoundly grateful.

Though we still went some places together, after the rubbers' episode my father and I really didn't trouble each other very much. We were still on a first-name basis, but there was a distance between us. He made many efforts to win my confidence, hinting at terrible things he had done in his youth, thinking no doubt to draw from me a recounting of my own debaucheries. He told me that anything I may have done he had done ten times over, and worse. That was unsettling to me, and, after speculating a bit, I decided that I didn't want to exchange my secrets for his. I didn't want to know that much about him. And I really didn't want to reveal my private thoughts to him, because he had the dismaying habit of repeating the most intimate confidences of his friends at the first opportunity. It seemed that he was so pleased with being trusted that he wanted to prove to his family that people held nothing back from him. It frustrated Frank that even strangers would confide in him more readily than most members of his own family. I respected him for his warmth, compassion, and charisma, and for his ability to give wise and helpful counsel, but I distrusted his ability to keep a close rein on either his temper or his mouth.

One thing Frank and I had very much in common was a love for his fiction. I think that we both fantasized to a degree that we were his fictional hero. We differed, however, after the sun went down, for he probably found more pleasant things to dream about than the hard-wrought fiction he had been working on all day, whereas I liked to relive the heart-pounding action that was always plentiful in his stories. While I suffered from insomnia, my father snored the whole night through.

In my bedtime fantasies, I would feel a horse between my knees, watch its ears bobbing up and down, and see the foam on the rippling neck muscles as we crashed through the brush at the entrance to a canyon. I would look at the butt of my rifle and touch the smoothly worn handle of my six-shooter and then ride into a valley where the still air was soon punctuated with (silent) gunshots. I knew that there would be a tall, slender girl who would have to be rescued from a greedy range boss, and I was the man for the job. I usually fantasized myself as more than thirty years old, six feet tall, and—well—exactly like my father. And it was look out greedy range bosses! Adrenalin pumping in my veins, I got ready for action. I never really hurt anybody in my dreams, but I did shoot a few guns out of some thugs' hands.

Being Frank C. Robertson's son had its advantages and disadvantages. I was patted on the head a lot to the tune of "So, you're Frank's son?" This was followed by "We've got to fatten you up, boy" and "Do you write stories like your daddy?" There were irritations, but mostly I was pleased that my dad was welcome wherever he went.

He did prove a liability at times, though. For example, once I won a high school essay contest. While pumping my arm with hearty congratulations, my school principal asked me what my father did for a living. I replied that my father made his living being a professional writer. The principal abruptly turned on his heel, and never spoke to me again, nor I to him.

As far as help at home was concerned, it seemed to me that I gave more than I received. I was an unpaid typist who, assisting my mother, typed manuscripts by the hundreds, but I also embellished as I typed. One story I expanded won an award. Another story that was really mine brought a letter from an editor, mostly to the effect that this was the best story he had written to date. I thought we worked well together and made a good team. Frank was lavish in his praise of me—too lavish, really—but one thing he never offered to do was to split a check. His money was my money was the way he saw it. I never saw it that way. Winnie had the same problem; she wanted some money of her own. I went off and made my own money, but she never did.

There were pluses and minuses for my mother also in having a well-known writer for a husband. It would seem to many that she was an extremely lucky woman not to have ended up a farmer's wife. But not necessarily so. I love both my parents, but I have concluded that, though they often formed a united front and could be fiercely loyal to each other, they didn't really belong together, and Winnie might have been a happier woman had she married an orphaned Mormon farmer.

In my reading at about age five of my father's western stories, one detail bothered me. The heroine did *not* resemble my mother. That was odd, because the hero in most instances was exactly my father, every single inch of him. I remember wondering if Winnie might not take offense, but she never said anything, and the years went by without anyone but me seeming to notice. I kept wondering if I was overly sensitive.

But then I noticed something else. The heroines *did* very closely resemble a number of women whose company my father seemed to greatly enjoy, including a young, unmarried next-door neighbor woman. I noticed a lot of teasing, tumbling, tussling, good-natured camaraderie with lots of laughter, in which my mother did not participate. My mother called what was going on "lollygagging," and she clearly disapproved. Of my own knowledge, I don't know if Frank ever went beyond lollygagging, but I can certify him to have been at one time a lollygagger.

I think my mother would have been happier if her husband hadn't lollygagged so much. That's where being married to a farmer and living on a remote farm might have been better for her. There were just too many pretty, young writer groupies around Frank, to say nothing of hired girls, and they really liked him. But then, almost everyone liked Frank. If my mother was not hurt, she should have been. I was, for her.

Winnie had still more rivals for Frank's attention. Our house was always overflowing with people, including permanent residents. Through all the years that I spent with my parents, I can't recall a single day when—my sister Nellie being institutionalized—the family unit consisted of just my father, my mother, and me. Those who came to stay with us usually came to *stay*, like five, ten, or twenty years or until they died. My father's big economic umbrella never came down. If my mother complained of the extra work, Frank's invariable response was "Hire a girl.'" Since our house was already nearly full, it should be clear that Winnie felt her real complaint was not being addressed.

Another reason for my mother's unhappiness had to do with religion, though she might have stoutly denied it. My mother's religious beliefs were her secret, but I think if she had some to begin with—and she surely did—Frank argued her out of them. He was such an enthusiastic Ingersoll man that he couldn't wait to make her an Ingersoll woman. To the extent of pulling away from the church, she obliged him. Frank was forceful in his reasoning, very persuasive, and he had the endurance and zeal of his missionary dad. But in dropping out of church, Winnie sacrificed something she enjoyed—the Mormon Church's social life. This is why I think she might have been happier with a Mormon husband. Besides, she was not really at ease—especially when she went to New York City—with writers and agents who brandished cocktails and cigarettes at her as if they were weapons. Winnie was intimidated and eventually succumbed to the smoking convention and, at last, to emphysema. Poor Winnie. Yes, she might have fared better with an orphaned Mormon in a remote, one-bedroom log cabin like the one in which she was born.

Poor Frank, too. Few appreciate what he went through. I don't mean when he was a young man—that is well documented—but after his initial success, when people thought that life would now be soft for him. I have a wish for Frank also, and it is not for him to have married someone more sophisticated than Winnie. I suggest that Winnie might have been happier with someone else, and the same might have been true for Frank. I think my parents had a number of very good years filled with love, so I wouldn't change their marriage at all. My wish for them both is that they could have lived one year over and over again.

In the movie *Groundhog Day*, the central character relives a single day endlessly. I think 1926 would be the year I'd like my parents to repeat. That was a good year. Snapshots taken at about that time show Frank standing legs apart, tall, strong, and confident. If he seemed that way, that's because he was, and that's the way I would have him stay forever. He had the world by the tail and he was king of the hill. (A nom de plume he used on some of his books, King Hill, was appropriate.) His dental problems—those old black teeth—were gone, along with hunger, cold, pain, and humiliation. Now he had good-looking false teeth, a full stomach, and a world that looked very much like his oyster. Unknown to him then were the personal tragedies that lay ahead, those unbearable sorrows he had to face. Nellie was already doomed in 1926, but nobody knew that then. She was still a sweet little girl, and there was a vague hope for her complete recovery. Frank had vigorous health, he could identify with the heroes in his stories, and to his amazement, he could write much the same story over and over again with variations and get a check nearly every month. In his lifetime he would get thousands of checks, but in 1926, the thrill of opening a letter and pulling out a check was still there.

I have a photograph of my father as a child at school in Moscow, Idaho. It was sent to me by Chuck Tyrell of Missoula, Montana, whose family is mentioned in *A Ram in the Thicket*. It's hard for me to imagine my father ever having been the tyke in the photograph, looking like a refugee from Dickens's *Oliver Twist*. At the time this picture was taken, who could have predicted that this boy would write so many books that, stacked up, they would be taller than the boy himself—even taller than the boy become a six-foot-tall man and maybe even taller than the man and the boy together?

And my mother was so proud of him. At that time they were in love. But 1929 faded and gradually everything else began to fade, too, all the health and glory and old friends. He began to pine more and more for the past, and "I'm not half the man I used to be," from the song "Yesterday," became his refrain, expressed in various ways throughout the latter part of his life. Frank would try his best to be perfect, but there was no denying the clay feet, the weakening eyesight, and the temper that betrayed him time and time again. He carried on his unequal struggle with mortality until the end came in 1969 at Las Vegas, Nevada. He liked to gamble, and he had had some good luck before he cashed in his chips. A day or so before the end, he pointedly told me, "I'm not afraid of death." Ingersoll would have been proud of him, agnostic to the end, undaunted. And in one of those spooky coincidences, Frank had mailed in, just before his fatal heart attack, his final "Chopping Block" column for *The Provo Sunday Herald*, a weekly column that he had vowed to keep writing as long as he lived

A Ram in the Thicket was the jewel in his crown. He made it as honest as he possibly could, and the reprinting of it nearly a half-century after it was written, curiously predicted with accuracy by Erle Stanley Gardner in a letter I have carefully preserved, attests to the enduring quality he hoped it would have. Ostensibly, it was about his parents—his father is in every chapter—but it is also a summation of his life and philosophy. He recorded a place and time for the benefit of future historians, and I know how hard he worked on it to make it both true and readable. I appreciate having it for a family record. For a hundred reasons I am glad he wrote it, and not the least reason is that it made him feel good about himself and his family and his place in time.

The lens through which I saw the people of *A Ram in the Thicket* was narrower and fuzzier than the lens through which my father saw them. I saw with my own special bias, but then so did Frank. I owe my grandmother Mary a great deal, for she guided my education in my early days, and inclined me to become, like her, a schoolteacher. I remember her kindliness, one particular incident being especially vivid, for it aroused anxiety in me for her. My ball had rolled under a bed, and my grandmother retrieved it for me with perceptible creakiness. This was a woman of notable frail dignity for whom crawling under a bed did not come easily as even I, young as I was, could tell. I will never forget her nearsighted peering for that ball. It is an odd memory, but to me it is the epitome of Mary.

My view of my grandmother came to be modified over the next forty years by my mother, who saw Mary from another perspective and never neglected an opportunity to besmirch the icon.

What exercised my mother, besides the usual wife/mother-in-law tensions and Grandmother's constant presence, was one single expression, always pronounced piously between pursed lips: "Mebbeso," usually spoken when my mother offered an opinion. My mother enjoyed attacking reputations as much as my grandmother enjoyed defending them. The two women were destined not to get along.

From the beginning, Frank repaid with interest Winnie's criticism of his mother by loudly denouncing *her* mother. According to him, any difficulties he was having in his marriage could be attributed directly to *that woman*, Nellie Bowman. His complaint was that after a visit to Chesterfield, Idaho, where "Gramma" Bowman lived, Winnie behaved differently. It was as though Nellie had told Winnie, "Stand up to him!" If that was indeed what she had said, it was bad advice. How could Winnie stand up to someone who was far more eloquent than she in both speech and writing, who was bigger and stronger, who controlled the purse strings, who had to win at everything, and who made a far greater volume of sound? Winnie, of course, went down after each initially spirited encounter.

But during the nightly winter card games, Winnie would take a particular delight in vanquishing Frank at cards. Frank was the type who whistled through his teeth when he was winning but complained bitterly and loudly when he lost, while Winnie never changed expression except that her eyes sparkled if Frank ended up the loser, which was usually the case.

Ironically, Winnie pretty much approved of Frank's father, while Frank's main interest in having his father around seemed to be the satisfaction he took in seeing him firmly under the son's economic umbrella and in no position to wield any kind of authority whatsoever. Winnie, on the other hand, admired Will for being neat and clean, actually tidy. Furthermore, he was more often than not away on church business. His frequent absences really endeared him to my mother and, as I come to think of it, to everybody else as well.

I had mixed feelings about my grandfather. We clashed quite often, and my mother said we were "like oil and water." Frank must really have achieved dominance over Will, or I could not have escaped the consequences of my undoubted impudence. Grandad must have recognized the fact that the reins of power now rested firmly in his son's powerful hands. It is not surprising, therefore, that Grandad was away from home so much on the church business, which made him feel in control again. As Frank sardonically liked to put it, second fiddle was not Will's favorite section of the orchestra.

Yet, though we wrangled a lot, I really admired Grandad, not for his neatness but for the way he sat a horse. I remember him dressed in his Sunday-best clothes mounting a horse to demonstrate some point of horsemanship. He cut quite a figure, and I had no trouble believing that he rode the Chisholm Trail at its peak of activity in 1871.

The feud between Will and me may have saved my life on one occasion. The whole family was heading for Archer City, Texas, in two cars to see Will's younger brothers, Horton Lee and Chauncey Burr Robertson, and their families. Obe, Grandad, and I were in the second of the two cars, I on my old foe's lap. We were well on our way on a graveled road when Grandad decided he couldn't stand me any longer, so we pulled up and he shunted me into my parents' car. Soon afterwards, Obe lost control of his car on the gravel, and a serious accident resulted. I would surely have been pitched through the windshield, for there were no car safety seats for children then and no safety glass for windshields.

If Grandad didn't care much for second fiddle, there was another Robertson who had an equally strong aversion to that role, Will's oldest son, Chancy. The spelling "Chancy" is no mistake. I know Frank spelled his big brother's name "Chauncey" in *A Ram in the Thicket*, but I have to disagree with technical correctness in this case. The connotation of "chancy" is perfect, for Chancy was always willing to take a chance, gratified if danger came his way. No one who knew him ever *pronounced* the name as "Chauncey." No one would have dared.

As a boy, Chancy once pushed his little brother's head into a bucket of water and held it until Frank thought he would drown. Frank more than once told me that as a result of that incident, he had frequent nightmares and panicked if his face got near water. That was apparently not just one isolated prank by that dominating brother but one of scores, and that may have been why Chancy was the only other Robertson besides Will that Frank could bring himself to criticize—though it was usually on the grounds of Chancy's cavalier indifference to his responsibilities. Work always came first with Frank.

But Chancy was not lazy; he was just as competitive as Frank, and deferring to his younger brother was not his favorite pastime. We sometimes went during my school vacation to Chancy's ranch near Leadore, Idaho, where Frank, though flabby from the sedentary life of a writer, would offer to help with the haying. Of course, the result

1

School photograph, Moscow, Idaho, circa 1900. Front row, left to right: Mandle Erickson, Nellie Meeks, Frank Robertson, Lottie Sage, Arthur Showalter, Mary Rodgers, Craten Guff, Willis Sponsler, Vernon Ustler, Milton Rogers, Bertie Sage; middle row, Clara Levie, Doll Levie, Arie Staley, Nettie Sponsler, Vernon Ustler, Ode Grey, Luther McCarty, Ester Erickson, Hattie Staley (teacher); back row, Harold Staley, Bish McCarthy, Philip Showalter, Maurice Stepheson, Ruth Potter, Grace Cole, Daisy Matthews, Claude Cole, Willie Rodgers, Usless Showalter, Vernin (?), Johnnie Rodgers. Courtesy Chuck Tyrrell.

2

The family picture taken in 1926 shows Glen on his grandfather's lap, an odd juxtaposition, for the two didn't get along very well. Front row, left to right: Winnie, Russell, Grandad (holding Glen), Kelly, Grandma, Myrtle (holding Mary). Back row: Frank (holding Nellie), Obe, Chancy. Courtesy Glen E. Robertson.

3
*Glen and Frank.
Courtesy Glen E. Robertson.*

4
Frank, always a lover of the great outdoors, with his admiring son Glen.
Courtesy Glen E. Robertson.

5
Glen and sister Nellie, who showed early signs of precocity but whose mental development was permanently arrested at a very young age
Courtesy Glen E. Robertson.

6
Frank before the lightning of writing success struck.
Courtesy Glen E. Robertson.

7 & 8

Frank Robertson in 1927, when the world seemed to be his oyster.
Courtesy Glen E. Robertson.

9
*Frank and Glen, June 1934. The dressing alike was no coincidence.
Courtesy Glen E. Robertson.*

10

Taken a year before Frank's death, this was the last picture of Frank and Glen together. It seemed like a good photo opportunity since Glen had just finished attending his junior college graduation.
Courtesy Glen E. Robertson.

The Chopping Block

8-10-69 My birthday? d. 7-29-69

Time to Put Away Axe

By FRANK C. ROBERTSON

For more than a quarter of a century the Chopping Block has appeared regularly once a week in this paper, and now it is time to say, "Thanks—and Goodbye." To those of you who have read it from time to time I hope you have had the satisfaction that I have had in writing it.

I have expressed my opinion freely on many subjects, believing that to be a major part of our freedom; equal to the right to refuse to listen. I have been by heritage and nature on the side of the underdog. Though perhaps not qualified by formal education I have tried as best I could to be a voice for the inarticulate. In so doing I have sprinkled a little birdshot at those who feel themselves competent to regulate the affairs and morals of others . . .

———————————————
Written by Frank C. Robertson prior to his death, this column was intended as his last after 26 years of writing the Chopping Block for the Herald. See Off-the-Beat column at right.
———————————————

I do not believe they are wise enough to tell others what to do or say, let alone how to think . . . There is no slavery worse than an enslaved mind, and so I have urged people to think for themselves, and I hope there is a little more intellectual freedom in my state than there would have been had I not lived here.

The majority have seldom agreed with me, but even if they have read the column so they can refute it I have made them think, which is the only victory I have even wanted.

What people think is not nearly as important as that they do think for themselves. Not liking the onesidedness of any "cause" I have seldom adopted one. But I have given it my best, and no opinion of mine has ever been for sale.

I have no charity for people who practice cruelty whether it is to people or animals. I realize why they do it and have ridiculed sportsmen. They don't mind inflicting pain on helpless animals so I haven't minded making them squirm mentally a little. Bigotry and pomposity are a married couple and I have tried to ruin their smugness at every opportunity.

For myself I had rather be wronged than to be misunderstood. I hate to have my motives challenged for reasons that are not valid . . . I think that is largely what is driving the kids into rebellion today. It is not so much that they want more, as that they want people to understand why they want it. The generation gap is not caused by the younger ones running too fast, but by the older ones pulling back too hard.

I have seldom been mistreated because of my age, and I believe the way to achieve dignity is to recognize that of others, no matter how unimportant they may be. "Without regard to race, creed, or color," are words frequently used and seldom practiced. Those who object to the color of another's skin are somehow unaware of the darkness of their own minds.

The value of the old virtues have changed or they are governed by new rules. The older generations were proud of their stability; the younger ones boast of their adaptability to change. I doubt that one lifetime is long enough to determine which is best, but I have never feared to speculate about it.

These have been exciting years, and I am grateful to the Herald for having permitted me to express my opinions without censorship. The Chopping Block has been only a medium of opinion—mine—but none of them have been dishonest. They have seldom been popular, for my observation has been the popular side has been the wrong one and it is easier and safer to accept the popular view than to oppose it.

The Chopping Block has brought strangers to my door, as well as letters from all parts of the world. I shall miss them, but as I creep toward my eightieth birthday and physical debilities catch up with me it becomes harder to keep up with the events of the times. The only gospel I have tried to spread is that of tolerance and good will.

11

Frank's last column in the Provo Herald *appeared just after his death in 1969. Courtesy Glen E. Robertson.*

was that the two brothers would almost kill each other because neither would allow himself to be outdone by the other. Their wives chided them when they came in soaked with sweat, but it didn't do any good. Frank would be so stiff and sore the next day that he could barely move.

Even though Frank couldn't compete that way with his brother Obe, who, unlike Chancy, always maintained the same steady pace and couldn't be goaded into a race, Frank would invariably turn fieldwork into a life-and-death struggle if it involved competing with a "pretty built" man, that is, someone who had wide shoulders. My father was sensitive about his narrow shoulders. If he encountered someone with wider shoulders in a physical work situation, Frank would win whether the other fellow knew he had been in a contest or not. I think Frank would have preferred death by exhaustion to being outdone by a broad-shouldered man. Luckily, Frank was able to prevail because he had strength, prodigious energy, and a boundless will. Also, the other fellow may not have objected to Frank doing the lion's share of the work, if indeed he were in the least aware there was a contest.

Chancy, like his father, was not comfortable with being reduced in the pecking order, but he was realist enough to recognize the economic umbrella as a fact of life, and he uneasily accepted Frank's writing money to buy a ranch. He also let some of his children pursue their educations under Frank's aegis. The little guy had become the big guy, and, in fact, that's what Chancy often used to call Frank, ostensibly because of his size. It was big boy now, no more little guy. Chancy could recognize economic clout when he saw it, but he didn't have to like it.

Chancy was a likable man, engaging really, and I know my father envied him—envied him and probably resented him out of envy. Chancy was disposed to enjoy himself, and he gave pleasure a high priority. Putting work first and foremost, Frank was irritated that Chancy seemed to be having such a good time. My father respected Chancy, admired him, and liked him, but he would have preferred to change Chancy into a workaholic businessman. That wasn't going to happen, however, so relations between the brothers remained tense.

Although Frank fought those negative feelings about Chancy, the resentment wasn't suppressed entirely. Despite his claim to have modeled his fictional heroes on Chancy, I think he created heroes based on none other than himself and pointedly lacking the qualities that dismayed him in Chancy. I think unconsciously he also extended his negative feelings to Chancy's children. With pride and satisfaction, he saw them as Robertsons, possessing mostly good Scot characteristics, but with repressed anger he also saw in them the person who had played grasshopper to his thrifty ant and who had nearly drowned him once besides.

Kelly fared the best, because Frank seemed to feel that under his tutelage some of Chancy's sharp edges had been worn off. Frank and Winnie regarded Kelly more as a son than a nephew, and he toiled many decades ramrodding their fruit ranch. But once when he wanted to put in concrete irrigation ditches, financed in part by a government agency, Frank erupted. It was a sensible, farsighted project with no financial disadvantages, yet Frank insisted it would bankrupt him. I think Frank for a moment saw Chancy in Kelly, and he wanted to take his older brother down. He angrily refused to make the nominal investment, grumbling about "trying to do it the *easy* way," as if the easier way was always wrong. "What's wrong with a shovel?" he wanted to know. He loved shovels—and axes and picks—and couldn't understand why they weren't universally popular. Frank was very wrongheaded about the concrete ditches and surely realized it afterward, but it wasn't his style to apologize.

Chancy's other children, Russell and Mary, both stayed in our house in Mapleton, Utah, at the fruit farm, Russell going to college and Mary going to high school. They also came in for some Robertson criticism, and I feel bad for having been too timid to speak up for them when Frank—and Winnie, too—attacked. Even then, I clearly saw a double standard being applied, one to me, and another to them. At six feet two inches and 130 pounds—with rocks in my pockets—I was underweight to the point of emaciation, while Mary *may* have been (and this is disputable) a pound or two overweight, yet my father needled her with sarcastic comments about her "avoirdupois," by which he meant fat, as he tried to persuade her in a heavy-handed way to lose weight. I think he also saw his beloved dead daughter Nellie in her, for the girls resembled each other with big, luminous, dark eyes. It made Frank angry, I think, just to look upon Mary, Chancy's daughter. Where was his own beautiful daughter? But where was similar barbed criticism directed at me? There was none.

Like his brother Kelly, Russell in many ways was like a son to Frank, but Frank did criticize—and, again, unfairly. Russell's offense was that he would sometimes sit and read, and that looked like pleasure to Frank. He infuriated Frank to the extent that when Russell was offered a job stacking peas—a really hard job—Frank let him take it, an unprecedented decision on Frank's part, for that sort of thing could lead to independence. Frank may have thought the risk was worth it to stamp out a playboy tendency that reminded him of Chancy. He certainly wasn't trying to make Russell fiscally responsible, for no more thrifty person than Russell ever lived. He was like his grandfather Will in keeping careful records of every penny spent.

Russell was a hard worker; I, on the other hand, was completely devoted to indolence. My father wanted to give me what to him was the most precious gift on earth—time—thinking that I would make the same good use of it that he would. What folly. Anyway, I didn't speak out for Russell or Mary, partly because I didn't want to draw attention to myself. This, after all, was a man who almost beat me into jelly because of a pair of rubbers.

As exempt from Frank's criticism as I was, Obe was, if possible, even more so. Unfortunately for Obe, my mother, who considered Chancy the only good brother, noticed the omission of criticism aimed in Obe's direction and determined to rectify it. Though Frank did his best to deflect criticism aimed at the brother he considered the good one, Obe was constantly under fire from Winnie.

From the beginning, Winnie wanted Obe out of the house. Jealous of his closeness to Frank, she may have viewed him as the biggest threat to their marriage. The age of Frank's parents meant that *those* in-laws would likely pass from the scene before long, but Obe, born Oba Alvin, was only seven years older than Frank. It was soon clear to Winnie, I'm sure, that her efforts to get Oba Alvin to go his own way were hopeless. Obe's chances of getting Winnie kicked out were probably considerably better than Winnie's chances of getting him out.

Late in her life, my mother told me that she had once threatened to leave Frank. In fact, she had packed her bags and taken me in her arms to go out the door. Frank coolly called her bluff. Not only did he make not even the slightest move to stop her, he told her "Go!" Winnie could see that he meant it. She had gambled and lost. Winnie learned then and there that Frank's parents had done their work well in convincing him that he should provide an umbrella for them in their old age. They may have done their work too well, for Frank, with fanatical zeal, was convinced that family loyalty compelled him to provide eternal protection from sun and rain to the young and strong of his family as well as to the old and weak.

Obe, unlike the warier Chancy, never had any problems using another's shade. He may not have realized at first how reluctant Winnie would be to share the umbrella space with him, and when he did realize how jealous Winnie was, he hunkered down out of sheer stubbornness. Also, he may have thought it was payback time for having played mother hen when Frank was at the bottom of the pecking order. For whatever reasons, Obe stuck firmly at Frank's side, with unconcealed delight at their success (for he considered himself part of it). There was little that Frank did that he didn't consult Obe about first, knowing that a hearty endorsement was certain, for there was virtually nothing that Frank could say or do that Obe would not enthusiastically approve.

Winnie had her work cut out for her, but she had a stubborn streak, too, and when she realized that open combat would be counterproductive, she waged a cold war. She treated Obe correctly but with a complete absence of warmth, and it made for some chilly evenings. I tried to keep out of it, and Frank and Obe tried to keep me out of it, but my mother wanted me for her ally, so it made for some interesting battles through the years.

Obe never by word or expression revealed to me that he was distressed by Winnie, but Winnie had a great deal to say about Obe, very little of it good. I must admit that she had some reason to complain, particularly about Obe's smoking, for he was a very heavy smoker. Although my eyes watered sometimes from the smoke, it was easier for me to tolerate Obe's smoking habit than it was for my mother. Obe played ball forever with me, he was my pal, and he gave me countless empty Prince Albert tobacco tins. But Winnie resented the butts, the odors, the spit can, the cleaning up, and even his yellow teeth and stained fingers. She just plainly didn't like to clean up after her rival for Frank's affection and attention. On the other hand, she found Grandad's room always clean and tidy and smelling hospital clean, and the contrast with Obe's room was duly noted. It is sadly ironic that Winnie, after watching Obe die of lung cancer in 1944 and surely understanding the cause-and-effect relationship, took up smoking herself and died of emphysema at the age of sixty-seven in 1967.

I'm sure Obe had a lot of other bad habits that I was blissfully unaware of. He was what everyone called "an old batchelor"—not "bachelor," for that would have been too fancy for plain people like us. Sometimes Winnie's relatives called him "an old batch," in a not particularly friendly way. My mother seemed torn by a fervent desire for him to get married and an equally powerful fear that he would then bring his bride home for her to cook and clean for. Obe came quite close to marriage a couple of times, a whisker close once. In the circle of Utah writers that the Robertsons associated with was a tall, slender, beautiful woman with an infectious laugh, who delighted in Obe's humor. They used to stay up late, cigarettes glowing close together in the dark. She would "have him in a minute" my mother often said, if only Obe would "pop the question." Even to me, unobservant as I was, Obe seemed clearly head over heels in love, and almost everyone, it seemed, saw them as a couple that had been destined for each other.

But at Obe's age—pushing fifty—to come out from the comfortable shade of the umbrella into God-knows-what could have seemed a bit daunting. He knew what life under the umbrella was like, and, except for a certain chilliness, it was good. And if it got too cold, he could always head for a bar or a ball game. Even though Obe knew that he could absolutely count on financial support wherever he went, there was the problem of explaining such need for outside support to his woman, who had undoubtedly accepted at face value Frank's glowing appraisal of Obe as a writer far more brilliant than he could ever hope to be. But I absolutely knew the truth, which Frank tried so hard to avoid confronting in *A Ram in the Thicket*: Obe had a lot of special talents, and he had had a lot of experiences—but he was no writer. Obe's style—and I'm not exaggerating much—was to peck out about a few words in an hour and then strike out most of them, after which, exhausted, he was off again to a ball game or to some other unannounced destination.

The novels and short stories attributed to Obe under his own name or the name of Robert Crane were, as far as I could see, ghostwritten by Frank. Since I did the typing, I saw both the original stories and the rewritten versions, and there was no doubt in my mind that Obe supplied only the names of a few characters and perhaps a hint of plot, leaving Frank with much to do to create a salable story. It must have been hard for Frank, for he often was handicapped by what he had to work with, and he knew his brother would likely be shocked to see a new story in the place of the one he thought he had written. Obe was sometimes nettled, though he usually said little in my hearing.

Obe, however, was quite a man, and he had been through a lot in his life. He had many good qualities, and he worked hard on Frank's fruit farm. There was nobody better to work with, for he liked to stop and smoke, giving the rest of us a break and nearly always a taste of his acclaimed wit. His persona was of the kindly old uncle. We were sorry when his ladylove got away, but it may have been for the best. We heard later that she had died in San Francisco of lung cancer. Obe's fate was to remain with Frank and die of lung cancer. It was not quite Romeo and Juliet, but it did have overtones of tragedy. Had this couple married, the tragedy would have been compounded and their ultimate fate no different.

The only time Frank ever mentioned the tense home situation was in a letter in 1955. He confided, "Obe would never have tried to live with us had not Winnie made it a battle from the beginning, and he was too stubborn to admit defeat, so he stayed on." In the same letter he said, "Winnie thinks we would have always got along fine had not Obe and my folks lived with us. I know better than that...." He declared that had he yielded to Winnie, his bitterness would have made their relationship no more harmonious. There was just no getting around the resentment in our house, and if Obe had brought in a wife, the situation would probably have been exacerbated to the exploding point. Although usually well-concealed, Obe's temper might have been hard for him to hold back had he ever felt his bride ill treated, and there is little reason to expect that Winnie would have welcomed Mrs. Obe Robertson into her house with open arms.

If Obe had a nasty temper held almost one hundred percent in check, Frank was notoriously easy to rile, and his daughter-in-law, a Czech I had married in South America, could ruffle his feathers without half trying. In Europe she had clashed with Nazis and communists and she did not submit easily. Vera and Frank had an affectionate but often volatile relationship. Vera was passionately devoted to being his daughter-in-law and insisted that we spend whatever free time we had on the fruit ranch in Mapleton. On one of these visits, while I was off the premises, Vera called the fire department because she saw a ditch bank grass fire moving toward our house and garage. To her it was an inferno. To Frank it ranked as an emergency somewhere between a leaky faucet and a broken-down fence. It could use attention, but not in a hurry.

Red of face and shouting, Frank declared to Vera that he had wanted to put out that fire with his shovel. "Why?" asked Vera. "Isn't that what fire departments are for, to put out fires?" Frank mumbled Robertsons kill their own snakes and ended with a vehement admonition to her never to do anything like that again. It did little to mollify Frank that a couple of neighbors had already been battling the fire with shovels for some time and came by with relief on their faces to thank him for the timely intervention of the fire department. Frank accepted the thanks with little comment.

On another occasion, Frank had a flat tire, and Vera walked across the highway and came back with a service station attendant to change the tire. Frank, meanwhile, had been busying himself in the car's trunk trying to find his tools. He was old, he had a bad heart, and it was an extremely hot day, but he was shocked that Vera would question his manliness by hiring help. There was the inevitable explosion ("I can still change a goddamn tire!"), and Vera helped matters very little by insisting, "It's only two dollars. I'll pay it!"

After the tire was fixed, they went on, Frank still seething, until Vera helpfully told him not to try to pass a truck because cars were approaching. Boasting that he had been driving for fifty years without an accident (not true, by the way), and employing a number of goddamnits, Frank did the only thing he thought a man could do in that situation. He pulled out to pass and floorboarded the accelerator. This was an error of judgment that was nearly fatal. Disaster was averted by the width of a coat of paint, give or take a fraction of a millimeter, and Frank and Vera ended up on the side of the road with Vera screaming and Frank shaking. He silently handed her the keys and, as far as I know, never got behind the wheel again.

All that was left for them to tangle about after that was food. As a diabetic and heart patient, Frank was supposed to take various pills and watch his diet. He took his pills, but he had his own ideas about diet. Theoretically, he was restricted to fruit, vegetables, lean meat, and low-calorie desserts, but friends brought him candy bars, which he hid beneath his bed for snacks, and, explosions netting him little, he turned crafty, taking us out for dinner so that he could order a T-bone steak. In another role-reversal, I found myself trying to hold my temper as he ate every bit of fat from the meat on his plate.

At the end, his umbrella was in tatters, writing markets had dried up, and he was concerned about ending up a "vegetable." Fortunately, his mind remained alert, but he no longer boasted of his strength, his driving ability, or his business acumen. While he had prophesied disaster for borrowers, he had seen many of them grow rich, a bitter pill for him to swallow. At one time he could have bought a good portion of Beverly Hills, for on a visit to Los Angeles, a realtor had taken him out to look at investment property. Frank had been aghast. "Who would want to live *here*?" he asked. He rejected as equally ludicrous many other investment opportunities that would have made him a millionaire many times over. While he avoided blue chip stocks out of principle, his socialist instincts telling him that he should not support greedy capitalist corporations, he did invest to his sorrow in local ventures. Deciding one day to drop by the main office of an insurance company in which he had made a sizable investment, he was shocked to find himself looking at a vacant lot.

He may not have been the world's greatest businessman, but all things considered, he was an extraordinary man who grew tall from the soil of Moscow, Idaho, and cast a long shadow. He was certainly a product of his environment, and he inherited some incalculable genetic mix, but he had one piece of extraordinary luck. What if his first story had landed on the desk of an editor who, taking one look at the unpunctuated, misspelled, and unpolished manuscript, had returned it with a curt rejection slip? That is a big what-if, but I suspect there would have been no reprinting of *A Ram in the Thicket* and no prolific and internationally known author. Quite a few lives would have been changed in ways I shudder to contemplate, for mine would have been one of those lives so drastically altered.

I called him Frank. Whatever I called him, I knew he was my father, very human, full of contradictions, great and small at the same time, but a warm-hearted man who loved humanity and language, an idealist who really wanted to be part of building a better world (he even ran for office on the Socialist ticket). My memories of him are many, but I remember him most comfortably in his mellower days as a fruit farmer or "gentleman farmer" as he facetiously termed himself.

That gentleman farmer was a busy man, for he was a lot more farmer than gentleman, and he had a hands-on approach to the business of farming. His Mapleton farm was mostly planted to cherries, but there were also apples, raspberries, apricots, peaches, and peas, and a few cows and horses. On a typical day in summer, he was up at about 4 a.m. to milk cows. With his big hands he coaxed huge streams of milk from his rotund favorite, Sukey, and the other cows. I envied him those powerful hands, for I could manage only pencil-lead jets from that same old Sukey, who, I think, disliked me for not being my father. After the milking was done, he would haul cherry pickers from several nearby towns. He was always on hand to move the pickers' ladders for them so that they could safely devote their full attention to picking, and he moved the ladders with a calculating eye, concerned lest one of the pickers fall and get hurt.

Frank regarded those pickers as family, and he kept close watch over them and the number of pounds they picked each day, for he also helped to keep the books. He kept as close a watch on their poundage as he did on the daily baseball statistics, and he was a fan who knew the current batting average of almost every big league baseball player. Frank would argue with Obe and Kelly about the merits of each picker. I am surprised that he didn't try to choose an all-time, all-star crew or annual Most Valuable Picker.

After Frank had chauffeured the pickers home and checked the ledgers, he began his regular four-hour fiction stint, hunched over his Royal typewriter, but occasionally looking up and out over the orchard, perhaps trying to unravel some plot complication, although for thirty years he had gotten excellent mileage from the plot of a lone six-footer aiding a tall, slender girl in her struggle against a greedy range boss. Or perhaps he was thinking that all this work might net him nothing more than a rejection slip, for with the advent of television, the print appetite for westerns had waned. One of his stories did reach the small screen, "The Guardian" with Preston Foster, but he didn't recognize it any more than he had recognized the big-screen version of the novel *The Hidden Cabin*, of which not even his title remained. The medium of film was not kind to him. He had more success writing books based on current television shows, but it was a strange experience for him, contracting to write books that demanded that he use already established television characters like Rowdy Yates and Paladin. Fortunately, he had watched *Rawhide*, *Wanted Dead or Alive*, and *Have Gun Will Travel* often enough to know what was expected of him. Unfortunately, the police/crime genre began to displace westerns on television, and he used his typewriter more and more to commiserate with other western storywriters, like Nelson Nye, who saw their markets drying up. At least they had each other's shoulders to cry on.

Besides writing stories seven days a week, Frank carried on a voluminous correspondence. Because he didn't believe in short notes, he often wrote several pages, single-spaced, especially to his close writer friends. He corresponded with a regular who's who of authors, including Erle Stanley Gardner.

He had curious feuds with correspondents like the blind author Charles H. Snow of Napa, California. They were on excellent terms for a long time, and Frank wrote several newspaper columns about him when he came to visit, referring to him respectfully as "Mr. Snow" and praising him for his 387 western novels. (Charley was clearly more prolific than Frank.) Charley and Frank were competitors all the way. Once when a car salesman brought over a new car to sell to Frank, he had no more than opened his mouth when Frank said, "I'll take it." Charley quickly said, "I'll take two." He actually did, buying one car for himself and one for a companion. The car salesman was stunned as both men took out their wallets, peeled off some bills, and paid in cash on the spot, buying the cars as if they were ice cream cones.

I don't know what started the feud between the two men, but it became a bitter one. The two writers exchanged a series of long, angry letters in what has to be one of the oddest correspondences in history. Unless there was therapeutic value in writing, they might as well have saved their labor. Unable to read them himself and unwilling to involve a third party, Charley had Frank's letters burned upon receipt, and Frank couldn't make heads or tails out of Charley's gibberish. Charley had lost his eyesight at forty, and though he felt that all of his other senses had miraculously improved, they hadn't. He depended far more than he knew on secretarial assistance. So when there was just himself and a typewriter, the results were wildly random. If he thought his letters made any sense at all, he was mistaken.

In addition to his personal correspondence, Frank also wrote his newspaper column, "The Chopping Block," and that brought him a lot of both love and hate mail and also visitors, some of whom bore a passing resemblance to a lynch mob. While he pleased a number of readers, he managed to irritate an equally great number, including wardens, governors, and bishops of the Mormon Church. Because he seldom if ever checked his facts, he was often in hot water, and while he never apologized that I know of, he came close a few times. Once a woman whose husband had died as a result of a parking lot fight spurred Frank to write a fiery column that excoriated a vicious youth who wantonly left a family husbandless and fatherless. The day following the column's publication, a young man appeared at the front door and introduced himself as that self-same killer. There was an awkward silence, finally broken when the young man offered to give his version of what had happened in the parking lot. In his next column, Frank gave the other side of the story.

Frank also read. He loved to browse through bookstores, especially Sam Weller's Zion's Bookstore in Salt Lake City, and he was always adding to his collection of Western Americana. He subscribed to every prominent book club, and, because he felt he should keep abreast, he read all of the main selections. Where he found the time, I don't know.

He took a daily walk and a weekly drive to Salt Lake City, 50 miles away, and pitched horseshoes seven days a week. And he loved nothing better than a cesspool, the digging of which gave him an opportunity to use his beloved shovel. If he could use a pick, too, he was in seventh heaven, and, if an ax could also be involved, his gratitude was boundless. On a mostly tree-covered farm such as ours, where all kinds of occasions arose for the use of muscle and some simple tool, he was often a happy man. Frank never forgot about family. He faithfully kept genealogical information and reached out as well as he could to all branches of the Robertson and Bowman families. If he had ambivalent feelings at times about some members, he nevertheless took pride in them all, visited them, welcomed their visits, and did his best to keep in touch. This was no easy task. Winnie's brother Art never married, but her Mormon sisters did, and their numerous progeny were scattered far and wide. Chancy's children and grandchildren, though few in number, were also spread out with one notable exception. Kelly stayed by Frank, and in many ways he was more of a son to Frank and Winnie than I was. His marriage to a woman with a ready-made family brought Frank much joy, for he doted on the children, particularly Franky Win, a golden-haired child who was named for him and Winnie and whose family is still dear to me.

The Texas Robertsons, some with strange names and diminutive size, also filled him with pride. One Texas relative, a woman, was named John, and the top of her head reached only to his waistband. Here was a short branch of the Robertson tree over which Frank would have been glad to extend his umbrella, and, though he knew better than to insult those Texans by offering, he hoped, I think, they understood the umbrella was always there for them.

Being busy cost Frank, I think. He would have liked to attend a university, but he had to earn a living for his family. Besides, he probably visualized himself with a freshman beanie cap, hearing behind him snickering from wet-behind-the-ears classmates. He admired Wallace Stegner and seemed to feel that Stegner's advantage over him was related to education. Frank tried to put a reverse spin on the difference between himself and such writers as Stegner and Vardis Fisher by emphasizing how little education he had compared with them. He was sensitive to the possibility that because of his lack of education he might be the object of literary derision. Many people, he knew, looked down their noses at western storywriters and would scorn to mention him in the same breath with Shakespeare, who was "one hell of a writer," Frank often said with admiration in his voice. Shakespeare, who might have used Frank as a model for one of his characters, wrote in something like Frank's plain and simple style, "This was a man." That, in a nutshell, was my father. I am glad he had me call him, plainly and simply, Frank.